Punishment for Profit

Private Prisons/Public Concerns

David Shichor

Foreword by Gilbert Geis

SAGE Publications
International Educational and Professional Publisher
Thousand Oaks London New Delhi

For information address:

 SAGE Publications, Inc.
2455 Teller Road
Thousand Oaks, California 91320

SAGE Publications Ltd.
6 Bonhill Street
London EC2A 4PU
United Kingdom

SAGE Publications India Pvt. Ltd.
M-32 Market
Greater Kailash I
New Delhi 110 048 India

Printed in the United States of America

Library of Congress Cataloging-in-Publication Data

Shichor, David.
    Punishment for profit: Private prisons/public concerns / David
Shichor.
        p.   cm.
    Includes bibliographical references and index.
    ISBN 0-8039-7154-0 (cl).—ISBN 0-8039-7155-9 (pb: alk. paper)
    1. Prisons—Government policy—United States.   2. Corrections—
Contracting out—United States.   3. Privatization—United States.
I. Title.
HV9469.S55   1995
365'.973—dc20   94-42554

This book is printed on acid-free paper.

95   96   97   98   99   10   9   8   7   6   5   4   3   2   1

Sage Production Editor: Tricia K. Bennett

Contents

Foreword

The privatization of services traditionally provided by the state is a movement with momentum. The collapse of the economic systems in the former Soviet Union and its satellites is taken as a testament to the superiority of the capitalistic marketplace for best meeting citizens' needs. Privatization is said to be less costly and more efficient. Throughout the world, more and more tasks that once were performed by the state have been transferred to private business.

There are, however, significant issues regarding the proper boundaries of the privatization drive. In the United States, private operation of, say, telephone services seems to have produced a system that is superior to those found in countries where the state assumes responsibility for telecommunications. Competition keeps prices in line, there is no need for state subsidy, and rivalry for customers fuels the search for better and more consumer-friendly equipment.

On the other hand, nobody seriously recommends that the military be privatized, that wars be fought by soldiers and sailors employed by IBM or, say, Fighting Forces of America, Inc. If death and disaster on a considerable scale are inevitable products, the rule seems to be that this responsibility is the business of the government. The government is at least responsive to the will of the electorate, and it presumably will not declare or wage war with profit as its major goal. No one is likely to be persuaded to opt for the privatization of the military on the grounds that private industry can run military campaigns more efficiently and with less expense than the government, with its unwieldy bureaucracy and unnecessarily high salaries and benefits.

Issues regarding the privatization of prisons fall somewhere along the continuum between telecommunications and management of the military. Like the latter, prisons involve people, and in their case the people almost invariably are poor and powerless. Prisons also have, with justice, acquired a loathsome reputation; in fact, they are very likely much worse than most people appreciate. The beginning argument for the privatization of prisons has to be that nobody could do any poorer a job of dealing with the floods of people crammed into America's prisons and jails than is being done today.

If you read David Shichor's comprehensive critical analysis of the evidence that has been advanced regarding prison privatization, you may be led to the conclusion that desperately needed reforms must be mounted within the present operational structure and that the system should not be abdicated to private enterprise. Shichor stresses that his is not an examination only of economic issues, although he devotes considerable attention to claims that private companies can save taxpayer money. He is also deeply concerned with moral issues—such as those involved with the delegation of coercive power—and he is adept at taking statements advanced in favor of prison privatization and stripping them to their essentials to demonstrate that they do not stand up in logic or in terms of available evidence. Often he concludes that what is claimed is not necessarily wrong, only that it is not satisfactorily demonstrated by the evidence advanced for it. Although there is no question where the author comes down on the matter of privatizing prisons, readers seeking a full review of what is known and thought about this important public policy issue should be pleased to have before them a full and fair portrayal of every matter of importance on the issue: the historical record, legal issues, management concerns, expense data, monitoring matters, and outcome measures, the last concerned with whether private operations show a better result than the present system in terms of reform of inmates.

It must be stressed in this debate that, unlike telecommunications, garbage collection, and the post office, prisons deal with captive human populations. Two prison vignettes epitomize for me the essential characteristics of what today is euphemistically called "corrections." The first took place during a visit to Folsom, California's maximum-security prison. As one of the officers and I walked through the prison yard, I noticed that inmates lounging on the ground, with their backs against a wall, would pull in their feet whenever we came near them. The officer told me that this was a precautionary move. "This is a place that contains a lot of violent people with low ignition points. If purely by chance you were to fall over their feet, you might accuse them of deliberately trying to trip you. And then there would be a fight. There are a lot of weapons around here, and they could get killed. They pull their feet in, they don't take any chances."

The other incident is reported in *Prison Exposures*, Robert Neese's (1959) pictorial essay about the penitentiary at Fort Madison, Iowa. An inmate had spent endless painstaking hours training a cockroach to walk in a straight line. Everyone wanted to know why. "Well," the prisoner explained, as if the matter were obvious, "You never know when you might be able to make use in this place of a cockroach who can walk in a straight line" (p. 84).

The first story talks to the instability and the awful omnipresent threat of violence that marks prison existence; the second, to the monotony, the boredom, and the frustrations and despair associated with being locked up behind a wall often for many years and deprived of things most people take for granted.

Prisons have been with us for a long time. As early as 525 B.C., Plato, writing in *The Laws*, recommended imprisonment for theft, assault and battery, and as part of the punishment for the crime of "impiety." We also have early historical records of offenders being placed under house arrest. But imprisonment was used only sporadically to deal with criminals until comparatively recently. "It was not common to keep men in prison," Frederick Pollock and Frederic W. Maitland (1898) write of the medieval period, explaining that "this apparent leniency was not due to any love of abstract liberty. Imprisonment was costly and troublesome" (p. 585).

Prisons remain costly and troublesome. In the United States, as throughout almost all of the world, they are terrible places. They also are very expensive to run. Today, in the name of incapacitation (fueled largely by the emotions of revenge and retribution) Americans are demanding that more and more offenders be incarcerated. But they balk at the cost, and this provides the rationale for the entrance of cost-cutting entrepreneurs into the marketplace. David Shichor dissects the element of that movement in terms of the history of imprisonment and our early experience with privately operated programs, such as the rental of convicts to farmers.

At the heart of Shichor's estimable treatise lies the question he poses in his third chapter: "Whether private for-profit companies, their administrators, and line employees should be involved in handling the two most precious possessions of every citizen—their liberty and their life." It is a vital question and the answers he provides are the result of a painstaking review of available evidence and an examination of diverse claims advanced by those on both sides of the debate.

With crime standing in public opinion polls as the single most important concern on the minds of citizens, it is essential to examine thoroughly and with sophisticated analytical skill the merits and deficiencies of the press toward privatization. It is well to keep in mind in this regard the words delivered by Winston Churchill to the House of Commons almost a century ago.

> The mood and temper of the public with regard to the treatment of crime and criminals is one of the most unfailing tests of the civilization of any country. A calm, dispassionate recognition of the rights of the accused, and even of the convicted criminal against the state—a constant heart searching by all charged with the duty of punishment—a desire and eagerness to rehabilitate in the world of industry those who have paid their due in the hard coinage of punishment; tireless efforts towards the discovery of curative and regenerative processes; unfailing faith that there is a treasure if you can find it, in the heart of every man. These are the symbols which, in the treatment of crime and criminal, mark and measure the stored up strength of a nation and are sign and proof of the living virtue in it.

Churchill was correct. And what he said tells you why this is such an important book on such a significant social and moral issue.

Gilbert Geis
Department of Criminology, Law and Society
University of California, Irvine

Preface

The issue of the privatization of correctional institutions started to interest me in the early 1980s when I first heard of plans to build and operate prisons by private companies or to transfer the management of existing institutions to private corporations. Since then, I have been reading, thinking, and talking about this subject, and I have tried to write about it as well, although not enough. Frankly, I found in my discussions that most people I talked to were not extremely interested in this issue, a fact that sometimes annoyed me. At the same time, I may have bored them with bringing up my pet subject at various occasions.

A recent discussion at a party with a social scientist from another discipline is fairly characteristic of the reaction I have encountered in talking about this subject. After finding out that I am a sociologist-criminologist, he asked me casually about my professional work, what I am involved with at the moment. I was glad that he asked this question because I felt that now I could present some highlights of the subject on which I have been working on and off for several years. After mentioning to him the topic itself, he assured me that it was a very interesting subject. His reaction encouraged me to start into a more detailed presentation of the various aspects of this issue. However, at the first pause in my discussion, he managed to interrupt me, very politely, by pointing out that whether the privatization of prisons should or should not be implemented is basically a "pragmatic question" that boils down to economic feasibility. With this profound statement, he indicated in a subtle manner that his interest in *my* work was satisfied by turning to someone else at the party.

Yes, I have realized that many people consider this issue to be basically a pragmatic one, boiling down to the question of whether private corporations are able to operate prisons cheaper and at least at the same level of quality of service (whatever "quality" means) as public agencies do. Often, this question is underpinned by a general attitude asserting that currently the incarceration cost is so high and the situation in prisons is so bad that any change in the operation of prisons can only improve the current state of affairs. I should have been ready for this comment after dealing with this subject for years, but for some reason I was not. It hit me again that a social scientist who himself is involved supposedly in the analysis of various social phenomena was ready so easily to make a judgment regarding this issue. Apparently, my "overreaction" was the result of the accumulation of this kind of opinion and responses that I have encountered during the years. I guess everyone involved in a long project tends to lose some objectivity concerning the importance of the subject matter and the complexities of the issues involved. I am sure that I am not an exception. Nevertheless, I believe that the general lack of awareness that the privatization of human services (not only corrections, but corrections more so than most others) involves ethical, legal, political, and theoretical issues besides pragmatism is somewhat dangerous. It is especially so when it involves a clientele that generally is not considered to be desirable and is socially and politically vulnerable, such as the poor, the elderly, the mentally ill, and the criminal offender. I believe that the privatization of prisons raises very fundamental questions pertaining to the society we are living in; among others, What are the functions of the state and the government? What are the limits of civil liberties? What are the bonds holding members of society together? To a large degree, it questions the relevance of the extreme utilitarian approach to punishment, social control, and ultimately to social relations. In other words, it poses questions that reach to the core of our value and normative system.

I do not want to sound immodest by claiming that I am the only one who raises all these questions. In recent years, the professional literature dealing with correctional privatization has grown rapidly, and many aspects of this issue were dealt with. In this book, I try to address these various aspects of the subject; review the historical roots of private prisons; deal with the pros and cons of this policy; and formulate my opinion about it based on principles, facts, and policy implications, not on personal preferences and gut feelings alone. Obviously, I recognize that it is not possible to be completely objective, and my presentation and analysis of the various issues, opinions, and even facts will be influenced by my subjectivity. This is a reality that all social scientists have to face even though we were taught to strive for a value-free science.

Acknowledgments

It is very difficult to pay intellectual debts after being in the "academic business" for more than a quarter century. There are so many people that one learns from in various ways and to various degrees that it is impossible to recall and list all of them without the risk of major omissions. Therefore, by necessity, I confine my thanks to those who were involved with the current project and in one way or other had an impact on it.

I am indebted to Rita Simon at American University and Gilbert Geis at the University of California, Irvine, for providing me with material on privatization. Gil Geis also reviewed and commented on a recently published article of mine that is related to and partially incorporated into this book, and he was gracious enough to write the introduction as well. Robert Lilly at Northern Kentucky University made valuable comments on the above-mentioned article. The manuscript of this book was read by Solomon Kobrin at the University of Southern California, Simon Dinitz at Ohio State University, and two of my colleagues at California State University, San Bernardino— John Heeren and Dale Sechrest. I have benefited from their comments even though I did not always follow them completely. Also, two reviewers for the publisher were helpful—Doris MacKenzie and Harold Williamson. I am thankful to all of these individuals for sharing their knowledge with me and for dedicating their time for this project. Because of their great contribution to this work, the responsibility for the shortcomings obviously lies with them; however, for the merits of the book, I am ready to take all the credit. I also would like to thank C. Terry Hendrix from Sage and his staff for the very professional handling of this project. Lynn Rudoff and Karen Michelle Gray did a great job in deciphering my handwriting and typing the manuscript.

My late parents, Jacob and Malka, would have been proud and happy to see this book in print. Finally, my immediate family—Pnina, Nomi, Nadav and his new bride Iris—helped me in so many ways, just by being there and just by being themselves. I am grateful to them.

1

Introduction

The United States and several other industrialized countries show a major interest in privatization, "the systematic transfer of government functions and programs into the private sector" (Adam Smith Institute, n.d., pp. 17-18). This interest has been stimulated by increasing government budgets and expenditures and in some cases by ideological commitments (especially during the Reagan administration in the United States and the Thatcher government in Great Britain). The interest in privatization is prompted partly by the concern

> that the federal government has become too large, too expensive, and too intrusive in our lives. The interest also reflects a belief that new arrangements between the government and the private sector might improve efficiency while offering new opportunities and greater satisfaction for the people served. (Linowes, 1988, p. 1)

In the 1980s "privatization came primarily to mean two things: (1) any shift of activities from the state to the private sector; and (2) more specifically, any shift from public to private of the production of goods and services" (Starr, 1989, p. 21). Although at first "hard services" such as garbage collection and building maintenance were targeted for privatization, in the increasingly conservative sociopolitical climate of America and other Western countries (England, Canada, and Australia), a growing number of "soft services . . . performed for or on people" (Nelson, 1980, p. 431) such as public welfare and human services were considered for privatization (Carroll, Conant, & Easton, 1987; De Hoog, 1984; Earnshaw & Normandeau, 1986; Kamerman & Kahn, 1989; Linowes, 1988; Papadakis & Taylor-Gooby, 1987; Savas, 1982; Talbot, 1981).[1]

This book focuses on the privatization of prisons. Private prisons are defined as prisons and other institutions of confinement (jails, immigration and nationalization service facilities, detention centers, and secured juvenile justice facilities) operated and managed by private corporations for profit. The various aspects of correctional privatization are reviewed and the arguments for and against this policy are analyzed.

First, a brief overview of the idea of privatization is presented.

Philosophical and Theoretical Aspects of Privatization

Laissez-faire economics based on free markets and free competition is a cornerstone of the American ethos. The "classical liberal" philosophy framed the American republic. In this context the main emphasis was on the existence of individual freedom and the upholding of individual rights to their fullest extent. Accordingly, there was a major concern with private property that was conceived as an "absolute right" (Bell, 1976, p. 280). The major American political traditions "have shared a belief in the rights of property, the philosophy of economic individualism, the value of competition; they have accepted the economic virtues of capitalist culture as necessary qualities of men" (Hofstadter, 1974, p. xxxvii).

Historically, the liberal foundation of the American political and socioeconomic philosophy is strongly tied to the Protestant theology of the founding fathers. According to Weber (1958), this heritage was essential in the emergence of a new kind of ethic in the 16th century, "the earning of more and more money, combined with the strict avoidance of all spontaneous enjoyment of life" (p. 53). This ethos is referred to as the Protestant ethic, which became the core of the spirit of capitalism, a new value system that related to money not as a means for achieving material goals but as a goal by itself.

> Another major philosophical source of the modern capitalist ideology was rationalism, "a cluster of ideas that add up to the belief that the universe works the way a man's mind works when he thinks logically and objectively; that therefore, man can ultimately understand everything in his experience" (Brinton, 1950, p. 82).

Rationalism, as a major philosophical orientation, emerged during the 17th and 18th centuries in Western Europe and became the foundation of the intellectual movement of the Enlightenment, which championed individual rights.

Another cornerstone of Enlightenment philosophy was humanism, which questioned the authority of custom and rebelled against the clerical tradition and its stifling influence on everyday life. The humanists promoted the idea that human beings themselves make their own standards and emphasized the importance of human beings, their capabilities, interests, and achievements and—through these—their individual rights. There was a strong belief "in the perfectibility of man and society and, accordingly, the belief in the progress of the human race" (Bierstedt, 1978, p. 5).

The Enlightenment movement became to a large degree the intellectual and sociocultural basis of modern Western civilization (Hughes, 1958). This tradition is reflected in the works of the classical liberals such as Hobbes and Locke, who were dealing with the nature of the state, and Adam Smith, the father of classical economics.

Thomas Hobbes (1588-1679), in his major work *Leviathan*, maintained that the political power of the monarch is ultimately derived from the people and is transferred to the ruler by an implicit contract. That is the basic idea of the "social contract" concept by which the commonwealth is established through the voluntary submission of a part of each citizen's personal rights:

> The final Cause, end, or Designee of men (who naturally love Liberty and Dominion over others) in the introduction of the restraint from themselves (in which we see them live in the Commonwealths), is the foresight of their own preservation, and of a more contented life thereby. (Hobbes, 1651/1969, p. 115)

John Locke (1632-1704) furthered the concept of limited government. According to him, people enter into civil society to protect
themselves and their possessions. The role of the government is to
provide this protection; therefore, it is given coercive power but only
for this purpose. Otherwise, individuals have the freedom to compete
with each other without the interference of the government (Galston,
1986).

Adam Smith (1723-1790), a Scottish professor of philosophy, was
the pioneer of economic liberalism, and his ideas are among the most
influential ones in shaping American socioeconomic thinking. He is
considered to be a forefather of the pure liberal ideology that emerged
when the traditional social forces yielded to the increasing political
and economic power of the bourgeoisie. In *The Wealth of Nations*,
Smith (1937) promoted the ideas of free trade and laissez-faire economics at the decline of mercantilism, which was based on government regulation of the total state economy in order to secure a positive
balance of trade. In that system, major colonial powers (Spain, England, Portugal, Netherlands, and France) used their colonies for the
financial benefit of the mother country. In short, mercantilism en-
tailed government regulation of international trade often using subsidies and high import tariffs to protect the national economy from
competition. This policy, in less extreme forms, is still followed by
many countries today.[2] Smith strongly opposed government regulation and privileges for monopolies. He professed free competition as
the most effective economic policy. According to his theory, free
unregulated economy will provide to every citizen a fair and equal
opportunity to do what they do best. He argued that free competition
among private enterprises would result in greater income for everyone (McKay, Hill, & Buckler, 1983). Smith believed that everyone, in
following his or her own interest, would contribute to the common
good. In other words, the marketplace should be left alone because it
has the ability to guide the economic system and to secure the highest
material return (Heilbroner, 1966). These ideas may be captured in
the following:

(1) . . . that competition in economic affairs should be completely free;
only in this manner could a maximum productivity be achieved; and
(2) that the sphere of government should be correspondingly reduced;

natural forces will reconcile the requirements of both individuals and groups. (Martindale, 1960, p. 143)

Following this reasoning, Smith also claimed that if everyone would be allowed to follow free economic action, the competing individual interests, without any state intervention, would produce the most real wealth and happiness among the nations (Manuel, 1951). Thus he was against government interference in the market mechanism.

Lerner (1937), in his introduction to *The Wealth of Nations*, depicts three fundamental assumptions suggested by this major work: (a) "the prime psychological drive in man as an economic being is the drive of self-interest," (b) there exists "a natural order in the universe which makes all the individual strivings for self-interest add up to the social good," (c) therefore, the conclusion from the two previous points is that "the best program is to leave the economic process severely alone—what has come to be known as laissez-faire, economic liberalism, or non-interventionism" (p. viii). The state has, at best, only a peripheral role in society; the principal social dynamic is the "invisible hand" of the free market. Smith perceived the "morality inherent in capitalist production (free enterprise)" being "the social cement for society" (Carnoy, 1984, p. 27).

The view of human beings as creatures who are driven almost solely by their self-interest stems clearly from the rationalistic philosophy. This idea, coupled with the acceptance of the Protestant ethic, has deep roots in the American political, social, economic, and cultural heritage. In the American ethos, progress, productivity, and efficiency are associated with private enterprise, whereas inefficiency, stagnation, and corruption are tied to the public sector. This is reflected also in many contemporary social ideas; for example, in the preface to the "Report of the President's Commission on Privatization," David F. Linowes, its chairperson, illustrates the American credo by stating:

The American people have often complained of the intrusiveness of federal programs, of inadequate performance, and of excessive expenditures. In light of these public concerns, government should consider turning to the creative talents and ingenuity in the private

sector to provide wherever possible and appropriate better answers to
present and future challenges. (Linowes, 1988, p. vii)

The negative American view of the public sector and public administration is different from the Western European approach:

> In Europe the long term is controlled . . . by the specialized organs of
> government, which are imbued with a special sort of ideology, a variable
> mystique of the state of administration, or at least public service, an
> ideology whose guardians are the castes of high-level, carefully screened
> officials. (Crozier, 1984, p. 88)

The negative American approach to public management was reinforced during the 1970s and 1980s. It was strongly connected with
the revival of the conservative political and social ideology in American society. The disenchantment with the social turbulence of the
1960s, the Vietnam War, the declining American economic power,
and the public concern with drugs and crime prompted large segments of the American people to look for solutions in conservative
ideology; conservative leadership; and conservative political, economic, and social policies.

The traditional values of rugged individualism and aversion toward "big" and restrictive government were reinforced. This trend
gained a strong impetus with the election of President Reagan, whose
administration started to implement the ideas of the classical-liberal
socioeconomic ideology. The regulation/deregulation of the private
sector became a major issue. Regulatory agencies are government
bureaucracies that had been set up to regulate various aspects of
economic behavior. Their charges include everything from maintaining free competition to the protection of the health and safety of
workers and the general public (Coleman, 1989; Frank & Lambness,
1988). Regulation, at least theoretically, was established to protect
the public interest. "Regulatory law is an attempt to formally specify
constraints on how social benefits and damages will be distributed"
(Shover, Clelland, & Lynxwiler, 1986, p. 9). Government agencies
were to be armed with various carrots and sticks to ensure that the
companies' pursuit of private gain remained compatible with the
public interest (Shapiro, 1988, p. 63). "Deregulation," according to a

leading privatization advocate, "involves simply allowing the private sector to provide a service now monopolized by the government" (Butler, 1985, p. 21).

One somewhat simplistic approach states that regulations became necessary because industry failed "to provide willingly for the health, safety, and well-being of the public, consumers, and workers" (Clinard & Yeager, 1980, p. 214). Historically, in the United States, regulations came in three major waves: during the Progressive Era, as a part of the New Deal, and during the 1960s and early 1970s (Shover et al., 1986); these periods were socially liberal times and the main advocates of regulatory policies were progressives and liberals. During the Reagan administration, as an outcome of the conservative emphasis on small government and laissez-faire economics, a large-scale deregulation took place amid major attacks on government regulations. The most severe attacks came from libertarians. Some of them compared regulatory agencies (e.g., the Occupational Health and Safety Administration [OSHA]) even with the Gestapo (see Hospers, 1978). On the other hand, certain critics of the deregulation policy depict the deregulation during the Reagan era as the "dismantling of America" (Tolchin & Tolchin, 1983). The deregulatory policies resulted in some major economic as well as political scandals such as the debacle of the savings and loan industry, which may cost hundreds of billions of dollars to American taxpayers.

The conservative trend has taken effect in the public sector as well. A series of legislations and voter propositions aimed at curbing state and local expenditures were initiated and implemented (probably the best known is Proposition 13 in California, which drastically limited the increase in property taxes). These measures put pressure on government agencies to eliminate and reduce services or to contract them out to private companies. According to many, the private sector can offer an attractive option in the provision of services because it

faces less red tape and through competition can be motivated to drive down costs and improve service quality. Furthermore, private firms working in more than one location can take advantage of economies of scale and are better able to develop superior management information systems. (Gorham, 1983, p. xi)

Those who are against big government in principle and others who lost their confidence in the efficiency of the bureaucracy want to see major cutbacks in the size of government. These attitudes are reflected in the various alternative strategies for the delivery of services suggested by the critics: (a) some services that became supplied by the public sector during the past few decades should revert to their original status and be supplied by the marketplace; this is referred to as "load shedding," an arrangement under which both the financing and the delivery of services are divorced from the government (Bendick, 1989); (b) government involvement in delivery of public services should be reduced and limited; (c) user fees for services should be levied wherever possible; and (d) competition for service contracts should be used to a great extent (Savas, 1982).

These arrangements, according to the proponents of privatization, may include maintenance services such as trash collection, janitorial services of government buildings, public transportation, and social and human services such as health, welfare, child care, law enforcement, probation, corrections, and even courts.

The modern theoretical basis of the privatization of public services is greatly influenced by the "public choice" school, which follows a utilitarian approach examining public bureaucracies and services through the application of economic models. Public choice theorists argue that "the competitive marketplace produces goods and services efficiently, whereas monopolies, whether public or private, tend toward both inefficiency and unresponsiveness" (DeHoog, 1984, p. 4). This school negates public ownership and management completely and declares unambiguously that "government should not be in business" (Linowes, 1990, p. 3). It claims that the major benefits of contracting out public services to private contractors stems from free market competition. According to this school, at least three conditions are essential for successful contracting: "(1) competition in the environment and in the government's contracting procedures; (2) government decision making to attain the goals of cost reduction and service quality; and (3) an effective watchdog role by government" (DeHoog, 1984, pp. 18-19).

In reality, the watchdog role of government came under heavy attack during the Reagan administration in the United States and the Thatcher government in England when accelerated privatization became public policy. Simultaneously, as mentioned, there was a strong push for deregulation of various industries. Critics of this trend emphasize that these policies led to the erosion of government authority to protect the public. They point out, for example, that deregulation had a negative effect on airline safety (Dempsey, 1991) and among other effects, resulted in phenomenal losses and brought the savings and loan industry to an almost total state of anarchy (Benekos & Hagan, 1990; Calavita & Pontell, 1990). With the diminution of regulation, the caveat emptor (let the buyer beware) ethos of American business has returned to the marketplace.

The general sociopolitical atmosphere of the 1980s has affected criminal justice as well. There was an increased privatization trend at the various levels of the system, for example, in private security; preparation of probation presentence reports; operation of halfway houses, diversion programs, and juvenile detention facilities; and in the running of juvenile correctional programs. In some of these services, the private sector was involved for a long time, for example, private security and juvenile corrections, but this involvement became more significant (see Krisberg, DeComo, & Herrera, 1992), whereas in other services privatization is more recent.

Lately, as mentioned, the idea of the private operation of adult prisons has gained popularity and started to take place to a modest extent. It is important to review the historical antecedents of private involvement in prison management to understand some of the basic issues concerning the operation of correctional facilities by the private sector.

Changes in Penal Policies

For several decades during the 20th century, rehabilitation was the leading goal of American corrections. Rehabilitation became a major influence in the Progressive Era and continued to be an important factor in American penology until the early 1970s. Since that time, there has been a growing disillusionment with and criticism against the idea of rehabilitation. This was not only a result of the growing recognition that rehabilitation efforts have failed to either reduce crime or change offenders but also a result of a growing number of

TABLE 1.1 Prisoners in State and Federal Institutions in Selected Years

Year	Number of Prisoners	Rate per 100,000 Population
1971	198,061	96
1975	240,593	113
1980	315,974	139
1985	480,568	200
1990	738,894	292

SOURCE: Flanagan and Maguire (1992).

criminologists and social scientists arriving at the conclusion that there is a need to develop new penological strategies in light of the increase in crime rates and the changing sociopolitical climate. Some of these declared not only that rehabilitation does not work but that it should not be even a major purpose of punishment. These opinions were voiced both by liberal and conservative scholars (see, e.g., American Friends Service Committee, 1971; Fogel, 1975; Martinson, 1974; van den Haag, 1975; von Hirsch, 1976; Wilson, 1975). This perspective has represented an important turn in American penological thinking and was in line with public opinion demanding harsher punishment for convicted criminals. It also led to the development of an "antirehabilitation" trend in penology (Ingraham, Evans, & Anderson, 1978; Shichor, 1987). Although the rehabilitation approach (with its focus on individual offenders and their reformation) did not disappear and has maintained some public and professional support (Cullen & Gilbert, 1982; Gendreau & Ross, 1987; Shichor, 1992b), it was replaced by the emphasis on the protection of society. The leading principles became incapacitation, which in its modern version means locking up offenders for a certain period of time during which they cannot harm society (Hawkins, 1976) and deterrence. The major change in penal policies, coupled with the public demand for law and order and the politicians' continued declaration of a war on crime, resulted in an unprecedented increase in imprisonment during the 1980s and early 1990s (see Langan, 1991). From 1980 to 1990, the number of prisoners in the United States grew by 134%, and the incarceration rate per 100,000 population increased from 139 to 292 (see Table 1.1).

In addition, by 1990 about 400,000 people were locked up in local jails, among them close to 17,000 state prisoners who were housed in jails because of crowded state prisons (Jankowski, 1992). The United States achieved the distinction of having the highest number of people incarcerated per capita in the world.[3] Subsequently, the cost of incarceration skyrocketed as well: In 1984 the total state expenditures on correctional institutions was about $6 billion, whereas in 1990 it was approaching $20 billion, a growth of 233% in 6 years (Flanagan & Maguire, 1990, 1992; Jamieson & Flanagan, 1989).

This rapid and large-scale increase in the number of incarcerated people has resulted in major problems of overcrowding in correctional facilities in spite of an accelerated effort to build more facilities and enlarge the holding capacities of existent institutions. In 1988, 39 states, the District of Columbia, Puerto Rico, and the Virgin Islands were under some kind of court order to limit their prison or jail population unless they could increase their prison capacity (McDonald, 1990c). Usually, judges have determined the maximum number of prisoners that could be housed in each facility. Among others, these orders led to contempt-of-court orders when the situation was not rectified and to the early release of inmates to ease overcrowding.[4] Austin (1986) estimates that from 1980 to 1983, this practice reduced the prison population by more than 10%. Zimring and Hawkins (1991) imply that these numbers would be even higher if informal early-release policies such as enhanced good time credits and accelerated parole board hearings are taken into consideration. This was a paradoxical situation because early release of prisoners hardly fits into the get-tough and war-on-crime atmosphere of the 1980s and 1990s.

Correctional Cost

Closely connected with the issue of overcrowding is the problem of correctional cost. Correctional expenditures also were rising rapidly. Calculating correctional cost is a complex matter. The total estimate includes (a) operating and capital costs, which are direct costs, and (b) indirect costs such as services provided for correctional purposes by government organizations other than the Department of

TABLE 1.2 Operational and Construction Costs of Prisons

Average operating expenditure (1989-1990)[a]	
Federal prison	$14,456
State prison	$15,604
Development cost, building of new prisons per bed (1988)[b]	
Maximum-security state prison	$71,000
Medium-security state prison	$53,000
Minimum-security state prison	$30,000

SOURCES: a. Bureau of Justice Statistics (1992).
b. Bureau of Justice Statistics (1988).

Corrections, such as public assistance to prisoners' families, litigation, and so on (McDonald, 1989). Estimates from the late 1980s of the annual operational cost per adult inmate and building costs are presented in Table 1.2.

The operational cost varied widely among states. It was highest in Alaska at $39,822 per inmate per year, and the lowest was in Mississippi at $8,501 per inmate in 1985 (McDonald, 1989, p. 17). Operating costs nationwide increased 470% between 1971 and 1985. Since 1985, correctional expenditures have continued to rise because of the substantial growth of the number of inmates and due to inflationary trends in the economy. Correctional expenses between 1971 and 1985 rose faster than any other category of government spending. The average state and local government spending rose at an average annual rate of 10.1% during the above period, but corrections costs grew 14.9% on the average each year; thus the corrections cost increased almost 50% faster than other government costs (McDonald, 1989). In 1984 the state and local governments' expenditure on correctional institutions was $5.9 billion; it increased in 1986 to $6.7 billion; by 1988 the cost of state and local correctional institutions had reached $15.3 billion; and by 1990 it was $20.0 billion. Thus the states' costs of institutional corrections increased between 1984 and 1990 by 237.4% (Flanagan & Maguire, 1990, 1992; Jamieson & Flanagan, 1989).[5]

Although correctional costs were still climbing in the early 1990s, government budgets for other services, due to a severe economic recession, were cut. Thus a paradoxical situation has evolved in which there were major reductions in public education, child care, welfare, health care, and other human services, but the budget for prisons was expanding. However, the resources devoted for corrections are not limitless. Taxpayers, officials, and politicians have demanded an increasingly get-tough approach to crime and punishment resulting in longer periods of incarceration for a growing number of offenses affecting more and more offenders, but they are less ready to accept the ever heavier financial burdens of these policies. Serious concerns about the spiraling cost of corrections have been heard. Bond initiatives for prison construction failed to pass in several states in the early 1990s (e.g., in New York, Michigan, Oregon, and California). In some other states, these kinds of initiatives and legislations have passed only by a low margin. As King and Maguire (1994) put it pointedly, "the willingness to increase public expenditure on prisons does not match the demand for punishment" (p. 2).[6]

Ironically, the very same political leaders and their supporters who are the most vocal in their demands for law and order and for getting tough on criminals tend to be fiscally the most conservative.[7] They fight against big government and call for fiscal responsibility, a demand that usually focuses on the reduction of government spending. Often contradictory criminal justice policies emerge as a result of this configuration. For example, in California during the 1980s, under Governor Deukmejian—a conservative politician who made his political career to a large degree on criminal justice issues, especially his fight for the death penalty—large numbers of misdemeanants were continuously released early from detention because of the overcrowding in jails and other fiscal problems. Historically, it seems that when there are widespread public concerns about rising crime rates and ever increasing prison populations and correctional costs, the search for alternative solutions becomes apparent. One of the attractive alternatives is the idea of the establishment of private prisons, mainly to curb public expenditures and to increase prison capacity.

Prison Privatization

In the search to find answers to the problems of rapidly growing cost and overcrowding, there has been an increasing interest in the privatization of corrections since the mid-1970s. A study, commissioned by the National Institute of Corrections, indicated that in the early 1980s, 38 states in the United States had some kind of contract with private companies for the supply of various services such as medical care, food preparation, educational programs, and so on (Camp & Camp, 1984).

Since the beginning of the 1980s, private for-profit corporations started to operate entire prisons. Although many juvenile correctional facilities and community-based programs are operated by the private sector (see, e.g., Krisberg et al., 1992; Shichor & Bartollas, 1990), only a few adult jails and prisons are managed currently by private corporations. In the mid-1980s, at least one state, Tennessee, seriously considered the transfer of the management of the whole state correctional system to a private corporation, an attempt that did not come to fruition. At a 1991 census of private corrections facilities, 44 facilities were operated by 14 companies, housing about 13,400 inmates (Thomas & Foard, 1991).

Currently, there are various kinds of arrangements for the operation of correctional facilities besides the usual government-operated institutions. There are facilities operated by not-for-profit organizations mainly for juveniles and by for-profit corporations, and lately there are cases in which county and municipal agencies (sheriff's departments, cities, and police departments) contract with the state to run correctional facilities for profit. Privately operated institutions that are managed by for-profit corporations were referred to as "proprietary prisons" (Logan, 1987), and facilities operated by municipal governments were referred to recently as "public proprietary" institutions (Sechrest & Shichor, 1993a, 1993b).

Major Forms of Private Involvement in Prisons

According to Sevick (1987), private involvement with adult correctional institutions can appear in three major forms. First, *private financing and construction of prisons* is being sought because in many states there are debt limits on the government and a need for voters' approval of any new bond issues to finance prison building. This procedure is time consuming, and the outcome of the voting is not always predictable. Obtaining private financing for the construction of facilities is faster and simpler than securing funds through public channels. To address the problems of overcrowding, efficient financing is essential. Private companies can finance and build entire prisons in the matter of a few months, whereas it may take years for the government to complete a building (Logan, 1990). Second, *private industry involvement in prisons* has a long tradition in American corrections. There is a renewed interest in bringing private industries into the prison (e.g., Burger, 1983). Many privatization proponents believe that the private sector could teach inmates needed skills for their reintegration into the community after release; that inmates would learn work habits and discipline that many of them are lacking and "from their salaries, pay taxes, room and board, restitution to victims and support for their families" (Sevick, 1987, p. 3). Thus, besides having a certain degree of educational and rehabilitative effects, private involvement also would lighten the public's financial burden of paying for corrections. Third, *the management and operation of a whole correctional facility by a private contractor* is the most controversial area of privatization, although it is common in juvenile corrections and community-based programs (e.g., halfway houses, drug rehabilitation centers, and various diversion programs).

An additional area of privatization of prisons exists: the rendering of various services to the prisons by private contractors. This is the traditional and most widespread form of modern privatization, but it is limited to the supply of specific goods and services, including meal, laundry, educational, medical, psychological, and similar services (Camp & Camp, 1984; Lilly & Knepper, 1991). Under this kind of arrangement, government authorities do maintain full control over the management of the prison. As mentioned, the focus of the present work is the private operation of prisons.

The Suggested Advantages of Privatization

Among the arguments for all forms of correctional privatization are the claims that privatization would increase incarceration capacity because more facilities would be built at a faster pace, would bring more innovations into the correctional system, would respond better to correctional needs (flexibility) by cutting red tape, would attract better quality workers than the public system does because they would be younger and more enthusiastic than public employees are, and all these would cost less than it does currently. Greenwood (1981) declared in this vein that there is a need for new approaches and innovations in order to address the major problems of the correctional system and to clear up the mess of the current system. He asserted that "when you're looking for innovators you don't look to government; you look to business" and underscored this contention by claiming that "there are no incentives for the government to control costs or do things better. And, under government personnel practices, there are few incentives for any but the least able people to make a career of correctional work. So it is time to get government out of the prison business" (Greenwood, 1981, p. 7).

An argument was forwarded by Mitchell (1978), who criticized the expansiveness of the correctional system, the high cost of its personnel, and the lack of attractiveness of this system for innovative professionals who can introduce new and creative ways to handle correctional problems. He concluded that if we want better and more efficient prisons, we have to establish private, profit-making institutions—talented people are drawn toward profitable projects.

Following this argument, Logan and Rausch (1985), relying on Drucker's (1973) thesis, suggest that public service organizations are inefficient and ineffective because of the way they are financed. The claim is that the public and private sectors are operating on different principles. The private sector is competitively motivated, thus in a free market system, it is dedicated to provide maximum satisfaction to its customers and clients at a minimum cost. On the other hand, the public sector being monopolistic does not have a similar motivation; bureaucrats are rewarded not according to the performance of their organization but according to the size and the budget of their agencies, thus they are more interested in "empire building" than in increasing their efficiency (Logan, 1990; Logan & Rausch, 1985; Poole, 1983). The conclusion is that

> bureaucratic organizations increase in size and budgetary resources on the basis of promises, intentions, and efforts, not strictly on results. Because they depend for support on their ability to appeal to a broad constituency, they must be all things to all people and alienate no one.

This compromises their effectiveness because they cannot concentrate their efforts successfully. (Logan, 1990, p. 84)

According to Savas (1985), the major difference boils down more to the issue of monopoly versus competition, rather than public versus private. When private companies hold monopolies, they also lose their efficiency and flexibility, like in the cost of public utilities.[8]

It is also claimed that it is harder for government agencies to scale their activities to the needs of their service areas because of the varying sizes of these areas. For example, most counties in the United States have their own sheriff's departments and operate their own county jails. The start-up cost and the initial overhead of a jail may be proportionately much higher per inmate for smaller counties than for larger ones because of the smaller inmate population being served. According to proponents of privatization, private corporations having centralized headquarters can provide administrative services for a lower cost without the duplication of personnel and equipment. These factors are counted as supporting evidence for privatization, demonstrating that the private sector can save money for the taxpayers. These claims will be reviewed in more detail when various aspects of the comparison between public and private sectors are analyzed. Here they are mentioned only as arguments for the interest in prison privatization.

Conclusion

Various factors have contributed to the revival of interest in the privatization of prisons during the 1980s and early 1990s. First and foremost, the tremendous growth of the prison population and the concomitant steep increase in correctional costs, due largely to the changing sociopolitical atmosphere, led to the rethinking of correctional policies. Also, the Western, especially American, historical and cultural perspectives that value private enterprise, the free market system, laissez-faire economics, minimal state interference in the economy, and the generally negative approach toward the public sector have contributed to this trend.

There are several issues that have to be taken into consideration when prison privatization is being considered and debated. Some of these are directly related to conceptual aspects of punishment and incarceration; others deal with legal, economic, organizational, and other problems of this subject. The future of private prisons is not clear. We do not know whether it will become a viable alternative to government-run prisons or remain a small segment of the correctional system as it is today, or if it will be only a temporary phenomenon. Nevertheless, it merits a systematic overview and analysis.

Notes

1. Historically, in the United States many public services were provided by the private sector. For example, in education, schools on all levels (elementary, secondary, and university) were private. They became publicly funded only in the mid-19th century. Currently, most hospitals and nursing homes are operating under voluntary or for-profit arrangements.

2. For example, the Japanese economic system has many features similar to the mercantilist policies. This contributes to a large degree to the continuous friction between the United States and Japan in trade violations.

3. Irwin and Austin (1994) have referred to this rapid and massive increase in imprisonment as "America's imprisonment binge."

4. These situations sometimes led to strange developments. For example, the sheriff of Orange County, California was caught in a situation in which whatever action he took, he violated a court order. Municipal court judges tried to hold the sheriff in contempt of court because he released some inmates early from jail; however, the contempt order was thrown out by a superior court judge. The same judge cited a federal court order requiring improvement of conditions, including minimizing overcrowding at the jail (Avila, 1992).

5. It is often stated semijokingly that it costs more to keep an offender in prison than to educate a student at a prestigious university.

6. The toughness-on-crime trend continues and the 1994 crime bills, including the "three strikes you're out" statute, will increase the prison population even more, costing additional billions of dollars. It is very likely that large portions of the monies to cover these expenditures will come from the reduction of various social programs.

7. Donahue (1989) quotes 1985 surveys from Kentucky, Florida, and New Mexico in which the majority of respondents were asking for stiff sentences, but only a relatively small percentage of them supported a higher level of spending for the strained prison systems.

8. This argument did not convince many conservatives in 1992, including President Bush, who tried to veto the bill that would regulate the monopolistic cable TV industry. That was the first time during the Bush presidency that the veto was overridden.

2

A Historical Review of Private Prisons

To understand the current debates about privatization of prisons, a short historical review of private prisons is presented.

Private nongovernmental involvement in various facets of criminal justice has precedents in Western and especially English-American tradition. In England during the Middle Ages, criminal prosecution was often initiated by private parties hiring private prosecutors. This practice was based on the idea that the best way to bring criminals to justice is by leaving the prosecution in the hands of the victims (Cardenas, 1986, p. 359). The use of private prosecution was also, in part, a sign of the limit to the power of the crown. The right to start criminal proceedings privately by the victims remained in effect until the 19th century. This practice also was used in the American colonies (Gittler, 1984). Many victims during the colonial and early post-Revolutionary War period settled with offenders directly if they were ready to pay restitution. One reason for this practice was logistic: Because the courts were located mainly in colonial capitol cities, it was a problem to travel from remote rural communities under poor road conditions losing several days of work to settle legal cases. Also, many citizens preferred to receive restitution from the offenders rather than having them fined by the courts because the fines would be paid to the government.

In the colonies, crime was seen primarily as an offense against individual victims, and not against society; therefore, often it was not the government's duty to pursue, apprehend, and prosecute offenders (Cardenas, 1986). Before the Revolution, the victim was a major decisionmaker in criminal justice proceedings. The enforcement of laws rested to a large degree with private citizens. Even if assistance was provided by the authorities to apprehend offenders, often victims had to pay for the services of sheriffs, attorneys, and prosecutors. In colonial America, crime was not considered to be a critical problem demanding major societal efforts of control and prevention (Rothman, 1971). Because of that, victims were mainly on their own if they wanted to apprehend, arrest, and prosecute the offender, and if it cost money, they had to pay for all these services (McDonald, 1977).

Private Involvement in Europe

Historical precedents of private involvement in criminal justice in Europe often influenced the colonies. In England, as in America, many of the criminal justice functions were handled by the victims. As the realization of the financial burden for victims became clear, an act was passed in 1752 in England, mainly to control crime in London that was giving power to the courts to order the county to pay the prosecutors. The cost was paid only in the case of felony convictions, to discourage prosecutors from pursuing frivolous cases (Beattie, 1986). Before the 18th century, jails in Western European countries were primarily holding places for pretrial detention. Defendants often spent several months in detention until their cases were completed. Living conditions in these jails were usually dismal. For instance, in England during the 16th, 17th, and 18th centuries, there were a few hundred jails that were in theory the king's prisons but were run by different entities. Usually, these facilities were not housed in separate buildings; some were located in castles, others in court facilities, market houses, or other public buildings (Webb & Webb, 1963). They were often operated by private citizens.

Jails

In England, jails (gaols) operated by private entrepreneurs date back to the Middle Ages. County sheriffs were responsible for guarding felony suspects. In fact, prisons were known during the Anglo-Saxon period before the Norman conquest of 1066. These were places that were used not merely for custody but also for punishment (Pugh, 1968).

The private involvement in gaols in medieval England is described by Pugh (1968):

> In some places in the thirteenth century sheriffs hired working gaolers and threw the costs upon the Exchequer, and in the same period the crown sometimes relieved itself of such expenses, together with the costs of maintenance, by requiring a subject to keep a gaol in return for land, or by selling the right to do so for cash. To a growing extent, however, . . . the crown, by-passing the sheriffs, bestowed gaolerships on minor royal servants as a substitute for pensioning them in any other way. This gave an impetus to the already existing system of allowing prison-keepers of all degrees and types, their deputies and servants, to make a living out of their prisoners by means of fees, lodging charges, and the same of drinks and victuals. That such a system was liable to much abuse crown, parliament, and municipal authorities knew well, but circumstances compelled its toleration and even those who saw its defects most keenly seldom did more than try to impose rules to keep the various charges within bounds. (p. 387)

Since the 14th century, there were efforts to set better standards for gaols and gaolers. However, because of the need in prison services, these standards were hardly ever enforced. The gaolers were making their living from fees extracted from the prisoners (Harding, Hines, Ireland, & Rawlings, 1985).

In 18th-century England, besides fees, the gaol keeper made money by providing special accommodations to those who could pay for them, sometimes even in his own private quarters. Most of the keeper's income came from selling beer, liquor, and tobacco to the inmates. Even visits by family members were usually arranged for pay. In addition to the fees allowed by the law, the lack of strict control by the authorities over the jail opened up a wide range of opportunities for the keeper to make more money. "The fact that he exercised uncontrollable power over his prisoners gave him practically unlimited opportunity for extortion" (Webb & Webb, 1963, p. 7).[1] Prisoners who could not afford the payments had to rely on charities and on county funds dedicated to the maintenance of convicted felons. Others who did not fit into this category, like debtors or misdemeanants, had to raise money by working, getting gifts, or even begging. The fees that the gaolers extracted from people in custody were not uniform and varied from gaol to gaol. Every activity in the gaol was done for a fee, including putting people in irons, taking the irons off, "first locking up," providing copies of court papers, various privileges, and even being discharged. Not only the keepers but also turnkeys (guards) charged for various services. Most prisoners were too poor to pay; in these cases the magistrates paid for the cost of incarceration, but these payments were well below the fees that the keepers could expect from the more well-to-do inmates (Ignatieff, 1978; Rusche & Kirchheimer, 1939; Webb & Webb, 1963). The differences in privileges and living conditions between inmates who could afford to pay the jailers and those who could not was great. The private profit-making nature of these jails was so clearly accepted and established that the office of being a jailer was subject to purchase and sale. Often, the administration of a gaol was a family business, and there were families who were involved in this occupation for generations (DeLacey, 1986). The actual and potential abuses stemming from differential handling of defendants according to their ability to pay the jailer became a point of criticism by reformers, and finally this system was abolished toward the end of the 18th century.

Dismayed by the conditions in the gaols of England, John Howard, the sheriff of Bedfordshire, traveled to the continent in 1775 to learn about the conditions of prisons and workhouses there. He found two institutions that impressed him greatly; one, the Maison de Force in Ghent, Belgium, was a workhouse. In this institution, there was an attempt to classify inmates and to separate them according to sex, age, and the type of offense. A work regime was established with the idea that through work people can be reformed. A strict, but not cruel, discipline was maintained. The other institution, the Hospice of San Michele in Rome run by the Roman Catholic Church, was designated to hold youthful offenders under the age of 20. The regime was monastic and although the inmates were working together strict silence was maintained in order not to contaminate their minds and divert them from repentance. The religious philosophy of expiation with its potential for repentance and rehabilitation impressed Howard. On his return from the continent, he published a pamphlet titled *State of the Prisons*. One of his recommendations was to abolish all fees in jails and pay the jailers a government salary rather than be paid by inmates or their families (Barnes & Teeters, 1959).

Workhouses

Other European forerunners of the modern prison, besides the gaols, were the workhouses or houses of correction. They spread over northwestern Europe beginning in the 16th century. The origins of these institutions started in England when, after the breakup of the feudal system, large numbers of disbanded soldiers and peasants, whose work was not needed anymore in rural areas because of the transformation from mainly agricultural production to wool production, remained without work and means of income. Many of these displaced people migrated to cities. This large migration also brought with it thousands of paupers, prostitutes, vagrants, and other undesirable elements that contributed to crime and the decline of public safety; the situation became so critical it had to be dealt with. As a response to the deteriorating conditions, the city of London established a workhouse in 1557 in an abandoned royal palace, Bridewell. The function of this establishment was to care for and discipline the increasing number of riffraff who were considered to be a danger to society (Barnes & Teeters, 1959). This segment of the population was the forerunner of the urban underclass, which was later referred to as the "dangerous classes." People sent to the workhouse were supposed to work in various assignments (spinning, baking, nail making, etc.) "in order to instill them with a desire for hard and honest toil" (Babington, 1971, p. 11). In 1576 Parliament passed an act providing for the establishment of "bridewells" in every county of England. One of the major differences between the gaols and the bridewells was that the latter, at least at the beginning, were controlled by the justices of the peace rather than by the sheriffs. According to McConville (1981), "Bridewell was an attempt to entrust imprisonment with reformatory and punitive objectives, which were to be secured by a closely regulated regime" (p. 22).

The workhouse concept spread to the European continent. In 1596 the Rasphouse (Rasphuis) was established in Amsterdam. This institution was set up originally for the confinement of vagrants who were uprooted by the war between the Spanish armies and the people of the Low Countries (Belgium and the Netherlands). Later, beggars and property offenders also were confined in the Rasphouse. Labor was a major component of the confinement. Soon after its opening, the main work in this institution became the production of dyes for the flourishing cloth industry in Holland. The dyes were produced by rasping hardwood logs into dust from which the dyes were extracted. The convict labor was done under the contract system with private entrepreneurs (Sellin, 1944, 1976). The inmate labor brought in enough money to offset the cost of incarceration and even "provided income for inmates whose production exceeded the cost of their confinement" (Durham, 1989, p. 110). In the 18th century, Villain established the earlier mentioned Maison de Force in Ghent, Belgium, and several workhouses were opened in Germany. The workhouses were tied into the growing textile industry in Western Europe. In many of them, there was private involvement in the management; for example, in England entrepreneurs contracted in many counties with the local authorities for the labor produced in the workhouse. Private entrepreneurs contracted for the preparation and spinning of wool; also brickmakers, candlemakers, iron traders, wood merchants, and mattress makers used workhouse labor. Ignatieff (1978) claims that although these contractors hardly made any profit because of the rapid turnover and low productivity of inmates, they learned quite a bit about the management of extensive division of labor. He goes so far as to state that "in many respects, these state institutions were the earliest prototypes of the factory" (Ignatieff, 1978, p. 32). In these cases the private involvement was limited to contracting of labor for industrial production. On the other hand, there was an effort to stay away from the profit-based financial system of the gaols, and there were strict regulations to be enforced by government inspections (McConville, 1981, p. 33).

Private Involvement in America

In the American colonies, generally, English criminal justice procedures were followed. However, government was decentralized, and
the administration of criminal justice was localized. Certain practices
had an American flavor to them. For example, private prosecution
was an accepted practice because of the fear of the tyrannical rule of
the English government; therefore there was an attempt to minimize
its reach into the everyday life of the community. More important,
this arrangement was considerably cheaper for the community than
using public prosecution. However, major changes were made in
prosecutional procedures during the 19th century. After the Declaration of Independence, with the growth of population and increased
urbanization, there was a constant growth in the volume and rate of
crime. With the increased complexity of everyday life, it became
harder for the victims to pursue, apprehend, and prosecute offenders.
This inefficiency led to demands for changes in this system (Cardenas,
1986). Also, government officials were interested in increasing their
authority in the criminal justice process because they were aware of
the developments in Europe, for example, the use of public prosecution in England.

Criminal justice in Europe at that time was influenced by the ideas
of the Enlightenment. Beccaria's (1819) work especially had a major
impact. He held that crime was not a private matter between the
victim and the offender but was a matter for the whole society. This
view was also adopted in America, and public prosecution became
the norm. Crime became a public issue handled as an offense against
the state by the officials of the state. In terms of legal sanctions,
whipping and fines were the norm in colonial America (Rothman,
1971). As in England, local jails were established; however, they were
used mainly for detention and only in rare occasions held convicted
offenders for confinement. In the jails there was no segregation
among various offenders. Women and children were held together
with violent criminals. Generally, the jails were grossly overcrowded,
there were bad sanitary conditions, and escapes were frequent. The
county paid the jailer (who often also served as the sheriff) according
to a system of fees, by submitting to the county government bills for

specific goods and services such as food, clothing, removing irons, and so on. In some jails the jailer sold meals and various privileges to the prisoners, who relied on family, friends, and charity for money. Corruption was widespread. Many jailers embezzled public funds, received bribes from prisoners, sold whiskey to prisoners, and physically abused them (Walker, 1980).

Penitentiaries

Toward the end of the 18th century, a new type of institution dealing with offenders, the penitentiary, was born in the United States. In this type of institution, offenders were locked up, not to wait for their trial; the incarceration itself became the punishment. The development of the penitentiary, according to many, was integrally related to rapid industrialization (see Cohen, 1985; Ignatieff, 1978; Melossi & Pavarini, 1981; Rusche & Kirchheimer, 1939).

The new prison or penitentiary carried in its very foundation the idea of repentance, penitence, and ultimately rehabilitation. The ideal was to change the beliefs and attitudes of the convicts through repentance and expiation, and it was assumed that a change in their behavior would follow. However, there were other purposes for the prisons such as deterrence and the protection of society from crime and criminals (Lewis, 1922/1967).

Two major systems of penitentiary emerged in America during the 19th century. In 1790 the Walnut Street Jail was opened in Philadelphia and became the model for the "Pennsylvania system." It incorporated some of the principles that were recommended by John Howard in his report to the British Parliament. The program included solitary confinement of men convicted of felonies. Later, labor was introduced, partly to provide inmates with something to do and also for its assumed therapeutic effects: "Even if the criminal did not find it a relief from his sufferings, it nevertheless would be necessary to force him to it. It is idleness which led him to crime; with employment he will learn how to live honestly" (de Beaumont & de Tocqueville, 1833/1979, p. 56).

The ideology that led to the rise of the penitentiary and the early policies followed by this institution were influenced by William

Penn's Great Law that was introduced to the Quaker colony a century earlier. The Great Law eliminated the death penalty except in cases of premeditated murder. Violent crimes were punished by imprisonment at hard labor in the "house of corrections." Each county was required to establish a "sufficient house, at least twenty foot square, for restraint, correction, labor and punishment. . . . Thus, the Quakers sought to use imprisonment for the multiple purposes of incapacitation, rehabilitation, and punishment" (Walker, 1980, p. 34). It was not an accident that Pennsylvania became a center of correctional reform at the end of the 18th century and during the 19th century. Prisoners were not required to support themselves or pay fees for their upkeep (Chitwood, 1961). Hard labor was seen as a more effective and humane punishment than physical punishment because it was assumed to have a reforming value. This approach was influenced by the Protestant religious belief in hard and continuous work for the glory of God (Weber, 1958). Idleness was considered to be a sin; salvation could be achieved only by work. The Great Law was repealed in 1718 on the death of William Penn, and the British law was reinstituted in colonial Pennsylvania. However, this law's impact was felt in the punishment policies of America, especially in the emergence of the modern penitentiary and prison.

In the Walnut Street Jail, the solitary confinement wing was designated for corrections to allow convicted felons to spend all their time to think about the crimes they had committed and to repent. Later, some work, mainly spinning, was added to the program in the segregated cells to maintain the physical and mental health of inmates because a large number of them went insane in isolation without anything to do in their cells. The prisoners were credited with fair pay for their work and were debited for the cost of their upkeep. The wages paid were either equal to or somewhat lower than the pay outside the prison for similar work (Lewis, 1922/1967).

The penitentiary movement continued to expand. New York State adopted the penal principles of Pennsylvania. The Newgate prison was established in New York City at the end of 1797. Labor was an integral part of the system, but its main function was not only the reformation of inmates but also having their contribution to the operational cost of the penitentiary (Lewis, 1922/1967, p. 47). Inmates were charged for their clothes and maintenance and accounts were kept of the proceeds from their labor. Those who compiled a good record on their release were given a share of the profits they helped to earn (Lewis, 1965).

In 1819 another penitentiary was opened in Auburn, New York. This institution abandoned the idea of complete solitary confinement. The prisoners slept in separate cells, but at daytime they worked and ate together under a strict rule of silence. It became known as the "congregate system" or the "silent system." The main emphasis was on silence because it was believed that conversation among inmates would contaminate their minds and souls and would divert them from concentrating on repentance for their crimes. In contrast with the Pennsylvania (Walnut Street Jail) system, "instead of reflecting the Quaker doctrine of the 'inner light,' the Auburn system exemplified the Colonist belief in the depravity of men" (Lewis, 1965, p. 57).

To enforce the silent rule, "it was necessary for prison officials to devise elaborate techniques for constant surveillance and to make unsparing use of coercion and intimidation" (Lewis, 1965, p. 81). Violators of the silence rule were disciplined with whipping and other corporal punishments. Auburn soon became the leading model for prisons in America, and it had followers in Europe as well. For instance, the silent system was adopted in many prisons and workhouses in England (see Babington, 1971; Ignatieff, 1978). One of the major attractions of this system was that it lent itself to the introduction of modern industrial production into the prison. According to Melossi and Pavarini (1981), the Auburn penal theory "puts forward a model of labor subordinated on industrial lives. Where the silent system prevails, labor saving machines and communal work are introduced along with factory discipline" (p. 136).

Prison Labor

Because the modern prison was developed during a period of rapid industrial development in the Western world, it fit into the system of mass production. Almost from its inception, it opened the opportunity for various forms of private sector involvement in the organization of prison industry. Often, manufacturers contracted with the state for various kinds of industrial production; they supplied the raw material to the prison workshop, which delivered the finished product to the contractor. This arrangement is described in the following: "The contractor enters the prison, efficiently organizes production, industrializes the workshops, partially pays for work done, manufactures non-craft goods and personally handles the distribution of these goods on the free market" (Melossi & Pavarini, 1981, p. 136).

The Auburn penitentiary, according to 19th-century reports, was not only self-supporting economically but was even producing surplus revenue for the government (de Beaumont & de Tocqueville, 1833/1979). This prison produced a variety of goods such as footwear, clothing, carpets, barrels, harnesses, and furniture (Lewis, 1965). In Sing Sing, the famous New York prison that followed the Auburn model, convicts worked in the marble quarries. In other prisons they were involved in construction work outside the prison. Newgate in New York contracted out its shoe industry in 1802 for $1,200 per month; 179 prisoners worked in this industry. Later, the nail industry also was introduced on a contract basis (Gardner, 1987).

Wines and Dwight (1867) emphasized the importance of hard labor that was attached to imprisonment in the following:

> The element of hard labor in the sentence is the dictate at once of justice and policy: of justice, because it is right that criminals, who put the state to more or less expense, should do something towards defraying the public cost of their crimes; of policy, because work is an essential condition of the prisoner's reformation. (p. 248)

Thus one of the claims was that prison labor could train and familiarize inmates with work habits, discipline, and often useful skills (Johnson, 1988). This arrangement put the manufacturers in charge of the inmates during working hours. Later, it was gradually changed to the "piece price" system (payment according to the finished products), in which the physical control over the inmates remained in the hands of the public prison authorities, but the payment for the manufactured goods was made according to the level of production.

The Auburn system illustrated how private, for-profit interest could be infused into the penal system. Prisoners were used in industrial production because of the increasing need for a steady and reliable source of workers at a time of great industrial expansion. Prisoner labor was cheaper than that of free workers and was a predominantly young and physically strong workforce. Prisoners also provided a stable labor market without the fluctuations of supply and demand. When workers started to organize into labor unions and were fighting for minimum wages and better working conditions, prison labor became even more attractive for private enterprise.

In this context Rusche and Kirchheimer's (1939) comment merits consideration: "The transformation in penal systems cannot be explained only from changing of the war against crime, although this struggle does play a part. Every system of production tends to discover punishments which correspond to its productive relationships" (p. 5).[2]

Through time, a major change occurred in the function of prison work as a component of corrections. At the beginning, prison work was introduced for purposes of repentance and institutional discipline to control inmates, but later it became an important source of income for the state government. Conley (1980) points out that "prison industries were a central feature of penal development in the United States, and that production and profit were the cornerstones of penal policy" (p. 257). According to this perspective, administrative procedures, physical structures, disciplinary measures, and institutional programming all were driven by the profit motive of state officials and businessmen who were eager to use inmate labor and to make a profit. State officials were interested in these profits to cover the expenditures of the penal institutions, whereas businessmen were looking out for their own financial gain. This practice resembles the adage to "both eat your cake and have it" at the same time. The officials, and many others, believed that they could punish the offenders, protect the community from dangerous criminals, and deter potential offenders without carrying the financial burden for these benefits, or even making some extra profit for the state (see Lewis, 1922/1967). Prison labor was also seen as beneficial for the inmates because idleness and the lack of good work habits were presumed to be a major source of criminal behavior and an impediment for adjustment in society.

Politicians and officials could easily justify these policies that put prisoners to work and earned money for the state:

State legislators and wardens found these notions attractive and were eager to implement them. Secure in the knowledge that they were acting in the best interests of taxpayers and inmates alike, that they were simultaneously furthering financial and reformist goals, they had no objection to making some contracts with private manufacturers to lease convict labor or to establishing a prison routine of long hours with little relief. Hoping in this way to make the penitentiary a self-supporting, even profitable venture while rehabilitating the offender, they favored a schedule that maximized work. (Rothman, 1971, pp. 103-104)

Private entrepreneurs also liked this arrangement because this provided access to a large pool of workers with whom they did not have to deal directly. Although there was a turnover of individual prisoners, the supply of workers was steady. The direct supervision over the workers by prison officials was built into the business deal and production costs were lower than in regular factories.[3] The entrepreneurs made handsome profits on the contract work system (see McKelvey, 1936).

Similar practices were followed in several Western countries besides England, mentioned earlier. In Canada, for example, shortly after the opening of the Kingston penitentiary in 1835, inmates were either leased out to farmers, or their work was contracted to provide industry with cheap labor (Gandy & Hurl, 1987). There was private involvement in forced labor in the Dutch prisons during the 19th century. It was under constant criticism "because of the alleged unfair competition with the free market" (Diederiks, 1992, p. 35). In 1886 this practice was discontinued. Also, France adopted the contract system, which was referred to as the "enterprise." This was a private arrangement, not only for contracting industrial production but also for the management of the entire prison (O'Brien, 1982). It was similar to the American lease system (Wines & Dwight, 1867).

There were several ways that arrangements could be made with an entrepreneur in France. One of these was the leasing of workshops set up on prison premises under the entrepreneur's supervision. When an entrepreneur became the manager of the entire prison, he became responsible for all the day-to-day operations, including discipline, labor, production, and procurement of all supplies needed. He was paid according to the number of inmates in the institution and the number of days of imprisonment. The quality of care of prisoners, such as food, clothing, health, and living conditions, were only infrequently monitored and controlled by state officials. This state of affairs provided ample opportunities for neglect and abuse. The entrepreneur made his profit on the discounted price of prison labor. The system was open for corruption; often state officials were paid off and received a part of the profit from the entrepreneur, who also made money by having a contract to supply the prison with goods (O'Brien, 1982). He also ran the prison store (canteen), and the proceeds from this business recouped the money that he paid the prisoners in wages. Various European reports (for instance, from Germany) indicated that many private entrepreneurs bought the cheapest food and cut the inmates rations to the minimum (Rusche & Kirchheimer, 1939).

Families of entrepreneurs were involved in this business for generations. Many of them amassed a sizable fortune in the "prison business." Some cited philanthropic reasons for their pursuance of this line of work, but these claims are questionable in light of the large profits they pocketed from prison labor. Under the lease arrangement, guards were also supervised by the entrepreneur. Even the disciplinary system was under his control. The goals of prison labor were to make punishment cheap for the state and profit making for the contractor and not the rehabilitation of offenders. There was no attempt to train prisoners in occupational skills that they could use on their release.

In France there were plans to change the common living arrangement of the prisons to single-cell systems for the night. Common workshops and living quarters were cheaper for the contractor (e.g., it was more economical for lighting and heating purposes). The alteration was supposed to be financed and implemented by the local administration; therefore these conversions usually were not carried out. Private entrepreneurs were outsiders to the correctional system, but by virtue of their control over inmate work and the financial power they derived from it, they exercised a major influence over the prisons and their administration. de Beaumont and de Tocqueville (1833/1979) emphasized the great influence of private contractors in the French system. These authors expressed a negative view of the private contractor who, according to their opinion, regards "the convict as a laboring machine, thinks only how he can use him to the greatest advantage for himself. . . . The extent of his privileges, more-over, gives him an importance in the prison, which he ought not to have" (p. 68). Finally, to retain control over the prisons, the authori-ties recognized the necessity of replacing the enterprise with state-directed production and did so toward the end of the 19th century (O'Brien, 1982).

As seen, the private for-profit involvement in corrections was a well-known practice in 19th-century America. There were several prisons in the Pennsylvania and Auburn systems, at the beginning of the 19th century, in which private contractors were in charge of vari-ous services, including prison labor. de Beaumont and de Tocqueville (1833/1979) were more favorable toward the American practice than the French one, where, to limit the influence of any individual entrepreneur, in several prisons each branch of the production was contracted out to a different contractor. According to these French authors, the American contractors were not given any formal say in the policies and implementation of prison discipline. They could interact with prisoners only to instruct them on their jobs and only in the presence of guards; therefore the contractors did not have a direct authority over labor. However, this situation started to change for several reasons. The contractors were ready to pay only low prices for the products. The guards were supposed to instruct the prisoners in their work, but it was hard to find guards who knew the trades as well. Thus the prison system, which was interested in making higher profits, had to provide increasingly more access for the contractors to communicate with and instruct prisoners. This was done amid concerns for the maintenance of strict prison discipline.

de Beaumont and de Tocqueville (1833/1979) were impressed with the prisoners' orderly work and quality in the American prisons. In contrast with the continent, prisoners in America did not receive any remuneration for their work. In spite of their generally positive impression, however, these authors deemed this system excessively severe; they believed that some earnings for inmates would provide positive reinforcement and also would have a positive effect on their community readjustment after release. However, they found one practice that they looked on favorably, that of Baltimore, where prisoners, after finishing their fixed task at work, could work for themselves for wages. At first, they could spend their earnings in the prison, an arrangement that increased their motivation to work, but this proved to be detrimental for the discipline in the institution; therefore, later, the money was accumulated and given to them on their release.

The contract system spread all over the country. According to Knepper's (1991b) historical analysis, "virtually every state relied on convict labor at some point" (p. 16). Following this practice, private contractors employed prisoners inside or outside the prison walls in the different states (Conley, 1980; Houghen, 1977; Keve, 1991). In the contract system, in which the contractor often assumed direct supervision of the inmates inside the prison, sometimes the contractor's supervisors "added to their petty graft by 'short-changing' the inmate in his work tally" (Barnes & Teeters, 1959, p. 527). The piece-price system, a variant of the contract system, was somewhat of an improvement in this respect because the prison provided its own supervisors, but there were many instances in which these officials were involved in corrupt practices to make money for themselves.

The Lease System

The lease system also became widely used in America during the 19th century. In this arrangement, private contractors took over complete control of the institution, including maintenance and the discipline of the prisoners. This system was adopted mainly in the expanding frontier areas because these were under pressure to develop their economic and institutional framework and were ready to shift prison operation, burdened by an increasing inmate population, to private contractors. The first lease arrangement in America is traced to the Frankfort, Kentucky state prison, which was not able to make money on convict labor and cost the state money at a time when the state was having a serious financial crisis (Knepper, 1991a). In 1825 a businessman, Joel Scott, offered $1,000 per year for the work of convicts in that facility, which would run under his management for 5 years. The authorities accepted the offer and were glad that the maintenance of the prison was taken off their hands and that they could even make some profit in this arrangement. Scott, realizing the need for discipline and security, built a 250-cell prison that followed the Auburn model (Sneed, 1860).

In some states, besides working in the prison itself, some inmates were leased by the prison authorities to work outside the penitentiary. In Missouri, for example, prisoners mainly built houses in surrounding communities. These convicts were compelled to work very hard, were treated brutally, and many of them escaped even though they were guarded by prison staff (Ayers, 1984; Sellin, 1976). Louisiana completed its first state penitentiary in Baton Rouge in 1835. The prisoners were put to work to manufacture cotton, leather, and woolen products. The operation was not self-supporting during a major economic depression in the state; therefore in 1844 the state leased out the penitentiary for 5 years to a private company for $50,000 per year (Carleton, 1971). Alabama did the same in 1846 because the prison became costly for the state. In this case, there was a strong opposition to this practice, "which undermined a fundamental principle of a republican institution: the restoration of the prisoner's sense of obligation to a just society" (Ayers, 1984, p. 68). There was a concern that the lessee will try to lengthen the sentences of good workers by giving bad reports about them and "would naturally spend as little and extract as much as possible" (p. 68). Texas built its prison as a textile factory and made considerable profits from its penitentiary (Ayers, 1984). There were other states that resisted the lure of profit that could have been made from leasing the prison to private contractors.

After the Civil War, there was a renewed impetus, especially in the Southern states, to expand the practice of leasing. The major reasons for this trend were socioeconomic: (a) the tremendous burden of the war and the devastation following the defeat of the Confederacy, which necessitated a major effort for the fast rebuilding of the economy, and (b) the abolition of slavery, which seriously affected the plantation system of the Old South by depleting its cheap labor force, prompting the search for a replacement of the slaves for its labor-intensive economy.

Right after the war, there was a great increase in the number of offenders who were sentenced to prison. A large percentage of them were blacks, who previously were handled at the plantations for their infractions. Now they became a burden on the state (Carleton, 1971). Describing the situation in the South after the Civil War, Sellin (1976) paralleled the ways that convicts were treated to slavery:

> Burdened with heavy taxes to meet the expenses of rebuilding the
> shattered economy, and committed to the traditional notion that
> convicts should, by their labor, reimburse the government for their
> maintenance and even create additional revenue, the master class,
> drawing on its past experience with penitentiary leases, reintroduced a
> system of penal servitude which would make public slaves of black and
> poor and friendless white convicts. (p. 145)

In the South, the leasing of convict labor became an important
economic and social arrangement during the Reconstruction period.
At first the leasing was initiated by army commanders mainly because
state penitentiaries were destroyed during the war and there was a
need to maintain control.

From the early 1870s, convict leasing became profitable when the
Southern states started to attract large-scale investments to exploit
their natural resources; the availability of cheap labor was a part of
this economic attraction. The fact that this arrangement almost exclusively involved blacks was an added benefit in the eyes of the
general public. By the mid-1880s, the development of this system
reached its peak. This was propelled by an increase of the convict
population after several Southern states (e.g., Georgia, Mississippi)
raised the stealing of relatively small items and amounts to felony
crimes (Novak, 1978). The convicts were exposed to worse conditions
than they were during slavery, and many of them died. For example,
in South Carolina the death rate of convicts leased to the railroads
was 45% in 1877 to 1879, in Arkansas it was 25%, and in Mississippi,
16% (Novak, 1978). The contractors hired a certain number of convicts, not individuals; thus, if a convict was released, he was automatically replaced by another one. This practice started to decline
beginning in 1893 when, due to a major depression, state authorities
had a hard time finding private contractors to lease the convicts.

The extensive use of the lease system served, at least primarily, as
a replacement for slave labor that was abolished after the Civil War
(Adamson, 1983). The Southern convict lease system after the war
appeared as a derivative of antebellum slavery, and a functional
replacement of it, but was "lacking its ameliorative features," that is,
the personal bond of master-slave relationship disappeared, and only
the economic exploitation and social distance between whites and
blacks remained (Sellin, 1976, p. 146). Most Southern states, even

those that did not have a strong tradition of slavery before the war, introduced the convict lease system.

There was also an important development regarding the lessees. In the antebellum period, private contractors in the Northern states were, in most cases, individual entrepreneurs. However, in the South after the war, industrial companies—many from the North—such as railroad and mining companies, leased convicts as well (Adamson, 1983; Ayers, 1984; Sellin, 1976). This is in addition to the plantations, which also leased prison labor.

According to Ayers (1984), "the penitentiary had become a Southern institution" (p. 188). In Tennessee, under the pressure of free tradesmen, the legislation rejected attempts to introduce the lease system in the antebellum period. However, the changing social and economic conditions after the Civil War presented a new reality. The state was heavily in debt; therefore, "leasing the labor of convicts to private parties was an attractive solution to the prison problem because it clearly was less expensive than refurbishing the old prison or building additional facilities. It even offered the tantalizing possibility of profit" (Cody & Bennett, 1987, pp. 831-832).

Prison authorities signed a contract in 1866 with a Nashville furniture company, leasing out prison labor. However, in 1867 there was a fire in one of the workshops, the lessee stopped making payments, and a long legal battle ensued. After years of litigation, there was a favorable ruling for the state by the state supreme court. This case alerted the authorities to the need for tighter control over the lease and the lessee's activities. Subsequently, Tennessee leased its prison labor to private companies on an economically profitable basis. Nevertheless, there was mounting criticism of this practice from free labor because of unfair competition, from citizens because of large numbers of escapes, and from some politicians because they felt that this practice was morally wrong. For example, three governors during the 1870s and 1880s expressed a negative opinion of the convict lease system but realized that the abolition of this practice would create a severe financial burden on the state, and therefore they continued, albeit reluctantly, this policy (Cody & Bennett, 1987).

As mentioned, Texas was another state that experimented with private involvement in corrections. In 1866 when the state had financial difficulties in maintaining its increasing inmate population, officials decided to hire out convicts for labor to private parties (Ethridge & Marquart, 1993). This practice was terminated in 1867 because

> the state discovered it could not easily guarantee that its provisions for the welfare and safekeeping of its prisoners would be faithfully adhered to by private parties who employed prisoners for private gain. State supervision proved especially difficult when prison inmates were scattered in work camps far from the scrutiny of the officials responsible for them. (Walker, 1988, pp. 21-22)

In 1869 it was proposed that the whole prison in Huntsville be leased out to a private party because it was not well managed, was overcrowded, and its operating cost was considered to be too high. The stipulation was that the inmates had to work in the prison facility itself.

The first Texas prison lease was awarded in 1871 to a company headquartered in Galveston. One of the principals of this company, Nathan Patton, had been politically involved in the state government and had previous connections with the governor. Although, at first, official reports were favorable toward the private management, there were also accounts of mistreatment, abuse, overworking (even on Sundays), malnourishment, and lack of health care for the inmates (Walker, 1988). When these horror stories were confirmed, including 382 escapes and 62 inmate deaths in 1876 (Martin & Ekland-Olson, 1987), the state reassumed a certain degree of control over the operation of the prison, for example, control over the hiring and work performance of the guards, food services, and health care (Rothman, 1980). However, the private contractor remained in charge of the prison in spite of these changes. Prison deaths remained unusually high, and there were indications that the brutal treatment of prisoners continued. In 1883 the state assumed responsibility for the prison system, but continued to contract with private contractors for convict labor (Martin & Ekland-Olson, 1987). The involvement of private contractors in the system in Texas ended in 1912, after a law was passed in 1910 to end leasing, partially as a result of pressures from agrarian elements and urban workers who saw it as an unfair competition in the labor market, but mainly from "civilian-minded activists from voluntary associations" in the growing urban centers (Walker, 1988, p. 195). This was in line with the emerging social philosophy of the Progressive Era, which sought to abolish the lease system primarily on humanitarian grounds.

There were also instances in which the initiative to cease leasing came from the private contractors themselves. For example, in 1893 an economic depression forced the entrepreneur contracting with Wisconsin's prison system to close up shop and to fire convict laborers. The state was caught unprepared to step in because it had become dependent on private contractors. It took about a decade to implement a new system of prison labor in that state (Durham, 1989).

Another historical example of 19th-century privatization of prisons in America, the California experience, is explored. It is presented in more detail reflecting on some of the major issues that may have relevance to the contemporary debate on prison privatization.

California gained statehood in 1850 in the midst of the Gold Rush. The new state experienced a rapid population growth. In the first decade of statehood, the population quadrupled. A large majority of the population were single males, many of them adventurers without strong roots in the community. They came to California with high hopes of becoming rich fast, but most of them remained with unfulfilled expectations. They were followed by a large number of people trying to make a living off the more successful explorers. The followers included professional gamblers, petty thieves, prostitutes, peddlers, con artists, paupers, and many others with questionable backgrounds and motives. Crime increased dramatically. For example, in 1854 the total number of known murders in the United States was 682; of these 64 (9.4%) occurred in California. Only New York (with 74 murders) exceeded California, which led the nation in the number of executions (15, or 17.8% of the total). At that time California's population was only 1% of the total U.S. population. There was a general lack of public confidence in the criminal justice system, which brought sporadic outbursts of vigilante activity, especially in San Francisco, the largest city in the state (Pomeroy, 1953).[4]

In this situation the establishment of a prison became a relevant public issue. California had to organize its government without substantial federal support in the midst of the Gold Rush. Many of the gold seekers were transients and, although great amounts of money passed through their hands, they were not easily taxable. There was a chronic budget deficit, and the government was on the brink of bankruptcy. As early as 1850 there was a proposal for the establishment of a private prison, which seemed very attractive to the state government. In 1851 the state leased its prison for 10 years to two private entrepreneurs. One of them, James E. Estell, was a member of the legislature and was considered to be one of the most powerful people in California, the other was Mariano Guadalupe Vallejo, a rich and politically influential landowner.

The state convict population was growing rapidly, from 35 at the signing of the contract to over 600 by the end of the decade. At first, a lack of adequate buildings and personnel contributed to a large number of escapes, which in turn prompted the rise of a vigilance committee in San Francisco. Later, a permanent prison was built at San Quentin on land that was owned by Vallejo amid strong controversy over political corruption and budget overruns. Estell, using his influence, gave a major share of the construction contract to his business partners through bid rigging, which was later annulled in the wake of a public outcry (McAfee, 1987). Because of budget constraints, the private management of the prison was not effectively supervised. Politics was mixing with business, and the situation was constantly worsening. For example, Estell employed Governor John McDougal as a prison guard on his retirement from office (Lamott, 1961).[5] The number of escapes was growing because prisoners were not well guarded on their way to work when they were hired out by contractors for profit. There was also a corrupt trusty system. Prisoner trusties were keeping the records, issued guns, and were strolling and drinking in the streets of San Francisco (National Center on Institutions and Alternatives, 1987). The quality of guards also was a major problem. Many of them became drinking partners of the prisoners and used female inmates as prostitutes (McKanna, 1987). The guards blamed their low morale on the fact that they were never paid on time.

There were increasing calls from the public and in the legislature for the removal of the lessees and the annulment of the contract amid persisting rumors of corruption, such as that Estell was selling pardons for $200. In 1857 the new governor, John B. Weller, a political foe of Estell, with the legislature's approval, personally took control of San Quentin in the presence of reporters. This was a popular move as the public was weary of the continuous scandals of the private prison. The governor was using this occasion for publicity because he was preparing to run for the U.S. Senate. However, there were legal problems with this action because the private contract was still in effect. A long process of litigation ensued, which ended with the California Supreme Court's ruling that the takeover of the prison was illegal. The prison was returned to private management. Estell died shortly after this incident in May 1857, and John F. McCauley and Lloyd Tevis took control of San Quentin as assignees of Estell's lease. McCauley was in charge of the prison, and by all accounts, he was even more opportunistic than Estell had been. In 1859 the state sued to regain control over the prison, alleging that

> McCauley ignored his charge both to treat prisoners humanely and to harbor them securely. Instead, by neglecting to clothe prisoners properly, by feeding them "unwholesome and insufficient food," and by refusing to improve their quarters, McCauley created a "state of dissatisfaction" so great that many prisoners "risked their lives in desperate attempts to escape." (Bookspan, 1991, p. 16)

In 1860 Chief Justice Stephen Field, in answering the claim—often heard nowadays—that the state's police and prison operation cannot be delegated to private parties, declared that the only constitutional restriction on the delegation of prison management is related to the issue of cruel and unusual punishment. He did not see the case at hand relevant to this issue. The state lost the legal battle. In 1860 a final settlement was achieved between California and the lessee, who received $275,000 compensation, a substantial amount of money at that time, and the prison was returned to state management. Governor John Downey stated after the settlement: "I would most seriously object ever again to allow the prison or its management to pass out of the exclusive control of the State" (California Senate Journal, twelfth session, 1861, p. 33). Many of the issues that emerged in the historical experience of California's private prison have a relevance to the contemporary scene in the United States (see McAfee & Shichor, 1990).

There are reports from other states of scandals and corruption connected to private involvement in prisons that raise serious questions about the ethical aspects of the lease system (Gilbert, 1992). For example, in the 1870s the lessee of the Kentucky penitentiary, Jeremiah Scott, who was considered to be one of the most influential persons in the state, was providing legislators with "cheap boarding" and "free drinks" (Kentucky Corrections Cabinet, 1985, p. 3). In 1882 the working conditions were so bad under the lessee that 25 convicts died in a camp. Convicts were forced to work in waist-deep water in winter, some were killed in cave-ins, and beatings were the "mainstay of discipline." The legislature's investigating committee recommended to abolish the contract leasing system, but the recommendation was not followed (Kentucky Corrections Cabinet, 1985, p. 5).

In the United States, private involvement in prison operation remained in effect until the early part of the 20th century although the convict lease system started to be phased out earlier, toward the end of the 19th century. This practice was replaced in most Southern states with the state use system, in which the prisoners were working either on plantations to raise crops for the state, or in public works (e.g., road chain gangs). However, this change did not improve the prisoners' lot considerably (Walker, 1980).

The discontinuation of the convict lease system in 1923 was a great victory for the reformers of the Progressive Era, but it created a major financial problem for state governments because "the contractors had paid the states handsomely for inmate labor and at the same time spared them all administrative costs" (Rothman, 1980, p. 139). The contract system, in which private companies supplied materials, machines, and foremen and manufactured in the prison using inmate labor, continued. In this practice, there were opportunities for abuses and corruption as well. Often inmates had to work longer than usual hours, bribes were paid to guards to allow the contractors to put more pressure on the inmates for getting more work done, and so forth. This practice declined during the Great Depression when few states were ready to accept prison products from other states. All available jobs were needed for the masses of unemployed. The private contract system all but disappeared by 1940. From then on, almost all prison labor was done in the state use system, in which all production was earmarked for supplying the needs of state offices and agencies. A variant of this practice was the public works system, which took inmates out from the prison to work mainly on roads and railways

(Melossi & Pavarini, 1981; Sellin, 1976). These practices did not make prisons very humane either, but at least they eliminated one potentially abusive factor, namely, the exploitation of prisoners by private entrepreneurs or companies for the purpose of profit making.

Conclusion

It is hard to summarize the accumulated historical experience of correctional privatization because of its diversity, and this review is not intended to conduct a detailed evaluation of this experience. However, some general observations can be made regarding the historical antecedents of privatization of prisons.

One observation is that private prison management was especially feasible in countries having a Protestant religious and cultural tradition, although as seen, there were inroads of privatization in the French penal system as well (O'Brien, 1982). Several factors contributed to this development: (a) The Protestant ethic placed a very high, almost mystic value on work as a goal by itself—it was practically a religious devotion to the work ethic and a strong belief in the spiritual, therapeutic, and cleansing power of it; (b) simultaneously, there was a strong belief in fierce individualism and a basic mistrust of government that was seen as a constant menace to individual freedom and well-being; and (c) the strong cultural support for the free enterprise, laissez-faire economics, which also had deep roots in the Protestant tradition, led to the decentralization and the limitation of government functions. These factors, in turn, opened the door for the private sector to be involved in the discharge of government functions and services. In time the public sector came to be seen as inept and corrupt, whereas the private sector was regarded as efficient and effective. This approach was also amenable to absorb some of the social Darwinist philosophical premises that were fairly popular in some circles around the turn of the 20th century. Social Darwinism held, among other beliefs, that "the positive function of the state should be kept to the barest minimum" (Hofstadter, 1967, p. 7), leaving many public services in the hands of the private sector.

The historical experience also revealed some warning signs that should concern us today. These included, among others, (a) the potential for exploitation and mistreatment of inmates by contractors; (b) lack of effective government oversight; (c) corruption between officials, staff members, and private entrepreneurs; and (d) legal problems confirming state authority.

Notes

1. Rusche and Kirchheimer (1939) refer to an English source, according to which some jailers, to make sure that they would have a flow of inmates to secure their income, were paying judges annuities "in return for a promise to deliver all their prisoners" to their establishment (p. 225).

2. During the mercantile period, many convicted offenders in maritime nations were sentenced to galleys because of the need to maintain a large volume of overseas commerce. During the colonial period, British offenders were sent to the American colonies and later to Australia and helped to establish and maintain the new colonies.

3. Historically, there have been individuals and organizations, especially during the 19th century, that showed great interest in what was going on in prison and what was happening with the prisoners. Various societies and associations were established by concerned and active individuals, many of them Quakers, to champion prison reform and the betterment of prison conditions, starting with the Philadelphia Society for Alleviating the Miseries of Public Prisons that was established in 1787. These included the Boston Prison Society, organized by Louis Dwight; the New York Prison Association, in which John W. Edmonds played a major part; and the activities of prominent humanitarians and reformers such as Dorothea Dix, Samuel Gridley Howe, and Francis Lieber. The activities of the above organizations and individuals culminated in the National Prison Congress held in Cincinnati in 1870. The most well-known organizers of this congress were Enoch C. Wines and Zebulon Brockway. The above personalities and organizations tried to raise public interest in prison matters and in the handling of prisoners, based on humanitarian grounds and on deep religious convictions (Dix, 1967; Lewis, 1922/1967; Lewis, 1965; McKelvey, 1936; Sullivan, 1989).

There were also similar efforts of prison reform and of raising public interest in prisons in Great Britain. John Howard's work about prison reform had a triggering effect, and it was followed by the activities of Elizabeth Fry, who formed the Prison Discipline Society in 1817, and William Allen, and others. As in America, in Great Britain most reformers also had deep religious convictions, and many of them were Quakers. Later, in the 1880s, the John Howard Society, dedicated to prison reform, was formed (Ignatieff, 1978) and is active to this day.

4. To curb the growing levels of crime, the legislation of gun and knife control laws and increased funding for education were proposed, just like some of the propositions suggested today.

5. The same John McDougal, while in office, appointed his brother to serve as a prison inspector. His brother George swayed the other inspectors to approve a contract to build a prison for the tremendous sum of $800,000. The contractor chosen was a business partner of Estell. This contract was recalled in 1852 by the legislation (*California Senate Journal, fourth session*, 1853; McAfee, 1990).

3

Conceptual and Theoretical Issues

The punishment of people who violate the law is one of the most intriguing social and moral issues. It has occupied the interests and minds of many philosophers,[1] jurists, social scientists, politicians, government officials, and large segments of the general public. Legal punishment has five basic characteristics:

It must involve pain or other consequences normally considered unpleasant.
It must be for an offense against legal rules.
It must be imposed on an actual or supposed offender for his offense.
It must be intentionally administered by human beings other than the offender.
It must be imposed and administered by an authority constituted by a legal system against which the offense is committed. (Hart, 1968, pp. 4-5)

Imprisonment is one form of legal punishment that, by definition, involves the deliberate causing of suffering for a convicted offender by the criminal justice system representing the state; it raises questions about the authority and legitimacy of the state and the morality of punishment.[2]

In the case of privatization, there are further questions concerning the delegation of coercive power, public-private domains in punishment, and punishment and profits.

45

The State and Punishment

One of the most controversial issues concerning the privatization of prisons focuses on the nature of the relationship between the state and its citizens. The provision of human services, including corrections, by the private versus the public sector cannot be dealt with apart from political questions (see Starr, 1989). This issue raises questions regarding the concept and the functions of the state. Privatization of any public service raises these questions to various degrees, but in the case of human services, particularly punishment, these questions are more pointed because punishment of lawbreakers is qualitatively different, on moral and ethical grounds, from garbage collection, janitorial services in public buildings, government's motor vehicle fleet maintenance, and other public services that, until recently, were targeted for privatization.

As seen, the definition of punishment implies that it must be imposed for the violation of legal rules and "administered by an authority constituted by a legal system" (Hart, 1968, p. 6). This definition involves the state because legal rules are created by a legislative body representing the state. According to the above definition, the authority implementing the punishment is also a representative of the state. The raison d'être of government is the provision of a legal order (van den Haag, 1975), which involves the exercise of formal social control. Punishment, including imprisonment, is meted out by the criminal law that is fundamentally a "governmental social control" (Black, 1976, p. 2), and it is administered by a governmental apparatus—the criminal justice system that represents the state. Therefore, to understand formal social control and the issues related to it, one has to learn about the state.

States usually emerge when the complexities of civilization are introduced (Hoffman, 1988). One of the main differences between a stateless society and the state is that "the stateless society has no single central symbol or instrument of rule . . . whereas a single headship is the mark of the presence of the state" (Hinsley, 1986, p. 7).

In the 17th century the state became the most important subject of analysis in European thought (Skinner, 1978). Hobbes, in his social contract theory, argued that individuals from their own free will transfer their rights to a powerful authority, to the sovereign (the head of the state) who can force them to keep their promises and contracts (Held, 1984). For Hobbes, the major task of the sovereign is to provide and ensure security, to protect every citizen (Mabbott, 1967).

> For by this Authoritie, given him by every particular man in the Common-Wealth, he hath the use of so much Power and Strength conferred on him, that by terror thereof, he is inabled to form the wills of them all. Peace at home, and mutuell ayd against their enemies abroad. (Hobbes, 1651/1969, p. 118)

This view, then, holds that the sovereign has the authority to ensure the security of the citizens by keeping order internally and by protecting the country from outside enemies.

Locke also views the state in terms of the social contract. Individuals give up their natural political power to someone else to secure order: Locke claims that this power still resides with the individuals who make up society.

> Political power is that power which every man having in the state of nature, has given up into the hands of the society . . . it can have no other end or measure when in the hands of the magistrates but to preserve the members of that society in their lives, liberties, and possessions. . . . And this power has its original only from compact and agreement and the mutual consent of those who make up the community. (Locke, 1692/1955, pp. 126-127)

If the state does not fulfill its task of protecting of the individuals (Locke included only male property owners in this category), the members of society have the right and power to dissolve the state (Carnoy, 1984).[3] The legislative and executive powers are transferred to the state conditionally on the state's adherence to its essential purpose, namely, the preservation of "life, liberty, and estate." "Sovereign power . . . remains ultimately with the people" (Held, 1984, p. 39).

The classical-liberal tradition viewed authority as bedded in the consent of citizens. Authority is granted by individuals having conflicting interests who have a free ground to act in the economic sphere but need to be coordinated and controlled by the state, which has the coercive power to enforce the rules and laws (Hobhouse, 1964; Lukes, 1978). Thus the establishment of the state reflects a large degree of centralization of power and indicates a fundamental change in the patterns of authority in society. The state has a monopoly over the use of legitimate force,[4] in other words, the use of coercive power that is acquired legally (Held, 1984).[5] The concept of the modern state, as seen above, includes the exercise of its powers by commanding obedience to its rules. The state both formulates the rules of society (legislative branch) and applies them (judicial and executive branch). The liberal theory of the state justifies the rules and their coercive enforcement, including punishment, only so far as they are aimed at protecting the equal autonomy of all citizens (Sadurski, 1991). In spite of this approach to the exercise of legitimate power, the liberal tradition is open for the development of less traditional views of the state and its authority as well.

One of the premises of classical-liberal thinking is that, despite a social contract, the political power still resides with the individuals who delegate the powers to those who govern (Locke, 1692/1955). Although the rights to legislate and enforce the laws are transferred to the state, this is conditional on the state fulfilling its essential function of safeguarding life, liberty, and estate (Held, 1984, p. 39). Thus the ultimate power remains in the hands of the people. These ideas have deep roots in American political philosophy.

This approach may lead to the ideal of the "minimal state," which is "limited to the narrow functions of protection against force, theft, fraud, enforcement of contracts and so on" (Nozick, 1974, p. ix). Nozick sees only a very limited use of coercive power by the state that cannot be applied, for instance, "for the purpose of getting some citizens to aid others, or in order to prohibit activities to people for their own good or protection" (p. ix).[6]

Privatization in general is related to the ideal of the minimal state. This concept, among others, questions the principle of the centralized state monopoly of crime and delinquency control. There are claims that the state has overreached its capacity to control and that it should loosen its grip over its citizens' actions. This claim, according to Cohen (1985), emanates from several different sources: (a) the pragmatists sound it on the basis that the control system is inefficient, slow, and irrational; (b) disillusioned liberals state that the benevolent, paternalistic state has violated civil rights and individual liberties, and therefore the time has come to limit the power of the state in order to provide greater autonomy to individuals; (c) neoconservatives are motivated to make this claim by aiming to cause less harm rather than more good through the limiting of the reach of state power; (d) antiprofessionals are determined to demystify the experts, that is, psychiatrists, psychologists, and social workers, and often replace them with self-help groups, hotlines, and crisis intervention centers instead of the state bureaucratic apparatus; and (e) "sentimental anarchists," who through the popularization of Rawls's (1971) and Nozick's (1974) ideas, influenced both left-wing (e.g., Tifft & Sullivan, 1980) and right-wing (Logan, 1990) versions of libertarianism. They generally claim that the state is increasingly usurping individual freedom. Therefore there is a need to scale down state intervention in many aspects of social life. One of the strongest criticisms of the competing views of government authority and exercise of coercive power comes from the libertarian tradition.

Logan (1990) elaborates on the *libertarian* views of governance, using this term "to encompass all political philosophies that give priority to the liberty and rights of individuals over the welfare and the rights of society or the state" (p. 239). The analysis includes the ideas of classical liberals, minimal-state libertarians, and some anarchists. The core ideas of his approach are the following:

1. Individual rights are natural, inalienable, and supreme.
2. The most fundamental of these are the rights to life, liberty, and property.
3. No individual or group may rightfully initiate the use or threat of coercive force against anyone else.
4. Within certain limits, individuals have the right to respond with force to the initiation or threat of force by others.
5. The state has no rights or legitimate powers not originally held by individuals, and therefore no unique claim to the legitimate use of force.
6. The proper function of government (if any) is to enforce and protect individual rights under the rule of law. (Logan, 1990, p. 239)

Following this libertarian perspective, "crime is seen as a violation of a particular individual's rights" (Logan, 1990, p. 241). Some even hold the view that punishment is the exclusive right of the victim of a crime.[7] The widely held validity of criminal law that considers crime as an act against society is challenged accordingly. The question becomes, then, who determines whether an offense occurred or not, and what should be the punishment if it did occur? Following this approach to the extreme, victims would be the only ones who could determine punishment. It would be somewhat similar to the situation that prevailed earlier in history when a primitive man "had to take the law into his own hands; in effect, he made the law, and he was the victim, the prosecutor, and the judge. He carried out the punishment in the form of revenge aimed at deterrence and compensation" (Schafer, 1977, p. 6). Obviously, this is an extreme position of the libertarian perspective. In fact, one of the main reasons that the punishment function was transferred to society was the inherent danger posed to society by the individual sanctions as they developed into blood feuds (Gilbert, 1992).

It is not clear how the above approach would implement crime control policies that have a utilitarian aim to protect society, that is, deterrence, incapacitation, and rehabilitation, because societal considerations would be considered relevant only as far as they would protect individual rights. Therefore retribution and restitution would probably become the major principles of criminal sanctions.

These views are integrally related to the idea of the minimal state that "sets stringent limits on the role of the state" (Anderson, 1986, p. 213). Consequently, the functions are the provision of security for "person, property and contract" (p. 213). This perspective was not only promoted by libertarians but also by neoconservative Reaganites and Thatcherites. One of the major motives of this approach is to look to the past to solve the increasing crime problem by reinforcing "traditional values" such as church, family, schools, and so on (Cohen, 1985). Paradoxically, this trend may lead to the shoring up of social control and to increased state intervention into everyday life such as the restrictions on abortion and on birth control information. During the 1980s and early 1990s, neoconservatives continued to restrict state involvement on the "soft end" of public policies (e.g., welfare, education). However, on the "hard end" (e.g., social control), they demanded and achieved an increased state commitment, which is reflected in stricter laws, increasing criminal justice budgets, and in the tremendous growth of the prison population.

The minimal-state concept that claims that all rights are individual and the state is an artificial construct having no legitimate authority and rights by itself, but only rights transferred to it by individual citizens, raises the issue of the delegation of coercive power.

The Delegation of Coercive Power

There are two approaches to the right of using coercive power by the state. One is based on the premise that the state has the sole right to use legal coercive power (e.g., Weber, 1964). The traditional definition of punishment maintains that punishment has to be administered for violation of legal rules and by the authority constituted by the legal system. The other approach follows the libertarian interpretation of the classical-liberal philosophy and claims that the source of legitimate power is in the hands of the individual citizens.

Because the main argument of this classical-liberal approach has been dealt with already, I shall relate it briefly and then I shall review the issue of delegation of powers by the state.

The classical-liberal/libertarian doctrine maintains that punishment is the exclusive right of the victim; therefore he or she can transfer this right to others. Accordingly, the protection of criminals from overpunishment would come from applying the principle of proportionality. The question is, again, who would determine what is proportional, and how would the punishment be enforced? Would the victim be able to supervise that punishment will be according to his or her specifications? Imprisonment, as a form of punishment, is seen by this approach as appropriate because "it defines, expresses, and upholds the norms of civil association, which crime violates and undermines" (Logan, 1990, p. 246). Because the victim is the "owner" of the right of punishment, its administration can be carried out by private entities.

Thus, although the criminal justice system is driven and directed by the representatives of the state, the authority to execute the punishment can be delegated to private entities through a contract. Accordingly, the libertarian approach would justify private prisons on the basis of the limited role of the state and the individualistic concept of punishment.

If the more traditional approach, maintaining that legal authority is integral to the state, is followed, then the question becomes, how

much of the legitimate coercive power of the state to punish criminals
could or should be delegated to private entities? According to this
thesis, it is an accepted principle that the "control of the means of
violence is par excellence the business of the state" (Beetham, 1984,
p. 213). How would this control be ensured if and when the delegation of some of this function takes place? Where should the line of
what can and what cannot be delegated be placed?

This issue relates both to external and internal security. For example, the U.S. armed forces have many contracts with private for-profit
firms. Not only are weapons, uniforms, and other equipment supplied
by private contractors but many other services as well (these services
can be related to food, medical emergencies, and others). The question becomes whether fighting units should be operated by private
companies if they can run them cheaper and in a more flexible
manner. This is somewhat parallel to the question of the operation
of the various agencies of the criminal justice system.

Furthermore, there is also the constitutional question of whether
the government has the authority to delegate to private entities the
power of such an important governmental function as the punishment of lawbreakers (Robbins, 1986). The American Bar Association
(ABA), on February 11, 1986, took a position oppositional to the
privatization of prisons. The ABA's criticisms of the private management and operation of prisons pointed out that "incarceration is an
inherent function of the government and that the government should
not abdicate this responsibility by turning over prison operation to
private industry" (Mayer, 1986, p. 310).

Many critics and even supporters of privatization (see Cikins, 1986)
agree that when a government deprives its citizens of their liberty, it
exercises state power. One of the questions is, How much police
power can be delegated to private parties to exercise this power? The
privatization of the operation and management of entire correctional
institutions entails a wider scale of delegation of state authority than
most other cases or private contracting. The issues arising from this
form of privatization are dramatically different than in cases such as
garbage collection, bus service, or mail delivery (DiIulio, 1990a; Starr,
1987). Besides the general issues of legal constraints on the delegation
of state authority of this scale, there are also questions whether this
policy is fundamentally a proper one (Mullen, Chabotar, & Carrow,

1985). Correctional personnel, by definition, have a major custodial and order-maintenance function that is clearly articulated in their authority to maintain internal discipline in the prison. The prison is a total institution having a near-total control over the inmates' lives (Wallace, 1971). It relies on the coercive compliance of its lower level participants (the inmates), which means that coercive power or the threat of it is applied to achieve compliance with the rules set by the authorities (Etzioni, 1961, 1964). Thus prison staff and management have the power to withdraw privileges, to initiate disciplinary measures that may involve physical force (e.g., breaking up fights and restraining enraged inmates), and in extreme situations, to use deadly force. In fact, Foucault (1977) saw in the disciplinary measures the very essence of incarceration. He stated that in the prison "disciplinary power . . . is everywhere and always alert" (p. 177). Foucault and a few other scholars (e.g., Cohen, 1979) have viewed discipline as "the focal concept in the emergence of prisons" (Bottoms, 1983, p. 175). Prison discipline covers every facet of institutional life. The disciplinary system includes both positive sanctions (i.e., granting privileges) and negative sanctions (i.e., punishments) and is aimed at obtaining cooperation from individuals who have good reasons not to be cooperative with the system because they are deprived of their freedom and kept in confinement against their will (Goffman, 1961). The great majority of reports come from line personnel who report to their supervisors in the chain of command (Schrag, 1961). Viewing this great amount of control over the inmates and the staff's capacity to exercise this control in the process of institutional discipline, it can be questioned whether this power should be delegated to private, profit-seeking parties.

A closely related issue is concerned with the quasi-judicial function that is vested in the prison administration. The length of imprisonment depends to a large degree on parole decisions; the good time computation and release dates take into consideration the recommendations of the prison administration and prison personnel. Disciplinary records and other accounts of institutional behavior are an integral part of this process. Thus decision making may be significantly influenced by the private administration and staff whose evaluations might depend on personal values, attitudes, and opinions reflected in institutional reports. The possibility to make profits from extended incarceration also may become a factor in the discipline process. As an illustration of this point, the ABA report (1986) quotes an employee who was in charge of reviewing disciplinary cases at a privately operated Immigration and Naturalization Service facility. This employee in an interview told a *New York Times* reporter: "I'm the Supreme Court" (p. 4). Also, the private contractor may put pressure on the staff regarding disciplinary policies.

Proponents of prison privatization claim that this issue can be addressed by proper government oversight and monitoring (Logan, 1990). However, the role of private staff members in this process cannot be completely eliminated. Staff members will continue to use their discretion by making decisions regarding what rule violations should be ignored, filed, or handled informally (Press, 1990). Monitors will not be able to be present at every encounter between staff and inmates.

These problems lead to the question of whether private for-profit companies, their administrators, and line employees should be involved in handling the two most precious possessions of every citizen—their liberty and their life.

The supporters of privatization approach the issue of the propriety of prison for profit through a constitutional analysis and arrive at a conclusion mentioned previously, namely, that the state, without totally abdicating its penal authority to private companies, may delegate power for the administration of penalties (Logan, 1990). This approach makes a crucial "distinction between the power to impose imprisonment and the power to administer it" (McDonald, 1990b, p. 183). Thus, although the legal authority to decide who and for how long to incarcerate rests unquestionably with the judicial system, the administration of this punishment can be delegated to private firms.

DiIulio (1990a), dealing with the private operation of prisons, raises a related question, namely, whether the "moral responsibility for given communal functions ought to be lodged mainly or solely in the hands of government" (p. 73). He concludes that on legitimate and moral grounds "the authority to govern those behind bars, to deprive citizens of their liberty, to coerce (and even kill) them, must remain in the hands of government authorities" (p. 73). Similarly, to the reasoning of Robbins (1986), he states that the whole symbolism surrounding punishment, that is, the uniform and badge of law enforcement and correctional officers and the robe of the judge, are expressions of the inherently public nature of punishment. This claim is discarded by privatization advocates and others who hold that it does not make much difference if the badge of an officer belongs to a public agency or to a private company (e.g., Logan, 1990). However, symbolism has an important role in criminal justice. The mere fact that a harmful act against an individual is considered to be a crime against society is symbolic. According to Janus (1993):

> Private involvement in corrections can affect symbolism in corrections in two important ways. First, it can serve to distance the state from the inmate (and vice versa), by introducing an intervening actor. Second, privatization introduces an important new political actor into the fundamentally symbolic public decision that takes place in criminal justice decisions. (p. 76)

Privatization supporters point to the fact that the substance of corrections is more important than the mere symbolism of the uniform. Probity and integrity are not the monopoly of the government. Whether a symbol such as a uniform or a badge will legitimize the organization will depend on deeds and the quality of service. The claim that criminal justice personnel (e.g., police officers, correctional officers, and other uniformed personnel) are representative of the people and symbolize the authority that was bestowed on the government is also being challenged; because these officers are not elected by the people or appointed politically, they cannot be seen as representatives of the public by virtue of their selection, only by virtue of their job (Logan, 1990).

The above view is contrary to the Weberian concept of legal authority, in which "obedience is owed to the legally established impersonal order. It extends to the persons exercising the authority of office under it only by the virtue of the formal legality of their commands and only within the scope of authority of the office" (Weber, 1964, p. 328). Correctional personnel in privately operated prisons receive their authority from the administration of the corporation, which in turn received its legal authority to handle prisoners from the state. This authority is more limited than the authority given to government institutions; for example, direct disciplinary actions are being curtailed in private prisons.[8]

Theoretically, the purest way to implement legal authority is by the employment of a bureaucratic administrative staff. The chief of this bureaucracy is appointed and functions according to a set of criteria that indicate the bureaucrat's separation from ownership. "The official works entirely separated from ownership of the means of administration and without appropriation of his position" (Weber, 1964, p. 334). However, administrators of private facilities are often on the board of directors of the corporations that operate the facility, many of them are shareholders, or they are in a profit-sharing arrangement; thus many of the managers, at least partially, are also owners.

According to Logan (1990), the core of the issue is "whether relevant legal values will be served more faithfully by public employees or by contracted agents" (p. 57). He sees this as an empirical question rather than a question of principle. Finally, he points out that the concern with symbolism by the opponents of private for-profit prisons belies the fact that their argument is not substantive. He claims that symbols should indicate legal authority, not government employment.

The point that is not addressed here is that public employees, wearing the government symbols, directly represent government authority. When a private company is contracted for the management of a prison, the employees are directly responsible to the private corporation and its executives. The employees receive their instructions from private executives, and ultimately their paycheck comes from the private company; they are hired, fired, promoted, demoted, rewarded, and disciplined by the management of the private company. If for any reason there is a discrepancy, be it a major or a minor one, between the goals of the government and the goals of the private company, or if there is any disagreement on a particular issue between these two entities, the personnel of the private corporation will answer to the direct orders of the private management. These employees, even if their company is under government contract, will have to follow the instructions of the private managers, and if they fail to do so, regardless of the nature of the instructions, they may be disciplined and ultimately fired by the private company and not by government officials. As mentioned, their direct responsibility and loyalty is to their employer and not to a government agency. Their dependence on the goodwill of the management is underscored by the fact that usually they do not have any union protection. Thus, by the delegation of legitimate power to the corporation, the government loses direct control over the correctional staff who deal with inmates punished by the criminal justice system that represents society.

The delegation of legitimate authority to private prisons is being done through contracting. In the United States and in a few other Western democratic countries (e.g., Great Britain), the delegation of legal and executive powers is well established in practice. For example, the power to arrest is delegated to various private police and security companies (e.g., Shearing & Stenning, 1987; South, 1988); often the handling of grievances between employees, unions, and employers is delegated to private arbitrators; the licensing to practice certain professions, for example, law or medicine, is delegated to professional organizations (Lawrence, 1986). A large number of criminal justice functions, besides prison operation, are administered by the private sector through government contracts (e.g., community corrections, diversion programs, electronic monitoring, transportation of prisoners, bail bonding, and presentence reporting). Logan (1990) claims that there is no limit to the type of government function that can be delegated to private parties, only to the quantity of it; in other words, "the question here is not what function can be delegated, but how much of it" (Logan, 1990, p. 59).

Regarding the legitimate use of coercive power, the state can give up some amount of it; however, if the state gives up all or a very large portion of coercive power, it ceases to be a state because it loses its sovereignty, which is a final and absolute authority (Hinsley, 1986). This is very important because "sovereignty concerns are at the heart of private versus public sector issues" (Johnston, 1990, p. 194). Obviously, the key issue is to determine the limits of the delegation of coercive power, that is, how much of it can be delegated. One of the problems is that the lack of clearly defined limits may create various definitions by different individuals, government agencies, and private entities. Of course, the major danger of the delegation of power is that "governmental power may be used to further private rather than public interests" (Lawrence, 1986, p. 662).

Private Domains

In the discussion of conceptual problems, a short review of the theoretical issues of public and private perspectives of state and government is in order. As seen in the classical-liberal model of state, "the notion of a self-regulating market which state power merely protects, is a model for the limited role of state elsewhere" (Cohen, 1985, p. 134). This is the opposing model to the totalitarian state, in which there is a total fusion between the public and private spheres of life.

Although the modern capitalist state, especially the United States, has tried to follow the laissez-faire classical-liberal model, it is questionable whether it has created a radical separation between the private and public spheres. State intervention in the economic and social life has been notable. Paradoxically, to maintain the laissez-faire economic model, a network of governmental agencies have been established; in other words, the private sphere has needed and has often requested protection from the public sphere. This is obviously contradictory, but as Becker (1945) pointed out, this contradiction is not new but a well-entrenched phenomenon in the United States:

> It would be a mistake to suppose that the people of the United States have ever really doubted that it is a proper function of government to promote the general welfare. Although Americans have commonly believed that government should never meddle in business, no class of Americans . . . has ever objected . . . to any amount of governmental meddling if it appeared to benefit that particular class. (p. 108)

The neoconservatives, at least in theory, object to government interference with business. They want to follow the conservative ideal of "economic freedom but moral regulation" (Bell, 1976, p. 275).

In crime control, the state intrusion is clear; judgments concerning the private lives of individuals have become an integral part of criminal justice procedures. There is an increasing boundary blurring between the private and the public spheres.

> "Privatization" hints at a diminished direct role of the state: the commodification of certain deviant populations and their management by private entrepreneurs; the massive growth of the private security industry with large corporations now regulating areas of public life previously controlled by the state. (Cohen, 1985, p. 136)

The public and private sectors have traditional distinctions between them; many of them are premised in legal principles that are related to accountability and authority, and not necessarily on economic or social theories. In certain types of privatization, "the public sector is being profoundly altered, and ultimately harmed by the deliberate blurring of these public and private characteristics" (Moe, 1988, p. 674). One of the problems with the diminishing public-private distinction is that the government delegates some of its powers and functions to parties whose legitimacy is not always clear (Moe, 1988).[9]

The trend of the shrinking role of government in society is buttressed by the general mistrust of government, which is embedded in the American tradition (see, e.g., Bellah, Madsen, Sullivan, Swidler, & Tipton, 1985). However, in reality there are often contradictions in this tradition. The laissez-faire and minimal-state rhetoric during the Reagan administration emphasized withdrawal and cutting back of state participation from social programs such as health and welfare, but in crime control the conservative agenda was to extend, to expand, and to strengthen the reach of law. This trend was reflected in the increasing number of laws, mandatory sentences, the conduct of the war on crime in other countries (e.g., Colombia, Peru, Mexico, and Panama), and more and longer prison terms. Paradoxically, the advocates of the curtailment of state power were using, as much as they could, the government to assist them in implementing crime control policies that fit their sociopolitical and economic agenda.

A more moderate vision of the declining role of the state is the pragmatic approach that does not follow the grand destructuring vision but rather tries to achieve the easing of the system's overload. This is a part of a wider trend often referred to as load shedding, which is an attempt to reduce "the social role and responsibility" of the government (Kamerman & Kahn, 1989, p. 256). This became a major social policy of the Reagan and Thatcher administrations during the 1980s (e.g., Bendick, 1989; Rein, 1989). In criminal justice the aim of this trend was to dislodge the soft "bits," such as status offenses and victimless crimes, from the criminal justice system and to concentrate on the "hard end," on dangerous crimes (Cohen, 1985). The agencies dealing with the soft end are dependent on and supported by "the selection procedures, discretion, financing, and back-up authority" of the criminal justice system (Cohen, 1985, p. 138). This is the aim of such strategies as "decarceration" (Scull, 1977), diversion, and dispute resolution. These developments are a reflection of the "bifurcation principle": The soft-end offenders are diverted out of the system whereas the hard-core offenders are targeted (Cohen, 1985). The bifurcation carries some contradictions in it as far as the minimal-state idea is concerned. First, the financing, classification, selection of offenders, and back-up authority remain in the hands of government. Second, a great deal of "net widening" is going on; in other words, more people come under some kind of surveillance as a result of the expansion of formal control, and many of these clients, without this policy, would not have been in the official system at all.[10] So, basically, the state's control is expanded rather than leading toward a minimal state.

The Expansion of Social Control

A perspective is emerging that views prison privatization from the vantage point of the expansion of the state's capacity to punish (Feeley, 1991).[11] According to this approach, most studies have failed to ask one of the most important questions, namely, to what degree does privatization expand the state's capacity to punish? This question may have a particular interest for classical libertarians as well as for civil libertarians. Feeley (1991) asserts in his historical analysis that correctional privatization always has resulted in "the generation of new and expanded sanctions and forms of social control" (p. 2). Thus privatization, instead of replacing public corrections, became complementary to it. This perspective has two variants: one that is supportive of privatization and another that is critical of it.

The perspective that supports privatization points out that the establishment of private prisons is not aimed at replacing the public correctional system, it is only meant to supplement it. It basically provides more options to the government to exercise its control. For example, the English government's intention to introduce privatization into criminal justice was interpreted in the following:

> Punishment for profit, by opening up opportunities for competition, contracting out services with private agencies, is seen as another way of making the system more efficient and finding new strategies for the

control of offenders in the community and outside the prison walls.
(Vass, 1990, p. 166)

This line of argument refers to community-based correctional programs (soft-end control), but it also has a relevance for private
prisons. For example, the promise of building prisons faster and
cheaper and the opportunity to ease overcrowding may enhance the
functioning of the whole criminal justice system. This perspective
sees a clear advantage in the variety that the private sector's entrance
to the hard end of corrections can provide: "Private prisons and jails
are not meant to be used in lieu of existing facilities, but to widen
and diversify the prison system. One purpose of competition, in
addition to cost containment, is to maximize choice" (Logan, 1990,
p. 10).

However, there is a traditional trend of expansion of formal social
control through mechanisms that were meant to be supplementary
to the existing criminal justice system (Cohen, 1985; Nelken, 1989;
Sparks, 1994). Because there is a general agreement from both the
advocates and the opponents of private prisons that the ultimate
responsibility for punishment of lawbreakers lies with the government, private prisons will help the authorities to discharge their duty
to punish. Following this view, there is an expansion of formal social
control because the government will be able to punish better and
handle more people in a variety of ways—for lack of space, many who
would have been released earlier or would not have been incarcerated
at all will be placed in privately operated institutions. Thus private
facilities will add to the government's ability to discharge its functions of punishment of offenders and to provide security to the
law-abiding citizens through incapacitation. This argument, coming
from those who support the minimal-state idea, is intriguing. Instead
of curtailing the power of the state, this expansion of its punishment
capacity will increase state control. Critics claim that the end result
of correctional privatization and the extended capacity to punish is
that large numbers of people who otherwise would not have been
sanctioned at all will be controlled. The iron rule seems to be that
once the penal system is expanded, it perpetuates itself and continues
to expand. Usually, if prisons are built, they will be filled up. In the
past many correctional reforms were initiated by entrepreneurs who

tried to accomplish what government could not or would not do. Often, after these entrepreneurs had developed innovations in dealing with offenders, the innovations were later incorporated into the government's repertoire of sanctions (Feeley, 1991). Similarly, private control programs, especially if they prove to be successful, tend to be co-opted and absorbed into the state's correctional system (Cohen, 1985). For example, the transportation of offenders as a penal sanction became important during mercantilism, and in a sense started a new punishment system. This policy gained importance during the 17th century and continued until the end of the colonial period in America, and later in Australia. It was strongly related to the British colonial experience and to the widespread perception in England that the criminal justice system was not effective. Transportation to the colonies "was a marriage of efficiency and effectiveness. Most of its costs were borne by profit-seeking merchants selling their human cargo and by planters who purchased it" (Feeley, 1991, p. 3). It was financed by private enterprise, and it served to a large degree the interests of a certain group of merchants and colonists who needed cheap labor (Rusche & Kirchheimer, 1939). Simultaneously, this policy helped to "solve" the crime problem in England and supported the colonial aspirations of the British government. This practice cost very little or nothing at all to the state, but it was profitable for the private entrepreneurs. It is claimed that thousands of offenders who otherwise would have been punished were sanctioned and sent overseas, supplying badly needed cheap (forced) labor for private interests (Linebaugh, 1992).

Feeley (1991) also deals with the privately managed factory-prisons of the 19th century, which have been analyzed earlier. Incarceration, which became the symbol of humanitarian progress during the 19th century, emphasized reform and humanitarian principles of punishment. The two major prison models, the Walnut Street Penitentiary and the Auburn Prison, with their new approach of discipline and corrections, became a major factor in shaping correctional policies even beyond the boundaries of America. In spite of the many unintended negative consequences of these institutions, they had at least one positive feature, namely, they did not cost much money because, at least partially, they could pay for themselves through work arrangements with private contractors. One of the convincing arguments of private entrepreneurs was that incarceration was not only a more humane sanction than physical punishment, the death penalty, or transportation but that it could also pay for itself. This argument was in line with the emerging utilitarian philosophy. The two major aims, humane treatment and cost-effectiveness of incarceration, were not necessarily seen as contradictory at that period for most of the reformers. It is suggested that the new penal policy, relying heavily but far from completely on incarceration (Smart, 1983), was a marriage of "conscience and convenience" (Rothman, 1980). Reformers and entrepreneurs were often one and the same. They not only promised a new form of punishment that seemed to be humane and cost-effective, but they also were serving industrial economic development and could benefit personally from the punishment as well. The idea that prisons can become factories—teaching inmates how to work in a disciplined environment, preparing them for life after release, and at the same time keeping the prison cost-effective for the state and profitable for the entrepreneur—remained very attractive.

As seen, the convict lease system in the South was especially important because it helped to replace the workforce of the freed slaves. It was also efficient in continuing to control large segments of the black population, with a relatively low cost. In the South private participation in the penal process was instrumental in expanding the capacity of the correctional system at a time when the states were not able to do so. Feeley (1991) concludes that

> each of these policies represent an extension and an expansion of penal policy—entrepreneurs inventing new forms to respond to immediate crises which, in turn, were incorporated into the fabric of an expanded and more effective criminal justice system. (p. 6)

Currently, the private sector is most active in the development of intermediate punishments such as drug treatment, diversion, halfway houses, and electronic surveillance of probationers and parolees. These relatively new programs are related to the traditional functions of probation, and they create new conditions to be imposed on the probationers. They also help to widen the net because many minor offenders (often juveniles), who before the introduction of these programs were released back to their families, are now placed under some kind of organized control. Participation in supervised treatment programs is often imposed as a condition of probation. These include substance abuse and even job training programs. Almost all of them are run by private corporations, many of them by for-profit companies. These became an integral part of the criminal justice process and provide an additional control mechanism over the client population, even though they are often exempted from the due process standards that more traditional methods of control are required to follow. Lately, the use of surveillance programs based on new technologies operated by the private sector for the control of parolees, probationers, and house arrestees has increased (see, e.g., Ball, Huff, & Lilly, 1988; Williams, Shichor, & Wiggenhorn, 1989).

Moral and Ethical Issues

In dealing with the various aspects of private prisons, there is a need to examine the moral and ethical issues involved as well.

Punishment is a moral issue because it is a "deprivation or suffering, imposed by law" (van den Haag, 1975, p. 8). It is a deliberate action by agents of society, thus it poses the moral question whether it is right to cause suffering to an individual in the name of society and if it is so, under what circumstances and to what degree. Punishment, as seen, involves suffering, which is a "moral embarrassment" (Packer, 1968, p. 59). It can easily become an outlet for feelings of revenge. The questions involving the morality of punishment place a major burden on the shoulders of society to make sure that people who are punished (a) deserve to be punished, and (b) that the punishment is administered in legally correct ways. The concern here is with the second issue. Because punishment was designed to be painful, it has the potential of being evil (van den Haag, 1975), in other words, it may be administered to a person who does not deserve it, or it may become abusive and/or excessive.

Moral and ethical questions of punishment in general, and their impact on private prisons in particular, are framed by the various rationales of punishment.

Four major theoretical principles are used to rationalize punishment. They are mentioned here briefly. First, *retribution* is based on the principle that an offender has to be punished because he or she deserves it. This rationale is in line with the social contact perspective of the state (Pollock, 1994). It considers punishment to be just because it restores the moral balance that was hurt by the offense (Ezorsky, 1972). Second, *deterrence* focuses on the preventive aspects of punishment, on the offenders themselves who supposedly will refrain from committing crimes again because they have learned the negative consequences of their crimes (special deterrence) and on prospective offenders who will be hesitant to take the risk for fear of punishment (general deterrence). Third, *incapacitation* justifies the use of punishment to remove criminals from society so they cannot harm law-abiding citizens. The modern method of incapacitation is incarceration; however, capital punishment and various forms of mutilation have been used in the past to achieve this goal (Samaha, 1983). Last, *rehabilitation* rests on the notion that punishment ought to prevent crime through changing the behavior and attitudes of individual offenders (Allen, 1981; Samaha, 1983).

Retribution is often referred to as the "justice model" because its only aim is to dispense just deserts, whereas deterrence, incapacitation, and rehabilitation are often seen as utilitarian punishments because their rationale is the achievement of a desired social goal, namely, the prevention and reduction of future crimes (see, e.g., Singer, 1979).

One of the basic controversies between the retributionists and the utilitarians focuses on the question of whether punishment aimed at achieving utilitarian results, such as the protection of society, is morally justifiable. The classic retributionist claim is that the only morally justifiable punishment is the one based on retributive principles. If they have any utilitarian effects such as deterrence (special and/or general), incapacitation and rehabilitation are fine, but they cannot be the major intent of punishment (Mabbott, 1939). On the other hand, utilitarians claim that the important point is the maximization of utility. In other words, it is more important to make the majority of people secure than to be concerned whether the punishment of the individual is more or less severe than the actual harm caused by it. Smart (1991) states in this vein that "notions such as those of rights, fairness, and equal distribution have no place in the fundamental ethical concepts of utilitarianism" (p. 363). The argument between retributionists and utilitarians is a continual one. Lately, utilitarian ideas have gained more influence with a public concerned with violent crime than has the retributive ideal seeking just deserts for criminals.

Interestingly, and at the same time sadly, ethical issues historically were not given a major role in the field of criminal justice (Silvester, 1990). Most of the attention in this respect was given to police behavior (see Johnson, 1982). However, the increased move toward correctional privatization opens the door to more ethical concerns. The concept of morality is a social one because it is concerned with how people relate to each other (Kleinig, 1991). Morality is also an instrument of society for the guidance of its individual members in defining what is "good" and desirable and what is "bad" and undesirable behavior (Frankena, 1963). The moral question in this context can be framed in a utilitarian and quasi-hedonistic form—namely, whether the privatization of correctional facilities will produce a greater good than evil for society. It also can be perceived as a deontological issue, which looks not at the consequence of an action but only at the motive or the intent of it, versus a teleological issue, which results in a moral judgment on the basis of the end result of an act or the consequences of an action (Pollock, 1994). I believe that it is morally questionable whether a corporation should make money from the punishment of lawbreakers. However, as I implied earlier, most people look at this issue on a purely pragmatic level. The privatization advocates' attempt to create a sharp distinction between the determination of punishment and its administration directs the focus of interest to the operational aspects of imprisonment, such as cost savings, effective monitoring, and contract specifications, and neglects the ethical and moral issues (see Sparks, 1994). Even some opponents of privatization reject symbolism and ethical considerations as major reasons to object to private for-profit prisons. "Ideological critics of privatization are right when they point out that corrections is a particularly important and delicate public task; they err when they conclude from this fact alone that only government can perform it" (Donahue, 1989, p. 157). In other words, according to this view, the privatization of correctional institutions has to be objected to on pragmatic or utilitarian rather than on ethical and moral grounds. I do not argue that issues of quality, economy, legality, and others are not valid, but I do believe that issues of morality and symbolism have to be considered as well.

One of the fundamental questions is whether the public good and the private companies' good are identical. It can be argued that there is at least as much, if not more, propensity toward the idea that private corporations are "more interested in doing well than doing good" (Robbins, 1989, p. 816). By definition, private corporations were not established for serving the public good; they were established to generate profit for their owners and stockholders. Why should we burden them with demands that are not in the purview of their original organizational goals? Because organizations are rationally constructed to attain their prescribed goals, those that have to serve multiple and sometimes conflicting goals become problematic and, more often than not, fail to perform any of these goals satisfactorily. Prisons fall into this category.[12]

In the case of private for-profit prisons, an extra conflicting goal is added to the equation, that is, profit making on punishment, a fact that may exacerbate the situation even further.

The core ethical question in the privatization of prisons, as seen, is whether it is proper that private parties will make a profit (will benefit) from the infliction of pain on others. Proponents of private prisons do not see any major ethical problem in this vein. Logan (1987) justifies forcefully the "propriety of proprietary prisons" (p. 38). He dismisses the importance of the motivation for involvement in corrections:

> The motivation of those who apply a punishment is not relevant either to the justice or to the effectiveness of the punishment. It is true that for punishment to be a moral enterprise, it is important that it be done for the right reasons. This, however, is a stricture that applies more to those who determine and decree the punishment than to those who carry it out—to legislative and judicial more than to executive agents. (Logan, 1987, p. 38)

Advocates further claim that even if the motives of involvement in private corrections are taken into consideration, profit making as a

motive should not be attributed only to private corporations nor
should they be the only target for criticism. The motives of all parties
working in prison, whether public or private, should be scrutinized.
These include state agencies, public employee unions, prison reform
groups, and even public interest groups. Logan (1987) poses a series
of questions concerning this issue:

> Is it wrong for state employees to have a financial stake in the existence
> of a prison system? Is it wrong for their unions to "profit" by extracting
> compulsory dues from these employees? Is it wrong for a state prison
> bureaucracy to seek growth (more personnel, bigger budgets, new
> investment in human and physical capital) through seizing the profits of
> others (taxation) rather than through reinvestment of its own profits?
> Are the sanctions of the state diminished or tainted when they are
> administered by public employees organized to maximize their personal
> benefits? If not, why would it tarnish those sanctions to be administered
> by professionals who make an honest profit? (p. 38)

Those questions are legitimate and should be asked in order to deal
with a major issue that not only involves efficiency and expediency
but is concerned with ethical, moral, philosophical, and political
principles as well. The contention of privatization advocates is that
the profit motive, in various forms, is universal, thus objecting to it
only in relation to the private sector is discriminatory and prejudicial
(see Logan, 1987, 1990; Savas, 1987). However, critics of privatization
question some of these contentions. They ask, for example, does
working for a salary as a prison employee entail the same motive as
that of the management of a private correctional corporation that has
to produce a profit for its shareholders and can increase its personal
benefits by increasing the income and/or lowering the cost of the
operation (e.g., Rutherford, 1990; Ryan & Ward, 1989)? The privatization proponents' argument fails to distinguish between the employees' motive of self-interest and the profit motive of the corporation.
Individual motives are always present regardless of whether the
organization is private or public; however, there is a fundamental
difference between wages in exchange for labor and profit earned
through capital investment (Gilbert, 1992).

The normative (ethical and moral) questions stemming from the
private operations of correctional institutions may become very thorny.

As seen, even scholars who are not favoring the privatization of prisons suggest that the emphasis should not be on the motives of the private sector and whether private firms should or should not profit from the punishment of inmates (see DiIulio, 1990a). DiIulio (1986) clearly states that "the profit motive of the privatizers is irrelevant" (p. 5).

However, the motives of the contractor cannot be neglected. As known, the motive or intent is a major variable in criminal justice; it may influence the definition of crime and the nature of punishment. If a private correctional corporation sets profit making as its major goal, profit making will influence its operations and policies. For example, profit making will determine the priorities set for its employees and the standards according to which they will be evaluated.

Private Prisons and
Laissez-Faire Socioeconomic Theory

The classical-liberal tradition is the major philosophical justification of private prisons. It focuses on the free market system, competition, and profit maximization in its economic doctrine. Profit seeking, according to this model, should take place through free competition, which leads to maximum productivity. It is increasingly recognized that the pursuance of profit by a corporation may pose ethical and moral questions (see, e.g., Machan, 1988). The best way to ensure free competition and to achieve maximum productivity is to reduce government intrusion into the economic marketplace. Accordingly, the state's major function is to ensure that the laissez-faire system will work and will not be endangered by those who oppose it (Held, 1984). The state would also have the tasks of suppressing fraud, keeping property safe, and helping to enforce contracts (Hobhouse, 1964). In its 19th-century version, this theory became the basis of the utilitarian philosophy forwarded by Jeremy Bentham and James Mill; it posed that the main task of government is to ensure the achievement of the greatest happiness for the greatest number of people (Held, 1984).

During the 1980s the Reagan administration, the Thatcher government, and several other Western governments adapted classical-liberal philosophy by substantially easing government regulations and by abolishing many regulatory agencies or severely diminishing their authority and effectiveness (e.g., Calavita, 1983). During this period the idea of invisible hand as a governing principle of society largely prevailed. This doctrine, as suggested by Adam Smith (1937), states that self-interest motivates the actions of individuals, and they often aid society even without intending to do so (Anderson, 1989).[13] Critics have pointed out that regulations are important because they provide a protection against the avarice of the marketplace and should serve as a check against extensive greed. Regulation is supposed to correct market failures, when for various reasons, like monopolies or lack of adequate information, the free market does not operate with full efficiency (Frank & Lambress, 1988). The large-scale deregulation of the 1980s, according to critics, played down the importance of protecting the public (Tolchin & Tolchin, 1983) even though the protection of the public was supposed to be a major function of government, according to the classical-liberal school itself (Hobbes, 1651/1969). Deregulation had far-reaching political, social, and economic impacts in the United States, in England, and to a lesser degree, in other Western capitalist societies as well. In America, to a large extent, it brought back the caveat emptor principle as a major driving force of free competition and the laissez-faire economy. It also resulted in several deregulated industries to the demise of free competition because of an unprecedented wave of mergers and bankruptcies (see, e.g., Dempsey, 1989).

The Correctional Triad in Private Prisons

Another related issue is worth consideration, namely, the classical-liberal philosophy based on the idea of an unregulated free market system in which the economy operates on the play of supply and demand of the market. Theoretically, economic competition is considered to work for the general social good. "A confidence that pursuit of private gain serves the larger social order leads to approval for both self-interested behavior and private enterprise" (Starr, 1989, p. 18). In accordance with this model it is assumed that customers shop around for the needed merchandise or services using their best

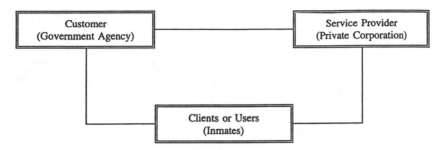

Figure 3.1. Customer-Client-Provider Relationship in Private Prisons

judgment and interest. However, in certain social services and particularly in corrections, there are some major problems in applying this model. In the case of correctional programs, prisons, and other human service organizations for profit, where government agencies place individuals who are under their control and pay for the services received, there is a more complex relationship than in a buyer-seller or provider-client situation. There are three parties—the provider of the service, the customer who pays for the service, and the client who receives the service—that have to be taken into consideration, and their interrelationships have to be analyzed. The provider is usually a private for-profit corporation, the customers who choose and pay for the services are government agencies, and the users or the clients who receive the services are the inmates or welfare recipients (Garsombke & Garsombke, 1987). Thus the traditional client-provider or customer-seller relationship is altered and becomes more complex because, usually, those who pay for the goods or services are the ones who benefit from the purchase, whereas in this situation the buyers of the services (government agencies) are not identical with the recipients of the services (clients). A client-provider relationship assumes a long-term, personal, and mutually dependent interaction between the provider of a service and the recipient of it, whereas a customer-seller relationship is based on an economic exchange of money for goods and services (Parsons, 1970).

However, in the case of private providers of public human services (including corrections), there is an additional relationship. This relationship is between the service recipients (inmates in prison) and the government agency that is paying for the services provided by a private entity. The nature of this relationship and its effects on the services should be researched and explored more extensively in the future. In the case of private prisons, inmates have a more complex web of relationships, in which they are dependent on the government agency, the officials of the entity that is bestowed with the legal authority to punish, and the "hired hand" private company that executes the punishment. In this web of relationships, inmates do not have the same direct control over services as customers have in their commercial activities; they cannot pick and choose, or "take it or leave it" (Palumbo, 1986). Because of their inability to go out and shop around in the marketplace, inmates are more dependent on the organization than the clientele usually is in other bureaucracies. On the other hand, the service providers in this relationship are much less dependent on the clients than on the customers (government agencies) for their economic success. It is more important for the providers to satisfy the customers than the needs and wishes of the clients. This implies that the clients (inmates) have little or no control over their fate in the correctional system, and this situation is amplified by the fact that they are kept in the institution against their will (Hasenfeld & English, 1974). In sum, the nature of relations is complex in the triad of the criminal justice agencies, the private correctional companies, and the inmates. Important questions may be asked regarding who is responsible for what, who handles complaints, who evaluates the services and on what bases, who makes final decisions regarding institutional conditions, who is judging inmate behavior, and so forth.

A related issue concerns the clarification of who is the primary beneficiary of this arrangement, namely, whose interest should be the determining one regarding the nature, the quality, and the cost of the services. The needs and wants of the above three participants usually do not coincide; they are often conflicting. The situation is even more exacerbated by the fact that the clients or the users of services are to a large degree politically, economically, and socially powerless stigmatized and unwanted people. "Prisoners are declassé—they are the outcasts of society, exercising virtually no suasion upon public policy" (Geis, 1987, p. 78). They cannot even vote.

In terms of organizational analysis, there is a blurring of the cui bono—who benefits—analytical principle (Blau & Scott, 1962). Theoretically, in the case of public prisons the primary beneficiaries of the organizational activities are the clients (inmates) as in "service organizations," or the public as in "commonwealth organizations." However, in private prisons the primary beneficiaries are the owners and the executives of the corporations, a feature typical of business concerns in this analytical scheme. This difference seems to indicate a substantial change in the organizational context of the delivery of punishment.

Another analysis deals with the organizational differences between private product-producing organizations (PPOs), which are privately held and have a tangible product, and public human service organizations (PSOs), which are government agencies providing public services. The central characteristics compared are organizational values and goals, incentives, organizational structure, raw materials, power-dependency relationships, technology, revenues, accountability, and environmental constraints (Schiflett & Zey, 1990). Although correctional institutions are not mentioned among the PSOs, an argument may be made that they can be characterized as such mainly because their raw materials are human beings (see Shichor, 1978), and their clients "interact with the production processes meant to change them, thus determining their success" (Schiflett & Zey, 1990, p. 574) as in the case of the PSOs. Also, the relationship between the correctional organization and its clients is similar to that of the PSOs, in which the clients depend on the organization for services and the organization needs the clients for its existence. In contrast, in PPOs the relationship between the organization and its customers is basically an instrumental one between the seller and the buyer.

Schiflett and Zey (1990) come to the conclusion that due to the differing organizational characteristics, "attempts to privatize PSOs by applying business models . . . will be ineffective" (p. 580). Critics and opponents of private prisons may arrive at a similar conclusion.

Conclusion

The privatization issue in general, and correctional privatization in particular, is integrally related to the concept and theory of state.

The classical liberal, the libertarian, and the neoconservative economic and sociopolitical philosophies view the minimization of state authority as a major philosophical and pragmatic goal. They see government as the problem rather than as the solution to social, political, and economic problems.[14]

However, there are some questions regarding this approach. As Starr (1989) points out, privatization entails the "fundamental reordering of claims in a society." The concept of *public* invokes "claims of public purpose, public accountability, and public disclosure. To say something is private is to claim protection from state officials and other citizens." Thus the activities of private corporations operating correctional facilities (which are out of the limelight, anyway) may be pretty much hidden from the public. To a large degree privatization limits if not eliminates "the foundations of claims for public purpose and public service" (Starr, 1989, p. 92).

The symbolic meaning of privatization is important as well. It indicates a negative evaluation of the competence and desirability of public provision of services and reinforces the widely held opinion in American society that government agencies cannot perform well. In many instances, and probably in corrections more than in any other field, it is a vicious circle because there are many restrictions on the quality of public provision of services stemming mainly from budgetary reasons. American society limits public services both in quantity and quality mainly because the recipients are poor and powerless people, thus almost making sure that any private provision will be considered to be an improvement over the public service. The view of inferiority of public services is being promoted by the supporters of privatization.

This approach is unbalanced and one-sided. "Privatization raises questions exclusively about the adequacy of the public sector; the comparable questions about the private sector do not receive the same attention" (Starr, 1989, p. 44).[15] Privatization has a strong political undertone because it is a part of an effort by conservatives to enhance their own political power, by blurring the distinctions between the public and private spheres of social activities (e.g., Bozeman, 1988) and by attempting to create a minimal state. These attempts reach to the heart of the privatization of corrections because the state monopoly on the use of coercive force against law violators is being questioned.

In an era of increasingly complex societies the feasibility of a minimal state is diminishing. There are social, political, economic, and technological realities that require state intervention. Even Reaganite conservatives were supporting government subsidies for depressed industries, financial bailouts for certain corporations, and government tax credit policies to help industries and urban areas (e.g., enterprise zones); there are even conservatives who demand enforcement of trade restrictions against foreign countries that are involved in unfair trade practices with the United States. The provision of certain social services remains in the government's domain. In some respects, conservatives increased the government's role in crime control by pressing for more laws, more law enforcement discretion, and higher criminal justice expenditures.

In many spheres the government's role is indispensable. As Kamerman and Kahn (1989) point out, there is no alternative currently to government control of environmental pollution, consumer protection, or the government solution of problems like the 1986-1987 liability insurance crisis. Public health agencies can direct more social action than market dynamics can in the search for disease control and research for major health problems such as AIDS partially because they are more susceptible to political pressures from interest groups. Except for a relatively few archconservatives, not many question the government's role in the provision of Social Security and unemployment benefits. Most people seem to realize "that government cannot really leave social services to the free market—if only because the market can inflate costs" as it has demonstrated in medical care (Kamorman & Kahn, 1989, p. 267). Modern complex societies do need a viable government in a much more extended role than the minimal-state advocates would like to have. This does not exclude the involvement of the private sector in the provision of certain services, but privatization as an ideology and a general remedy for the ills of public administration does not seem to be the answer. Also, the implications of the expansion of social control through privatization should be considered, analyzed, and evaluated in detail.

Finally, there is always a strong possibility that "throwaway" people who are handled by institutions will be mishandled, neglected, abused, and exploited. That danger is present not only in prisons but in nursing homes, mental hospitals, homes for people with developmental handicaps, juvenile institutions, orphanages, and other similar institutions as well, whether these institutions are run by public agencies or by private contractors (e.g., Mendelson, 1974; Wooden, 1976). But again, in all cases considered, the temptation of extra economic gain generated by cutting corners may add an additional risk for violations and abuses in privately operated versus publicly managed facilities. "One of the main problems that must be faced in a situation where services are rendered by one party to a second party with payment made by a third party is the fraud that the system can generate" (Jayewardene & Talbot, 1983, p. 184).

Notes

1. The fact that a large volume of philosophical literature deals with the nature, justification, and problems of punishment is an indicator of the serious moral and ethical questions involved with this issue.

2. Morality refers to what is judged to be good or bad conduct by society (Pollock, 1994).

3. Locke perceived the state as a political society that receives its power from the members of society to receive protection of their lives, liberties, and property, but ultimately the political power remains in the hands of the individuals.

4. Power is legitimate when it conforms to rules that are rooted in the shared beliefs of the sovereign and the subordinate, and the subordinate consents freely to this power relationship (Beetham, 1991).

5. In the post-Enlightenment European philosophical tradition, the state was seen as a cohesive force that unified society, and its legitimacy was derived from its unifying ability rather than from the implicit or explicit consent of citizens. Hegel, representing this tradition, saw in the state the provider of overall purpose for both individuals and for society. He saw in the state the focal organizing principle overseeing and protecting the general social interest by providing a universal and ethical spirit (Jordan, 1985). The priority of the state over the individuals in his philosophy is seen by viewing men as "rational, orderly beings to the degree that they accept the order inherent in the state, which is a universal sphere cutting across the egoistic interest of human actions in civil society" (Giddens, 1971, p. 5). Hegel idealized the state as the "highest of ethical communities" (Martindale, 1960, p. 155) and as a moral idea (Russell, 1945). In this line of thinking, the state has the legitimate monopoly over the exercise of coercive power.

6. This perspective, based on philosophical grounds, would favor the elimination of "Good Samaritan" laws, and such laws as wearing seatbelts and motorcycle helmets.

7. This approach could lead back to the "golden age of the victim" (Schafer, 1977), and at the extreme may undermine the foundations of the state, reflecting an anarchistic position.

8. For example, disciplinary hearings in privately operated prisons are conducted by government employees, usually by the state monitors of the facility.

9. For example, in southern California during the 1970s some government-funded drug treatment programs were run by the "Mexican Mafia," which was using these programs for drug trafficking.

10. Net widening is often mentioned as an outcome of community-based programs, especially diversion (see, e.g., Krisberg & Austin, 1980). Cohen (1985) describes this aspect of the expansion of formal social control by using the metaphor of the Trojan horse. On the other hand, there are writers who claim that the criticism of expansion of control is too general and does not allow for trying out new innovative programs (e.g., Pease, 1983; Vass, 1990).

11. The capacity of an "overburdened" criminal justice system to punish became a major policy issue during the late 1970s and 1980s as a result of the increased number of cases dealt with in the criminal justice system and the overcrowding of prisons. In the criminological literature the "system capacity" model emerged, which dealt with the impact of crime rate on the efficacy of deterrence (see Pontell, 1978).

12. Prisons are expected not only to incarcerate offenders but also to deter them from future crimes (special deterrence) and to deter potential offenders from committing crimes (general deterrence), to serve retributive justice, that is, to give the amount of suffering to the convicted criminals that they deserve, and on the top of these to make an attempt for some degree of rehabilitation (e.g., vocational training, some level of education, psychological programs, and alcohol and drug abuse programs). As known, the large majority of prisons do not perform very well in most accounts; in fact, that is one reason the establishment of private prisons is seriously considered.

13. Nozick (1974) demonstrates that the invisible hand explanation can be used in a great variety of situations. He also makes a distinction between the invisible hand concept and the concept of "hidden hand" explanation, which presents a set of disconnected facts as the result of an individual's, group's, or organization's design.

14. However, they do not feel as contradictory to their philosophy to demand and accept government help when it is beneficial for that segment of society that they represent, for example, the bailout of Chrysler by the government or government subsidies to various industries such as the tobacco industry.

15. Amazingly, there were no major attacks on the private sector—its efficiency, accountability, sense of morality, and so on—in the wake of the savings and loan scandal, which cost more to the American taxpayers than any other scandal before. There were only criticisms of individuals who were accused of wrongdoing but not of the whole private for-profit sector. It seems that the American public tacitly accepts the caveat emptor philosophy, meaning that the private sector may try to make money any way it can, and it is the government's function to stop these attempts and if the government is not successful in doing so, it is the government's fault. Here, again, is a contradiction because, as seen, the government interference with business activities is opposed by many, a factor that obviously limits the government's ability to be an efficient watchdog.

4

Legal Issues

Constitutionality

One of the major questions in the privatization of correctional institutions in the United States is whether this practice is constitutional. In a thorough legal analysis, Robbins (1989) deals with three constitutional dimensions of private operation of prisons: "the delegation doctrine, the state-action requirement, and the thirteenth amendment" (p. 544). Generally, the federal courts have accepted the delegation of federal powers to private contractors. There is a difficulty in precisely defining governmental powers. Nevertheless, certain powers are recognized as basically governmental, such as "rulemaking, adjudication of rights, seizure of person or property, licensing and taxation." These powers are coercive, "making someone do something he does not choose to do or preventing him from doing what he wishes to do" (Lawrence, 1986, p. 648). Delegation of government powers by states is seldom a federal constitutional issue.

Although the Constitution is not explicit about the delegation of power of Congress to other entities, public or private, the U.S. Supreme Court has ruled against this kind of delegation (Robbins, 1986). The Constitution vests all the legislative powers in Congress. Congress is empowered "to make laws which shall be necessary and proper for carrying into execution the foregoing powers" (U.S. Constitution, Article I, S1). It also entrusts Congress with the means to execute its legislation. There are contrasting views in regard to the issue focusing on the phrase "necessary and proper":

1. The early interpretation of the Constitution on this point was that this phrase excludes a choice of means; therefore Congress is required to use the most direct means to exercise its constitutional powers. This interpretation was rejected in 1819 by the U.S. Supreme Court in *McCulloch v. Maryland*.
2. According to the Court, the meaning of the term *necessary* implies the employment of any means to achieve the desired results (Ellison, 1986/ 1987, p. 691).

Robbins (1989) observes that the Supreme Court tends to sustain the constitutionality of delegation of power to public entities when it is challenged. As far as delegation to state powers is concerned, the Court upheld the vast majority of cases that were challenged. The guidelines for delegation on the federal level do not seem to be very precise. "Commentators generally agree that the Supreme Court has not stated a satisfactory theory of principles governing the delegation doctrine and has failed to articulate a precise test to distinguish between statutes that properly delegate and those that do not" (Robbins, 1989, p. 550).

For our discussion suffice it to say that on the federal level the delegation principle is generally not accepted when the delegation of legislative powers is concerned. On the other hand, when administrative powers are concerned, the courts tend to accept the delegation (Evans, 1987). The administrative power is delegated "when the legislature entrusts the management of public functions to private institutions, or significantly support such institutions in their activities" (Liebmann, 1075, p. 713). The operation of a private for-profit prison would come under the delegation of administrative powers; therefore it is unlikely that there would be serious grounds to question the constitutionality of private prison management. However, a recent U.S. General Accounting Office (GAO) report (1991) to the Federal Bureau of Prisons concludes that "key legal and operational issues need to be resolved before privatization should be considered in the federal prison system. Our legal opinion is that BOP lacks sufficient authority to contract with private companies to manage adult secure facilities" (p. 29).

State Delegation of Powers

Most of the private prison cases relate to state governments rather than to the federal government. Federal prisoners are only a small minority of the total prison population, roughly 8%, whereas 92% of the inmates are in state prisons (Flanagan & Maguire, 1990). Robbins (1989) examines the issue of state delegation of power in detail. He distinguishes among three different types of delegation: delegation of management functions, delegation of rule-making authority, and delegation of adjudicative powers.

The delegation of management functions occurs when "a private entity exercises governmental power when it deprives a person of life, liberty, or property at the behest of government" (Robbins, 1989, pp. 558-559). This kind of delegation is fairly common. For example, private security guards in department stores are permitted by statutes to detain suspected shoplifters. Robbins (1989) argues that this and other examples he cites to demonstrate the delegation of the management function are examples of functions that the states commonly permit private parties to perform. Furthermore, in the United States private citizens have the right to arrest suspected offenders, that is, citizen's arrest.

Incarceration of prisoners, however, is traditionally a function that the states have fulfilled (Ellison, 1986/1987), at least during the past century. Therefore Robbins (1989) suggests that it may be handled differently by the courts than the regular administrative delegation cases. However, state laws on delegation of power tend to be confusing; therefore several state legislatures have legislated laws that authorize the delegation of corrections to private parties (McDonald, 1990b).

Delegation of Rule Making

One of the questions relevant in the case of private prisons is whether the legislature has the right to grant powers to a private company to make administrative rules for the correctional facility under its management. If these powers are granted, then the private company can affect the liberty of individuals who, at least formally, remain under government control. The constitutional problems in this case are, first, that only the legislature has the authority to "exercise rule-making governmental power in the public interest" and, second, that a private company might make rules that are detrimental to the public interest but serve its own financial and/or political interests (Robbins, 1989, p. 563).

In the case of private prisons, the question of rule making can become one of the focal issues. Prison inmates have to follow a large number of rules as a part of the everyday routine of the institution. Many of these rules are minor and pertain to minute instances of institutional life. In toto, they create a potential for constant rule breaking among the inmates, which may affect parole decisions, time being served, and everyday living conditions, such as withdrawal of privileges. This situation is furthered by the hidden nature of confinement because, since the creation of the penitentiary, punishment that before was a public spectacle became the most hidden part of the criminal justice process (Foucault, 1977). Thus relatively little attention is being paid by officials and the public to what is happening in prisons.

In assessing the Court's possible reactions to the constitutionality of delegation of power to private companies, it is likely that the delegation of management functions will be upheld (Robbins, 1989). This would include cell assignment, prisoner counting, scheduling of activities, record keeping, and similar routine activities—the authority for these functions would be delegated even though these may impact the decisions concerning the liberty of inmates. For example, cell assignment, which is a "low visibility decision" (McDonald & Weisburd, 1992), may have an impact on violence among inmates and as a chain reaction may have ramifications, not only for the everyday life of the prisoners but also for their disciplinary records and the length of their incarceration.

Discipline

According to Robbins, although private companies will have the opportunity to propose disciplinary rules, these will have to be sanctioned by the state legislature or Department of Corrections. Courts would not allow disciplinary hearings to be conducted by the personnel of private companies in which a determination would be made whether an inmate had violated institutional rules and therefore should be subject to disciplinary action. This would come under the rule-making function. It also would be opposed on the grounds that the private prison corporation is not considered to be a neutral decisionmaker in these matters.[1] The profit that the corporation makes on its services is usually based on the number of inmates housed each day in the institution; thus there is a vested interest for the company in keeping the institution full at all times. Furthermore, the contractor also may benefit financially from the denial of certain services and privileges to inmates because these measures may reduce the operating cost for the corporation.

These arguments concerning the disciplinary measures come under criticism by Logan (1990). First, he points out, correctly, that in the situation of the 1980s and early 1990s there should not be any worry about the companies' profit motivations to keep prisoners in the institutions for longer periods of time because the supply of newly sentenced convicts is so great that the problem is how to find room to place them, rather than to try to cling to inmates who are already serving time in the prison. This situation, however, may change in the future if and when prison admissions start to level off or even drop.[2]

Second, he claims that

> the argument that private prisons will have an incentive toward unfair and improper denial of good time assumes that such decisions will confer only benefits and carry no costs; no commercial company with a competent legal staff would make so unrealistic an assumption. (Logan, 1990, p. 67).

However, this point should be clarified and some concrete examples should be given to show the relevance of this argument. For example, what are the possible costs of denial of good time that the author refers to? Does he mean legal steps? Would inmates be able to sue in every disciplinary case? Would they be able to provide proof for their claims? How would inmate actions weigh against the potential gains that these practices may provide to a private for-profit prison corporations? Third, Logan points to the fact that only about 10% of the disciplinary cases result in the revocation of good time, impacting on the length of sentence. The vast majority of disciplinary actions involve sanctions other than the revocation of good time. However, this 10% of revocation cases may involve thousands of inmates and large sums of money. And also, as mentioned, the denial of certain services and privileges may have financial consequences benefiting private companies.

Logan counters privatization critics' claims concerning the disciplinary process further. He asserts that Robbins, and probably other critics as well, assume that employees of private corporations are biased in ways that government employees are not. He posits first that everyday actions and decisions of employees in any company "are guided largely by personal motives, interests, and incentives that are often quite different from, and may even conflict with, those of the employing organization" (Logan, 1990, p. 68). Although this assertion may be correct to a degree, it does not necessarily mean that corporate pressure or directives from management and supervisors cannot or do not influence the actions of lower level staff at all. Research on organizational deviance indicates that corporations, by setting performance standards, often can "indirectly initiate deviant actions by establishing particular norms, rewards, and punishments for people occupying lower level positions" (Ermann & Lundman, 1982, p. 7). Executives often realize that the violation of certain laws, regulations, and norms are the shortest way to higher profits, and such violations can be mandated through policy directives to lower echelon workers and midlevel managers (Meyer, 1972). In a private prison low-salaried correctional officers who have few opportunities for advancement, lack job security, and have limited marketable skills for other employment may feel a pressure to follow deviant practices (e.g., write more disciplinary reports) to keep their jobs or get promoted.

Second, Logan (1990) claims that the potential for conflict of interest is not unique to private facilities. He mentions that many offenders from government prisons are released early under the pressure of overcrowding and court orders. Release decisions may be influenced by fiscal or other interests of the prison authorities and prison personnel. For example, "saving face and maintaining personal authority can influence both private and public corrections officers in disciplinary matters" (Logan, 1990, p. 69).

Accordingly, potentially biasing factors in organizations usually are not working in only one direction. "In the case of private prisons, the alleged pecuniary incentive toward delaying release in order to maximize revenue is counteracted by a second pecuniary bias toward early release in order to avoid prisoner litigation" (Logan, 1990, p. 69). He also claims that there is a motivation in the organization to maintain a good reputation, and this may be a factor in keeping up with all standards.

The state has an overwhelming interest in "retaining exclusive control over the power to order punishment" (Press, 1990, p. 35). Delegation of this power would be an abdication of authority. It also could open a legal Pandora's box, resulting in endless litigation. Press points out that there are alternative ways to deal with the issue of maintaining discipline in the private prison. One is to have the disciplinary committee as a fact-finding body and the description of the events leading to the write-up should be submitted to a state officer to determine punishment. The other way is to assign a state disciplinary officer to the private prison who would investigate the cases and mete out punishment.

This latter procedure is followed in California; however, there are some questions regarding this policy as well. Although disciplinary hearings in privately operated facilities are conducted by state correctional officials (except in minor cases), the complaints, write-ups, and narrative reports concerning infractions originate from the correctional workers of the private corporation. They determine the charges, they use their discretion, and they follow policies devised by the corporation. Investigations by a fact-finding body could be cumbersome and time-consuming, increase the possibility of friction between the private corporation employees and the state officers, be open to manipulation by prisoners, and undermine the status of the corporate employees in the eyes of the inmates.

The problematic nature of the prison disciplinary process is underscored by the 1974 Supreme Court decision of *Wolff v. McDonnell*, in which the Court laid down the foundation of due process in disciplinary hearings. These included (a) advance written notice; (b) a written statement by the fact finders, concerning the evidence and the reasons for the disciplinary action; (c) the right of prisoners to submit documentary evidence for their defense and to call witnesses; (d) providing counsel for inmates involved; and (e) having an impartial disciplinary board (Rhine, 1990).

Similarly, in England since the 1970s, prison disciplinary procedures were formalized and the courts were ready to interfere with disciplinary issues.

> These decisions recognized at last that what was at stake in disciplinary hearings was the liberty of prisoners, since, as one-third remission increasingly became a defacto right in post-war years, the major sanction of forfeiture of remission had become tantamount to a deprivation of liberty. (Fitzgerald, 1985, p. 31)

As earlier discussions have indicated, there is a strong claim that the motives of the individual officers or managers should not consistently be questioned. Due process policies can determine procedures for fair treatment, and they may be more important than the motives and character of the actors. Some suggest that due process in disciplinary procedures could be provided by ceding the initial authority to the officials of the private prison and providing arrangements for subjecting their decisions to independent review by government officials (e.g., Logan, 1990). However, as seen, the initiation of the disciplinary process may be influenced by corporate policies. These deliberations point to the importance of the contract, which, besides monetary considerations, should ensure due process procedures and inmate rights in private prisons.

Legal Liability

Another related legal issue is liability. In the everyday operation of private prisons, regardless of how much involvement and supervision will be exercised by government personnel, for example, in the disciplinary process, parole-related decisions, or use of deadly force, many everyday decisions will be made by the private staff and management. If any allegations of violation of civil rights occur, in connection with actions of the private corporation or its employees, the question of legal responsibility will have to be addressed. The plaintiff will have to show that the private party acted as a representative of the state to win the case under 42 U.S.C. 1983.

Most of the protections for individual rights and liberties specified in the Constitution apply only to the actions of government entities. Therefore when a private individual is sued for the violation of the civil rights of another person, it must be proven that the individual was acting "under color of state law," indicating that there was a "state action" in effect (Mayer, 1986; Robbins, 1986, 1989). Usually, an inmate in a privately run prison who is challenging an action of the management or an employee on the grounds of civil rights violations would file a lawsuit under 42 U.S.C. 1983. The claim would be that the inmate's constitutional rights have been violated by the private operator who acted under color of state law.

The above section of the law historically dates back to the period after the Civil War and the ratification of the Thirteenth, Fourteenth, and Fifteenth Amendments to the U.S. Constitution and it meant to provide protection against the unlawful deprivation of civil rights by the state.

Originally, the purposes of this section were threefold:

> To negate any state laws which sought to draw invidious distinctions between categories of citizens on the basis of race; to provide a federal remedy for those suffering constitutional deprivations in settings where state law clearly provided no adequate remedy; and to provide a federal remedy for those suffering constitutional deprivations in settings where state law, although arguably providing an adequate remedy on its face, was inadequate as applied. (Thomas & Hanson, 1989, p. 936)

This discussion then indicates that proving that a state action took place is a prerequisite for the application of Section 1983 because it establishes civil liability for those individuals who, while acting under color of state law, deprive others of their civil rights (Pellicciotti, 1987). Section 1983 was seldom used until the 1960s when its utility was greatly expanded in conjunction with the activities of the Civil Rights movement and the readiness of the Warren Court to deal with civil rights issues.

In corrections this section is likely to be used in cases where (a) the state acts through its own agents, (b) the state establishes arrangements in which private interest can deprive individuals of their constitutional rights, and (c) the functions traditionally performed by state agencies are delegated to private interests (Mayer, 1986).

Robbins (1986) posed the core question of this issue, namely, "whether the acts of a private entity operating a correctional institution constitutes a 'state action' " (p. 26). In other words, the question is whether the private company, which is alleged to be in violation of the plaintiff's constitutional rights, is acting under color of state law.

There are three basic tests that determine what constitutes a state action. First is the public function test. According to a U.S. Supreme Court decision (*Medina v. O'Neill*, 1984), a state action exists when the state delegates to private parties a power that traditionally was exclusive for the state authorities. Second is the close-nexus test, which tries to establish whether there is a close nexus between the state and the action against which a complaint is being submitted to consider the action to be that of the state itself. Third is the state compulsion test; this test tries to determine whether the state has an undisputed duty to provide the services that through their provision the plaintiff's rights were allegedly violated (Robbins, 1986).

It seems clear that on all three counts, the private operator can be considered to be acting under color of state law. According to Robbins (1986), (a) the state delegates to the private operators of prisons a power that was traditionally (at least in the 20th century) in the exclusive domain of state authorities; (b) based on several court decisions, there can be a close-nexus established between the actions of a private party operating a prison and the state; and (c) court decisions also indicate that the state does have an obligation to provide certain specific services (including incarceration of offenders) and, if a private entity under contract with the state provides these services, then the state is responsible for them.

The current perspective by opponents as well as by proponents of private prisons is that the government neither can discard its constitutional duties nor can it avoid liability for their provision, even if they are delegated to private parties (Logan, 1990). Joseph Fenton (the executive vice president of Buckingham Security Company, which is involved in private corrections) points out that after exhaustive legal research, the company's counsel came to the conclusion that there is very little case law available that directly deals with privately managed correctional programs. However, "that which exists suggests that the state can contract out duties, but it cannot contract away responsibility" (Fenton, 1985, p. 44). Other proponents of private prisons also agree that the liability for what is happening in the prison ultimately lies with the government.

It is feasible that many state departments of corrections would be ready to delegate the authority of handling convicted offenders together with the responsibility for managing correctional facilities. The major reasons for being ready to do so are related to the increasing pressures of the ever growing number of inmates, leading to unprecedented overcrowding, and the various court orders pertaining to the curbing of overcrowding. At the same time, there seems to be no relief on the horizon because federal and state governments are going through a severe fiscal crisis; therefore the continuous prison building programs seem to have slowed down. The public, which clamors for the incarceration of more and more dangerous offenders, appears to be reluctant to foot the bill and often defeats bond issue propositions aimed at financing the building of new prisons.[3]

Also, the high visibility of escapes and riots presented by the media could provide an impetus for the authorities to shed the liability for the management of prisons. However, it seems to be agreed on that "there is no legal principle to support the premise that public agencies and officials will be able to avoid or diminish their liability merely because services have been delegated to a private vendor" (Mullen et al., 1985, p. 9). As seen, not only the critics of private prisons but also the proponents agree on this issue. Logan (1990), for example, states that "government liability is a nonissue" (p. 184). In this case the question, according to him, becomes an economic one, namely, whether the liability for private prisons results in higher or lower legal costs for the government.

Another question is whether the fact that the government remains liable for private prisons is better or worse for corrections. Advocates of private institutions consider government liability a plus for the prisoners because, according to them, it emphasizes accountability and the protection of prisoner rights (e.g., Logan, 1990). This approach is noteworthy because it indicates that private prison operators want it in both ways; they want to operate the prison and make money on this endeavor, but at the same time they want an "insurance policy" backing them up in the form of government liability. This would mean that in the case of major legal problems, when a serious violation of inmate civil rights occurs, such as an inmate is severely injured, an escapee causes serious harm in the community, a riot "overflows" into the community, or one of the employees gets hurt, the government may become the main target of the lawsuit because even if the company carries a large insurance policy, the government remains the "deep pocket." That may occur under circumstances in which government agencies do not have full control over what is happening in the privately managed institution. Although the claim is that a detailed contract and monitoring system by the government will be safeguards from the above occurrences, the contention is that even the "best" written and most detailed contract and rigorous monitoring cannot provide full and complete government control over every action taken by the private management and its employees. Thus, although the ultimate liability would remain with the government, some of its control and authority in reality would dissipate.

Government officials who support privatization would like to get rid of the liability together with the responsibility for running the institution. This is in line with the Reagan era's policy of load shedding, which is basically aiming at the reduction of the social role and responsibility of government (Kamerman & Kahn, 1989).

Some analysts argue that liability laws do create incentives for private corporations to provide adequate services. They claim that in this respect inmates seem to be better protected in privately managed facilities because "the federal courts have clearly established that private correctional firms are liable for monetary damages if inmates' rights are violated, whereas public officials acting on behalf of public authorities are not" (McDonald, 1990b, p. 191).

These opinions are intriguing and illuminating because they involve both supporters and opponents of correctional privatization. It also indicates, as noted, that the private for-profit sector is interested in having a safety net in the form of government liability, which in the case of major legal or fiscal problems will be able to bail out private companies. On the other hand, government supporters of privatization want to privatize liability as well. Paradoxically, in the

true sense of privatization, these government officials are closer to
the ideal of privatization than are the promoters of private prisons.

On the practical side of the issue of liability, its importance can be
demonstrated by the increasing number of civil rights suits brought
by prison inmates during the 1980s. There were over 18,000 such
cases in 1985 alone (Ellison, 1986/1987).

According to Logan (1990), the fact that the liability for the private
prisons will remain with the government is a "very strong argument
for privatization, because it emphasizes that accountability and protection of prisoners' rights will not be compromised" (p. 184). This
seems to admit that private companies do not always enjoy a positive
public image; therefore, the government, which otherwise is criticized as inefficient and wasteful by privatization advocates, in this
case may fulfill a useful function in the furthering of the privatization
of prisons.

The fact that liability cannot be delegated by the government emphasizes the importance of contracts and their monitoring as major safeguards against legal problems that may affect the government.

Prisoners' Rights

Another important legal issue is related to prisoners' rights. There
is a consensus among many scholars, legal experts, and correctional
officials that privately operated correctional facilities will have to
abide by the same constitutional standards as the facilities administered by the state departments of corrections do (see Sullivan, 1989).
As seen, it was argued by many that government cannot shed completely or even diminish substantially its liability for the operation
of the prisons after privatization takes place (e.g., Mayer, 1986;
Robbins, 1986). These provisions also would cover the constitutional
rights of prisoners.

At the outset it should be mentioned that these constitutional rights
are protected by federal law. Since the 1960s prisoners "have besieged the federal courts with civil rights suits challenging every
aspect of prison programs and practices" (Jacobs, 1983, p. 33).

Historically, prisoners were considered to be the slaves of the state.
The well-known case of *Ruffin v. The Commonwealth of Virginia* in

1871 stated that a prisoner "has, as a consequence of his crime, not only forfeited his liberty, but all his personal rights except those which the law in its humanity accords to him. He is, for the time being the slave of the state" (quoted in Bartollas & Dinitz, 1989, p. 463; Hawkins & Alpert, 1989, p. 366). The Constitution did not dwell much on the rights of prisoners. The constitutional document itself in 1787 affirmed the basic right of habeas corpus (the right to challenge confinement). The Bill of Rights of 1789 had only one phrase in the Eighth Amendment concerning the unconstitutionality of "cruel and unusual punishment" dealing directly with prisoners. The Bill of Rights was hardly used for providing rights to prisoners until the mid-20th century.[4] The courts preferred not to get involved with prisoners' complaints against the conditions of confinement; therefore it was virtually impossible for inmates to seek legal relief from abusive treatment and harsh or inhuman prison conditions (Hawkins & Alpert, 1989).

This judicial approach reflected the often mentioned "hands off" doctrine of the courts. It demonstrated the tendency to ignore inmate complaints concerning their treatment and to defer to the correctional authorities problems that occur in prisons under their jurisdiction. This pattern often led to a catch-22 situation because these grievances were handled many times by the same authorities who represented those against whom the complaints were directed (Shover & Einstadter, 1988).

As a modern version of the hands-off doctrine, Shover and Einstadter (1988) present the *Stroud v. Swope* (1951) case in which a federal circuit judge declared: "We think it well settled that it is not the function of the courts to superintend the treatment and discipline of persons in penitentiaries but only to deliver from imprisonment those who are illegally confined" (p. 159).

The lack of special attention to prisoners and their rights in the Constitution has provided the states with the opportunity to create their own approach to the rights of prisoners. As seen, Virginia, for example, made a very strong connection between inmates and slaves. Many states enacted civil death statutes, meaning that the prisoners were legally defined as dead, losing, among others, their rights to seek any remedies for their conditions in the courts. Civil death statutes meant that inmates had no standing in legal proceedings concerning their property, marriage, custody of their children, and any other personal matters outside the prison.

In most states the civil death statutes have been abolished; thus the inmates have gained a legal standing in civil cases regarding their private affairs beyond the prison walls. The major turns in this respect came in the 1940s. In 1941 the Supreme Court, in *Ex parte Hull*, provided inmates the opportunity to exercise their constitutional rights of access to federal courts. It determined that the states cannot prevent prisoners from applying to federal courts for a writ of habeas corpus.

The writ of habeas corpus (in Latin means "you should have the body") is a document that commands the authorities to show cause why an inmate should be confined in prison or jail (Champion, 1990). The roots of this procedure are in the English Habeas Corpus Act of 1679, which was enacted against the unlawful detention of individuals without the filing of criminal charges against them (Jones, 1981). Habeas corpus petitions provide a legal avenue for prisoners to seek their release.

Another major case that focused on the writ of habeas corpus was *Coffin v. Reichard* (1944). In this instance the court ruled that federal habeas corpus could be applied to the conditions of confinement, not only to the fact of it:

> A prisoner is entitled to the writ of habeas corpus when, though lawfully in custody [fact], he is deprived of some right to which he is lawfully entitled even in his confinement [condition], the deprivation of which serves to make his imprisonment more burdensome than the law allows or curtails his liberty to a greater extent than the law permits (*Coffin v. Reichard*, 1944, p. 445).

These rulings paved the way for the federal courts to look into the conditions prevailing in state prisons. However, until the mid-1960s, the courts maintained the hands-off doctrine concerning prisoners' rights.

The reluctance of the courts to get involved in the operations of prisons arose also from

> (a) concern about the separation of powers of the three branches of government, (b) the issue of state's rights to run their prisons, (c) the question of court officials' expertise in prison affairs, (d) a fear that

judicial intervention would undermine prison administrators and their methods of inmate discipline, and (e) the likely increase in petitions from inmates following the adoption of a "hands-on" policy. (Hawkins & Alpert, 1989, p. 368)

Several experts foresee an increase in judicial intervention in prison administration with the change of the hands-off doctrine (e.g., Palmer, 1985); however, the conservative social climate of the 1980s and early 1990s may have dampened this trend somewhat.

There are several avenues in which legal procedures challenging prison conditions and/or the practices of prison officials can be initiated. These include (a) state habeas corpus; (b) federal habeas corpus, but only if state remedies have been exhausted; (c) state tort suits, which are civil actions against an individual correctional employee; (d) Section 1983 of the federal Civil Rights Act of 1871, which was originally enacted to prevent lynching by the Ku Klux Klan, used to claim that one has been deprived of a right provided by the Constitution; and (e) the Civil Rights of Institutionalized Persons Act of 1980, which allows the federal government to pursue in civil courts equitable relief, but not damages, against state employees of any state office or institution (Hawkins & Alpert, 1989).

Most habeas corpus suits by inmates are challenging the trial procedures or the sentencing phase of their cases in the federal courts, usually after they have exhausted the gamut of state legal remedies (Knight & Early, 1986). Only about one third of the habeas corpus cases involve prison conditions such as revocation of good time, parole date setting, or disciplinary proceedings (Thomas, Keeler, & Harris, 1986).

Recently, the most frequently used avenue for challenging prison conditions is Section 1983 of the Civil Rights Act of 1871. Thomas and Hanson (1989) claim that originally it was intended to provide a civil enforcement mechanism for Section 1 of the Fourteenth Amendment. The use of federal intervention into prisons, as it is provided by this section, is important in the sense that federal supremacy is needed to uphold and protect federal constitutional rights (McCoy, 1981).

If one's civil rights are violated by the state, the individual has the opportunity to seek redress for the "constitutional tort." Inmates often prefer to litigate constitutional claims in federal courts rather than in state courts. The two major reasons for this are that (a) in most states officials are given immunity from being sued in state courts for their actions in their capacity as state officials, and (b) "prisoners perceive that federal courts possess an aura of justice and dignity that they find lacking in state courts" (Kay, 1987, pp. 868-869). Section 1983 requires the complainant to establish, first, that the prisoners were deprived of their constitutional rights and, second, that the deprivation occurred under color of state law.

Most problems that inmates have with institutional rules and prison staff are handled through grievance procedures in the institution. Relatively few cases go beyond the prison walls to state and federal courts; the majority of these are either habeas corpus actions or Section 1983 lawsuits. The latter became prominent during the 1970s for prisoners who were seeking to change certain prison conditions. The use of this section has increased after the 1964 Supreme Court decision in *Cooper v. Pate*, pertaining to the rights of Muslims in prison to have access to the Koran, to be allowed to have communication and visits with Muslim clergymen, and to attend Muslim religious services (Jacobs, 1977).

Since 1977, Section 1983 actions surpassed the number of habeas corpus cases. The popularity of this section among inmates stems from the following: (a) prisoners, by using Section 1983, can seek damages that are not available through habeas corpus; (b) because Section 1983 represents the federal Civil Rights Act, it allows inmates better opportunities to build their case—as Rudovsky, Bronstein, Koren, and Cade (1988) state, "a prisoner in a habeas corpus proceeding cannot request the production of documentary materials, answers to written interrogatories, and admissions from the defendant; if the lawsuit is based upon the Civil Rights Act, such requests would clearly be a matter of rights for the prisoner" (p. 139); (c) in the case of 1983 actions, class action suits seem to be more likely to be accepted by the courts (Hawkins & Alpert, 1989); and (d) the legal remedy provided by this section is in addition to any available state remedy and it is independent of the latter (Knight & Early, 1986).

42 U.S.C. Section 1983 and Private Prisons

Several issues concern the legal protection of prisoner rights in privately operated correctional facilities. One major question in this

vein pertains to the civil liability of the private correctional corporations in the case of prisoners' suits. According to Thomas and Hanson
(1989), the extent of liability of a private company under Section 1983
is not clear. The core issues are connected to the state-action and the
under-color-of-state-law requirements that allow plaintiffs to bring
suits against private parties as defendants only under limited conditions. When a case is pursued under Section 1983, the plaintiff has
to prove that his or her constitutional rights, privileges, or immunities
were deprived wrongfully, and this deprivation occurred by a person
acting under color of state law and the particular instance constitutes
state action in order to satisfy the Fourteenth Amendment.

The legal issues involved in the delegation of power and the private
companies' actions under the various legal tests (public function test,
close-nexus test, state compulsion test, and multicharacterization analysis) have been analyzed by Robbins (1989). He came to the conclusion
that "state action can be found in the private-prison or private-jail
context under any of the various tests" (Robbins, 1989, p. 604). This
means that the government's liability for civil rights violations in private
correctional facilities remains in effect. Pellicciotti (1987) reached the
same conclusion by pointing out that the Section 1983 liability of
correctional officials will depend on the nature of official conduct in
each particular case. The scope of liability includes three categories of
conduct that are wrongful: intentional conduct, negligent conduct, and
intermediate conduct. If prisoners' rights are intentionally deprived, the
Section 1983 liability will clearly apply. Unintended injury caused by
carelessness or negligence of correctional personnel will not trigger legal
action under Section 1983 and will not hold the government liable.
Pellicciotti (1987) relied on two 1986 cases that were Section 1983
claims for deprivation of liberty without due process: (a) *Daniels v.
Williams*, in which a prisoner sought damages for injuries received when
he slipped on a pillow left on a stairway by a correctional officer, and
(b) *Davidson v. Canon*, in which a prisoner was injured by a fellow
inmate when correctional staff negligently failed to take reasonable
measures to protect the prisoner from the attack. The Supreme Court
rulings in these cases stated that negligence by correctional officials
causing unintended loss did not invoke the due process clause.

The situation in intermediate cases between intentional action and
negligent action is unclear. It does not involve intent to inflict injury,

but it does involve a greater degree of wrongfulness than a simple failure to exercise reasonable care. Thus this category remains a gray area.

An analysis of the implications of Section 1983 in the case of privatization reaches the conclusion, on the basis of various court cases, that private prison operations should be seen as a state action. This opinion is based on *West v. Atkins* (1987, rev'd 1988), in which the Supreme Court:

> Instead of looking at whether the actors were state employees at the time they were alleged to have caused a constitutional deprivation, the Court focused on the nature of the service any person, whether a public or private employee, was charged with providing at the time of an alleged deprivation. If the service was one the state itself constitutionally mandated to provide and the state merely chose to meet its obligation via contracting with a private entity for the service, then those providing the service acted under color of the state law for purposes of Section 1983. (Thomas & Hanson, 1989, pp. 946-947)

It seems clear that the Supreme Court established the principle that both public and private entities can qualify as defendants in Section 1983 cases, providing that their actions satisfy the conditions of the state-action requirement of the Fourteenth Amendment and the under-color-of-state-law requirement of Section 1983 (Thomas, 1991).

Inmates have only a limited opportunity to obtain legal remedies from the courts in the case of their claims of violations of their rights. According to the Eleventh Amendment, individuals cannot sue their own state or another state in a federal court. Because a state can act only through individuals who are its agents or its employees, the immunity accorded by the Eleventh Amendment is extended to officials who are in a policy-making capacity acting as the state. Individuals may sue these officials to challenge the constitutionality of their actions, even though the suit is considered to be against the state. Thus, when an official acts in violation of the constitution, he or she loses the sovereign immunity and may become a target of a suit (Kay, 1987; *Ex parte Young*, 1908). The most compelling reason for having sovereign immunity is to enable government officials to function effectively without the imminent threat of being sued. There are states that abrogated this doctrine. Therefore the sovereign immunity defense depends on the laws of each state (Palmer, 1985). In these cases, the state official may be liable only for prospective injunctive relief. Because the Eleventh Amendment is relevant only for the state, lower level officials who do not personify the state for purposes of litigation cannot use the defense of sovereign immunity (Kay, 1987). In this vein, county and municipal governments, which do not personify the state directly, are not protected by sovereign immunity.

In the case of a private prisons, not only the employees but the corporation itself could be liable in a Section 1983 action. A private prison official can be held responsible for monetary as well as injunctive relief.

State officials in policy-making positions, in addition to the sovereign immunity available to them, may rely also on a defense of qualified immunity. Unless there was a clear violation of the law at the time of the challenged action, the court cannot hold the state official liable for monetary damages. Based on the analysis of several court cases, it seems likely that the courts would extend qualified immunity to the employees of private prison companies. However, in the case of the corporations themselves, it is possible that only firms that are contracted by the state, that is, operating state prisons, would receive qualified immunity, whereas firms running jails would not.[5] Kay (1987) claims that the qualified immunity will not necessarily be extended for employees of for-profit correctional firms. The doctrine of qualified immunity meant to encourage state employees to perform their jobs to the best of their abilities without fear of being sued. The doctrine assumes that these employees will have the good of the state as their goal. On the other hand, employees of a private prison corporation are responsible to produce profit for their company and owe their direct responsibility to the management of the company. They do not have to answer to the public at large as do state employees; they are responsible to their supervisors and ultimately to the corporation's stockholders. "Unlike state employees, corporate employees may be forced to choose between making money and safeguarding the rights of inmates. A defense of qualified immunity, if awarded to these private employees, might encourage them to cut corners to maximize profits" (Kay, 1987, p. 887).

It may be claimed that the private corrections companies voluntarily took on themselves a task that was previously the exclusive province of the state for profit-making purposes. Thus their workers have a different status than state employees have because the state is required to render certain services; therefore state employees' actions are not voluntary. Accordingly, "the liability of private contractors may be greater than that for public employees in comparable situations because the private party will be able to assert fewer immunity defenses" (Kay, 1987, p. 888).

Thomas (1991) seems to agree with the above analysis, but sees the situation as advantageous for the inmates housed in private facilities because, according to him, they have more legal remedies in the case of violations of their rights than inmates incarcerated in state prisons. On the local level, as in the case of county jails, government units have less immunity than state facilities do; they are open to the full range of Section 1983 remedies with the exception of punitive damages. Private companies operating correctional facilities at the local level would be open to punitive damages as well. Again, according to this analysis, inmates in privately operated facilities would have more remedies available to secure their rights than would inmates in publicly run facilities. Thomas's (1991) conclusion is that prisoners' rights in private facilities are better protected because private prison companies and their workers have less immunities guaranteed by Section 1983 than do government prisons and their employees, thus prisoners in private prisons have more legal remedies available to them in case of violation of their civil rights. Opponents of privatization seem to agree with this conclusion (e.g., Kay, 1987). However, they point to the other side of the coin, namely, that this situation will leave the government ultimately liable for the situation in privately operated facilities because the government has the constitutional obligation for the punishment of lawbreakers (Robbins, 1989). Thus, ultimately, the government will be held responsible for an operation over which it does not have full control and may end up paying for damages.

Nevertheless, the suggestion that prisoners in private prisons enjoy more vigorous legal protection of their rights than do those in public institutions because of weaker legal immunities available for private companies and their employees than for government agencies and their staff, is reassuring (e.g., Logan, 1990; Thomas, 1991). However, this optimism should be tempered somewhat by the fact that in a prison, there are many opportunities to violate due process rights of prisoners that do not necessarily result in court cases. It is emphasized by both proponents and opponents of privatization that the formal disciplinary process and other procedures affecting inmates have to be conducted according to the state Department of Corrections' policies, or if they are not in conflict with state policies, the American Correctional Association's (ACA) standards can be followed but have to be reviewed by the department that has the final authority over them. These major decisions include "classification as it affects custody level, discipline, grievances, allocation or revocation of good time, computation of parole eligibility, or discharge dates, and approval of work, medical, or temporary furloughs" (Logan, 1990, p. 27). Logan admits that to formally maintain state sovereignty does not mean that private prison officials should be excluded completely from the decisions and actions relating to discipline in the institution and the release dates. The limitation is that private prison officials should not have the final control over decisions in these areas.

> So long as the government retains final authority and the power of review over disciplinary actions or good time—decisions that affect the liberty of prisoners—delegation of responsibility for these functions would not be "excessive" because sovereignty will not have been lost. (Logan, 1990, p. 60)

It is obvious that at least formally, the state has to maintain exclusive control over punishment. Delegation of this particular power would amount to abdication of authority that the state cannot allow to happen.[6] As seen, it was suggested that this problem should be handled by either (a) the disciplinary committee of the private facility serving only in a fact-finding capacity and having a state officer make decisions regarding sanctions, or (b) the state appointing a disciplinary officer who would both investigate the facts and decide about the sanctions (Press, 1990). But these procedures, as was pointed out, are not going to eliminate the influence of private employees on the disciplinary process and its outcome. Similarly, there will be influences by private staff on the classification of inmates that may affect their institutional treatment. Classification

is often used for disciplinary purposes (e.g., Dauber & Shichor, 1979).
This can be seen when the major criteria used for offender classification are examined. Three major criteria are applied for this purpose:
(a) offense criteria, which is concerned with the seriousness of the
offense committed; (b) risk criteria, based on the probability of future
criminal involvement; and (c) program criteria, based on the evaluation of the nature of correctional treatment needed for each individual offender (Clear & Cole, 1990). Prison staff and officials do have
the opportunity to influence the classification based on program
criteria, and likely, they can influence the risk criteria as well.[7]

Logan (1990) claims that classification of inmates in line with the
level of security or supervision they require is best made by those
who run the institution. According to him, in public institutions there
is a tendency to overclassify inmates because maximum-security
prisons have the highest status, the largest budget, and the largest
staff; therefore there is an incentive to place many of the inmates into
higher security levels. Privately operated prisons have a financial
incentive to hold inmates at the lowest security level. In this way,
they may be able to employ fewer correctional officers or build less
expensive physical plants because maximum-security prisons are
more costly to construct and operate. This claim is correct only if the
per diem paid to the private corporation is the same regardless of
classification levels. However, it is likely that the company can
charge a higher fee for higher security inmates. Privatization advocates using this analysis emphasize that biases in classification, that
is, putting organizational goals before the best interests of inmates,
may occur in any prison regardless of whether it is operated by public
authorities or by private companies. If that is the case, given the
findings that "classification that relates to human and environmental
variables can improve prisoner adjustment and prison management,
often quite substantially" (R. Johnson, 1987, p. 165), misclassification
by purpose for whatever reason may be considered as a violation of
prisoners' rights. In addition, it should be emphasized again that one
of the basic functions of classification is to facilitate organizational
control over inmates (e.g., Doran, 1977), and it is a question to what
extent this control should be given to a private for-profit corporation.

Use of Force

The issue of prisoners' rights and the maintenance of discipline in the prison also raises the question of the use of force, especially deadly force. Generally, the use of deadly force is a relatively rare occurrence, but it may happen, especially in cases of escape attempts and riot situations. In some states private prison employees are deputized as peace officers, thus while they are working for the private company, they are also licensed by the government and may assume public responsibility.

The use of force against an inmate in a prison is a sensitive and complex issue. It may be in violation of rights set by the Constitution (e.g., Eighth Amendment, Fourteenth Amendment). However, under narrow circumstances, the use of force may be justified. One of these circumstances may be the compelling interest in the maintenance of order and security in a correctional facility. The question is whether a private contractor, who has similar obligations to the government's in maintaining security and order, can use force legitimately (Robbins, 1989).

Robbins (1989) presents several alternatives in answering this question. One approach would prohibit the contractor from using any force against inmates, by retaining this power exclusively for the government. This does not seem to be a realistic option in the context of the day-to-day operation of correctional institutions. The potential use of force by correctional officers is an everyday reality in prisons. The banning of the use of force by correctional officers would endanger their own personal safety and would make it impossible for them to render any protection to inmates who are being attacked by other inmates. The staff's ability to maintain order in the institution would be severely impaired. Because, as mentioned, every correctional institution relies on various amounts and forms of coercive power to achieve compliance, there is a need to ensure that there will be the capacity to apply coercive force. If the employees of the private corporation are not allowed to use physical means to achieve compliance in extreme situations or to keep order and to prevent escapes, then government agents will have to be stationed in the facility to do so. That would not only defeat the purpose of privatization but also

would complicate the organizational structure by putting government employees under private management and making private
administrations dependent on public workers.

A second approach would allow private staff to use nondeadly
force under certain defined conditions but would reserve for government workers the exclusive right to use deadly force under limited
circumstances. Robbins (1989) suggests that the circumstances in
which force can be used by the private staff be defined clearly in the
contract, whereas, as said, only government personnel would be able
to use deadly force. This arrangement would result in a situation in
which only government employees would guard against escapes or
prison riots. That would necessitate, again, the staging of a certain
number of public employees in the privately operated facility and
could make the administration of the institution complex and confused, especially when the chain of command is concerned, not to
mention the fiscal aspects of this solution.

A third possibility would be to permit the contracting private
company to use deadly and nondeadly force under limited circumstances. This way the government would not have to do anything
with the use of force at the institution. The direct control over the
use of force probably would allow the smoothest operation of the
prison by the private administration because there would be an
opportunity to react immediately to any situation that may require
intervention. Robbins (1989) suggests that this approach, if adopted,
has to specify clear safeguards and guidelines in the contract, otherwise it may be abused. These guidelines should include adequate
staffing, staff training depicting the circumstances and places in
which force may be used, reporting procedures in case force was
used, and the specification of relationships between the contractor
and local law enforcement authorities regarding prison riots and
searching for escaped inmates.

Two major concerns in the use of force issue are adequate staffing
and proper training for the private prison staff. Because many believe
that one way that private companies will try to cut costs and increase
profits will be the reduction of the number of line staff and their level
of training, the use-of-force question is becoming more important.
Robbins (1989) recommends that the company be required at least to
meet the ACA standards of staffing and training. This requirement is

not objected to by the proponents of privatization; in fact, it is favored by them because by meeting the standards set by a known public organization, they can increase their credibility and public image.

Mayer (1986), in her analysis of this issue, points out that employees working for a privately operated prison already have the same limited arrest power and right to use force that any other private citizen enjoys in the United States. This right is codified in most common law jurisdictions; thus the use of ordinary force by private correctional officers to control inmates in a correctional facility emanates from the common law right of citizen's arrest power.

In regard to the use of deadly force, according to the common law tradition private citizens have a limited right to use deadly force to make an arrest or to prevent an escape (Mayer, 1986). However, in the *Tennessee v. Garner* (1985) case the Supreme Court held that the Fourth Amendment sets more stringent limits on police use of deadly force than do many state laws that are rooted in the common law. This decision eliminates the validity of many state statutes based on the common law.

> Since the right of a police officer to use deadly force is generally more extensive than the right of a private citizen, it seems clear that a private corporation guard's use of deadly force to prevent an escape would be restricted at least as much as the Garner Standard, and possibly more restricted. (Mayer, 1986, p. 318)

In situations other than escape, unless the correctional officer was acting clearly in self-defense or in defense of another person, deadly force would be considered to be excessive; the correctional officer would be liable under criminal law; and the officer, the private corporation, and the state would be liable under civil law.

The most pertinent case in this regard so far has been *Medina v. O'Neill* (1984). In 1981, in Houston, 26 stowaways were detained by the Immigration and Naturalization Service. At first, 20 of the detainees were held at the local jail and 6 of them were placed with a local private security firm. The private firm placed them in a cell designed to hold six people. A day later 10 of the 20 detainees held in the jail also were transferred to the private firm for custody, and they were placed in the same cell, which was already filled to its capacity (Logan, 1990). In this situation 16 illegal immigrants were held in a 12 ft by 20 ft holding cell. A day after the transfer of the 10 aliens to the private facility, the detainees tried to escape from the facility and a private guard in his attempt to prevent the escape accidentally killed one of them with a shotgun and seriously wounded another one. The private guard apparently was untrained in the use of firearms, and his intention was to use his gun as a cattle prod to force the detainees back to their cell (Dunham, 1986).[8]

This and similar incidents were largely attributed to the lack of adequate training of personnel in private companies, the low salaries paid to these employees (private detention personnel were reporting that their salaries were about half of what public correctional officers were paid), and also to the low staff-inmate ratios in private facilities (e.g., in Houston the ratio was one guard to 50 inmates) (Dunham, 1986).

The fact that, so far, private companies manage facilities that are not classified as maximum security, meaning that they tend to have less violent and less seasoned offenders than maximum-security prisons have, has underemphasized the problem of security, discipline, and deadly force. If private companies will enter the hard end of corrections and not only try to manage less troublesome soft-end facilities, as some critics claim, this problem may become even more important. In terms of legal liability for the use of force against inmates, private corporations have a greater exposure than the state itself because the private corporation "is not regarded as the state for the purposes of eleventh amendment immunity" (Spurlock, 1987, p. 1020). This may have a beneficial effect on handling inmates but, at the same time, may expose the state to a higher level of liability because it lies to back up the corporations if the financial claim against them extends beyond the amount of their liability insurance.

Bankruptcy and Mergers of Private Companies

There are legal questions concerning the economic and business aspects of private prisons as well. The problem of government liability for private prisons can shed light on some issues that are connected with the contemporary context of privatization. As seen, modern prison privatization is being done by companies that have been formed specifically for this purpose or are specialized branches or subsidiaries of large conglomerates.

One important issue in this vein that has legal ramifications is involved with the economic strategies of corporate managements to make their operations more profitable. During the 1980s there was an unprecedented trend for corporate mergers, takeovers (both friendly and hostile), acquisitions, and large-scale reorganizations, resulting in spin-off companies and divisions from the newly acquired corporations that were losing money or were less profitable than anticipated. The question of how the government's reliance on private prison management would fare in these kinds of situations is important. What are the legal guarantees for the continuous operation of the prison if a correctional corporation is bought out or sold by its parent company? Moreover, during the past decade an increased number of American corporations were acquired by foreign interests. What will happen if a corporation that owns a division or a subdivision that manages prisons is taken over by a foreign company? Is it acceptable that a foreign corporation handle and will have a certain degree of authority over American prisoners and will make a profit from it? (Shichor, 1993).

Another related issue having legal ramifications is concerned with the question of bankruptcy: What happens when a private prison company declares bankruptcy or goes out of business (Robbins, 1989)? This subject is very appropriate because the number of bankruptcies has peaked during the early 1990s as a "hangover" from the "rolling 1980s" when buyouts and takeovers financed by junk bonds reached formerly unseen proportions. Some issues in this regard concern the legal obligations of the government vis-à-vis the creditors of a prison corporation (American Bar Association, 1986). Others focus on the obligations of the private corporation itself in a case of bankruptcy and its effects on government agencies. How will it be ensured that the prison will continue to operate? Who is going to step in and continue the operations of the facility after the declaration of bankruptcy by a private contractor (Holley, 1988)?

The problems posed by corporate bankruptcies and their legal implications for private prisons should be seen in light of the complex nature of modern business practices. In the current business climate bankruptcies are used for various business strategies such as the alteration of bargaining positions, renegotiation of debts and contracts, stalling for time, and shifting the financial risk to other parties (Delaney, 1990). All these strategies are legal and can be used in dealing with government agencies as well. If the prison population will continue to increase and the government's reliance on private prisons will grow, corporations may use these strategies to try to change contract provisions without the government being able to forestall them.

Regarding the legal issue of bankruptcy, the major questions that have to be asked include

> whether the contract automatically becomes void upon filing for bankruptcy, whether the filing for bankruptcy constitutes a breach of the contract on the part of the private company, and whether the company may assign its contractual obligations to another company for subsequent operation. (Holley, 1988, p. 19)

If a company files for bankruptcy under Chapter 7, a court-appointed trustee has to manage the bankruptcy estate. The trustee may want to assume the contract later. However, the trustee is selected on the basis of economic and business considerations and not on the basis of correctional capabilities.

It is suggested that the state should incorporate several provisions into the contract to make sure that the rights of the state are protected. One of the problems that has to be addressed is that according to Section 365 of the Bankruptcy Code, which applies to the contracting of private prisons, the debtor's power exceeds the legal protections provided to the state. A question that may come up is whether the trustee through an executory contract is able to sell the contract to a third party, and whether this third party is acceptable to the state to fulfill the conditions of the original contract. Usually, the contract can be terminated also under the termination-at-will clause (Holley, 1988). In either way, the government will have a hard time ensuring that the private company will continue to operate the facility uninterruptedly on a satisfactory level under the original conditions.

One variant of bankruptcy under Chapter 11 would allow the existing management to direct the firm as "debtor in possession," as is the case in business and industry. However, again, the problem is that the government may have a direct liability for paying the bills, without regard to the legal type of bankruptcy declared.

Even before actual bankruptcy is declared, the state may be forced to bail out the corporation if it shows financial troubles and cannot meet its obligations. The state's primary concern and responsibility is that the facility will continue to operate, and basic necessities such as food and medical services will be supplied or that an alternative suitable arrangement will be found. To find another facility or another correctional corporation that can step in and operate the prison on a short notice may take some time. Because the government itself may not be equipped to step in by itself to take over the management, it is likely that the only short-run solution in this kind of situation will remain a government bail out.

The bankruptcy situation may become more complicated if a private prison corporation gets involved in a fraudulent bankruptcy procedure, which became an increasing problem during the 1980s and 1990s.

A related factor that should be given some consideration is the increased dependence of the corporate world on financial institutions that control their capital flow (Glasberg, 1981). Many corporations raise their money for their start-up from these institutions. They also need financial institutions in the case of expansion, mergers, takeovers, issuing of stocks, or in instances when they get into a difficult economic situation. Banks, because of their strong lending power, often are able to gain a seat on the borrowing corporation's board of directors. Banks and other lenders frequently dictate policies to the company that seeks financing (Mintz & Schwartz, 1985). Also, financial institutions tend to be the major holders of bonds, which are longer term loans. In the case of bankruptcy of a company, bondholders' claims have a precedence over stockholders' claims (Glasberg, 1989). Thus corporate entities, without any expertise and experience in prison management and without a direct contract with the government, may become involved in the running of a private facility. If a situation like that evolves, it could create legal confusion in the operation of the prison. This underlines the potentially strong influence and interest of financial institutions in the privatization of prisons even though they do not get involved in the hands-on management of facilities. The likelihood of actual involvement of the representatives of financial corporations in management is low. They are interested in profit rather than in actual day-to-day control (Useem, 1984).

As an example, we can mention the E. F. Hutton brokerage company, which intended to move into the private prison business during the early 1980s. Later, this firm was found to be involved in illegal financial manipulations reaching millions of dollars. Shortly after this affair, it merged with another brokerage firm. (See more details in Chapter 10, this volume.) A related facet of the corporate world that adds to the complexities of private management of prisons is the widespread practice of interlocking directorates among large corporations. Interlocking directorates relate to a network of corporate directors who simultaneously serve on the boards of two or more large corporations (Useem, 1984). This phenomenon emphasizes the interdependent nature of corporations and the impacts on corporate decision making. Although there are provisions in antitrust laws to regulate this kind of networking, the government lacks the means to monitor effectively these arrangements and their effects on the operations of corporations (Pennings, 1980).

In case of bankruptcy of a private prison company, because of the fact that only a handful of companies are involved in the management of prisons, it is unlikely that many corporations will be available to step in and continue operations.

Conclusion

It seems that there are no serious constitutional problems with establishing privately operated prisons. However, there is a general agreement among the students of correctional privatization regardless whether they are for or against it, that the ultimate legal responsibility for the private prison will remain with the government (Logan, 1990; Robbins, 1986, 1989). Under 42 U.S.C., Sec. 1983, the government will remain liable for any civil rights violations against inmates in a private prison (Pellicciotti, 1987; Thomas & Hanson, 1989). Prisoners confined in private facilities will have to retain the same legal rights as inmates have in public facilities (e.g., Elvin, 1985). In the case of private prisons there may be an increase in litigations because the government will not be able to use the sovereign-immunity defense in civil rights violation lawsuits (Robbins, 1989). Several students of this subject maintain that this problem should be dealt with by making certain that private corporations operating prisons will carry a high-liability insurance contract (e.g., Robbins, 1989; Thomas, 1987). Nevertheless, it seems likely that third-party suits against the government will increase with the growing trend of privatization in corrections because of the deep pocket that is being sought by lawyers in civil suits. Government agencies will have less control in avoiding such cases than they had before when the prisons were operated by government departments, and if the private corporations will not be able to pay the judgments against them, the government will have to do it.

Notes

1. In California's private correctional facilities minor disciplinary infractions are handled by the officials of the private company, whereas more serious ones that can affect such practices as good time and furloughs are handled by the Department of Corrections' staff stationed in the institution for monitoring purposes.

2. There were signs of leveling off of prison population in the early 1990s (Hurst, 1991), but the situation became unclear with the three-strikes legislations.

3. For example, California voters, after approving bond issue propositions in all the elections during the 1980s, voted down a similar proposition in 1990. Apparently, the economic downturn in the state dictated a more stringent fiscal public attitude even toward the correctional system.

4. After the Thirteenth Amendment was ratified in 1865, slaves were granted freedom and the only "slaves" remaining were the prisoners. This amendment declared: "Neither slavery nor involuntary servitude, except as punishment for crime whereof the party shall have been duly convicted, shall exist within the United States."

5. Even this can be questionable. For instance, California has held that the operation of a municipal or county jail is a governmental function; therefore an inmate may not sue these political entities for injuries that occurred during incarceration (Palmer, 1985).

6. This does not mean that publicly run prisons necessarily handle prisoners' discipline or grievances satisfactorily. Cavadino and Dignan (1992) point to the cumbersome grievance procedures in British prisons.

7. For instance, Crouch and Marquart (1990) describe how the famous court decision *Ruiz v. Estelle* (1980) in Texas, which was aimed at reforming the correctional system, after awhile became relaxed. They found that "the security staff learned how

to use the sanctions legally available to them for inmate control, especially the 'write up,' or report of rule violation" (Crouch & Marquart, 1990, p. 105).

8. In another case, not connected with the use of deadly force, a private firm in Florida that was hired to transport prisoners treated them unconstitutionally. For example, one prisoner was shackled to a bus bench for 15 days; this prisoner was suffering from hemorrhoids. Other prisoners were denied adequate food and health care by the same company (Dunham, 1986).

5

Contract and Monitoring Issues

The importance of writing a good contract and the close monitoring of it is a recurring subject of the private prison literature. This chapter deals with the various issues involved in writing a private prison management contract and the government monitoring of contracts.

The importance of the contract and its monitoring was underscored by the state delegation of authority to private parties to administer the punishment of lawbreakers and by the fact that the government cannot shed its legal liability for what is happening in the privately managed prisons.

The major impetus for privatization of prisons is economic.

Americans have always been far more willing to support policies aimed at increasing the certainty and severity of punishment for convicted offenders than they have been to pay the costs of incarcerating the influx of prisoners which result from such policies. (Ring, 1987, p. 1)

Contracting with for-profit companies for the provision of social services, including the management of prisons, comes from the analogy of government contracting in general. The contracting out of various services of municipal governments is a growing trend in the United States. It is usually "straightforward, immediate, measurable, amenable to monitoring, and technical in nature" (Bendick, 1989, p. 107). These services include, in the various municipalities, garbage collection, data processing, maintenance of public buildings, maintenance of automobiles, and many others. Well-entrenched practices of privatization can be found in the correctional field as well. As seen, many services such as laundry and food preparation in some correctional facilities are supplied by private for-profit contractors. There are also certain privatized human services in various prisons, such as vocational training, educational programs, and medical services. Regarding the operation of correctional programs, the private sector is traditionally involved in the management of a large and increasing number of juvenile institutions for delinquent, neglected, abused, and "problem" youth. In the United States by 1989, 67% of all juvenile correctional facilities were privately operated and handled 42% of the children in custody (McDonald, 1994). Many community-based, nonresidential programs, diversion programs, halfway houses, and drug rehabilitation programs (both for juveniles and adults) are administered by private companies.

Proponents of prison privatization often point to the economic benefits that were achieved through the privatization of other government services, such as various maintenance services. However, as several students of this subject have pointed out, the privatization of the management of entire correctional institutions is not only quantitatively but also qualitatively different from the provision of certain limited services in prisons (DiIulio, 1990b). Although partial privatization of services is widespread and well entrenched in the current system, full privatization, meaning the operation of entire prisons, is limited so far (Hutto, 1990).

The privatization of corrections involves the signing of a contract between the government and a private corporation. As mentioned, many agree that a clearly written and detailed contract is a key element in the success of correctional privatization (e.g., McAfee, 1987; Mullen et al., 1985; Woolley, 1985).

Major Issues of Prison Contracts

Mullen et al. (1985) list six major issues to be considered in the preparation and the signing of a contract between the government and a private correctional company.

Duration of the Contract. Usually counties and states limit the length of their contract by statutes to 1 to 3 years in order not to bind the next elected administration or not tie down monies for the next budget period. Potentially, short-term contracts enable the government to change private contractors if their performance is not satisfactory and "renegotiate contracts to reflect changing needs" (Mullen et al., 1985, p. 77). However, short-term contracts are problematic for the correctional corporations because it is difficult to plan revenues and budgets, develop programs and staff, and remain financially competitive when the contract is for such a short period. Therefore the short duration of contracts may force correctional companies to cover their costs by asking for higher fees than they otherwise would. In this way they may protect their investments if the contract is not renewed, but this may eliminate or diminish the financial advantage of contracting that was hoped for.

Appropriate Payment Provisions. Most private correctional facilities operate on a per diem basis, which sets a fixed price per inmate per day. This gives the government the ability to calculate how much the incarceration of a certain number of inmates will cost for the duration of the contract, and it minimizes the risk of cost overruns. This arrangement also provides the contractor with a good basis for occupancy projections. To provide a safeguard against an unforeseen drop in the number of inmates, usually minimum levels of occupancy are stipulated. Another kind of payment that is usually provided in the contract by the government is a start-up reimbursement, based on actual cost to the company (e.g., State of California, 1985). This payment covers the costs involved in starting a new correctional program or taking over an existing one.

Minimum and Maximum Capacity Levels. A minimum occupancy level, as seen above, is agreed on to minimize the risk of the contractor losing money if there are not enough inmates sent to the institution. Although in the current trend of incarceration this risk does not seem to be very realistic, nevertheless, a minimum capacity level is stipulated in the contract because the ultimate control over the numbers of prisoners sent to a facility is in the hands of the government authorities. It is not realistic to expect that a private corporation should invest money, time, and effort to start a program if the sole "customer," the government, does not commit itself to a minimum supply of inmates.[1] In California, for private community correctional facilities (CCFs), the minimum capacity level is set at 70% occupancy (State of California, 1985). Usually, there is also a maximum capacity level determined, which provides the government assurances that a certain amount of prison space will be available and the facilities will not be too overcrowded, and at the same time it protects the private contractor from liabilities for overcrowding. Some contracts include a higher per diem rate if the occupancy is more than 100% of the designated beds in the facility (State of California, 1985). The reasoning behind this practice is that there are extra expenses involved in the running of a facility above the numerical capacity designated, for example, the staffing will have to be increased, utility bills will be higher, and so forth.

Types of Inmates. An important function of the contract is to specify the types of inmates who will be housed in a correctional facility. This clause also has to include the definition of the private contractor's role in making transfer and release decisions. This is an important issue because there are many claims that most private companies are interested only in handling low-security-level inmates who do not pose much trouble, and they try to avoid troublesome cases. Also, often companies are interested in dealing with inmates needing special kinds of programs, such as drug, alcohol, or psychological treatment, that can be more profitable for the company. In the case of inmates who need special treatment, the institutional personnel may have a larger say in the discharge decision than in the case of other inmates. If government payments are dependent on occupancy rates, there may be a conflict of interest for the contractors if they have any authority to determine the release of inmates because it may affect their level of income.

Standards of Performance. The inclusion of clauses of well-defined standards of performance into the contract serves as protection for both parties. Without these provisions the companies' goal for profit maximization may conflict with the government's interest in maintaining safe, secure, and humane conditions in the facilities and the avoidance of legal cases and litigations brought on by or on behalf of inmates. Standards that are clearly stated in the contract also protect the companies from changes in government requirements without suitable financial adjustments. The major areas in which the statement of standards can be especially useful include personnel selection criteria, staff conduct, allocation of space, allocation of staff, safety and sanitation requirements, procedures for security and control, disciplinary procedures, supervisory practices, food and medical service requirements, standards for the availability and content of vocational and educational programs, the details of recreational programs, and the use of inmate labor. In addition, administrative rules such as accounting, bookkeeping, reporting, and monitoring procedures have to be stated. There are some suggestions concerning the setting of outcome standards such as recidivism and extent of rehabilitation as well (see Cullen, 1986); however, this is a complex issue and seems to be difficult to implement. Also, these kinds of standards are not set for public institutions; therefore it will be hard to request them from private operations.

Performance Incentives. Sometimes incentives to do a better job are stated, usually in monetary terms. This clause, according to Mullen et al. (1985), although not a necessary component of the contract, should be seriously considered. This could provide a positive reinforcement for good performance. At the same time, also, penalty clauses for the failure of performance should be considered.[2]

There seems to be an agreement among students of privatization that the crucial element in contracting is to devise and enforce "controls capable of ensuring that public safety and inmate care—not private profits—retain their paramount role in the formulation of corrections policy" (Ring, 1987, p. 39).

Several key issues deserve some elaboration. One of these issues relates to the contract terms. As mentioned, usually contracts are written for a short period of time, mainly because of procedural reasons (e.g., budgeting). Private companies have an interest in a long-term relationship because they need to make substantial up-front investments to be ready for the management of a facility. They need also the security and the stability provided by a long-term contract for further planning (e.g., employee training), and it may contribute to the smooth everyday operation of the institution. To recover their expenditures they will need several years of financial relationship with the government. From the government's vantage point, the long-term contract may have some positive aspects as well. First, changing contractors involves a large-scale administrative and financial burden. As noted, often because of the limited market for private corrections, not many suitable private corporations may be available at hand to make a switch over from one company to another on a relatively short notice. If a new contractor with satisfactory qualifications is found, there are many costs involved in drawing up the new contract, checking out the new company, negotiating new terms, and so on. Even if the renewal of the contract with the same company is considered, the negotiation process may be time consuming, and the new contract may cost more money because new conditions may be introduced by either party or higher prices may be demanded by the contractor. There is a genuine concern that the government will lack the ability to take back the operation of prisons because of the reliance on private companies. This situation may have an impact on the authorities' bargaining position to negotiate satisfying terms, and therefore they will be at a disadvantage vis-à-vis the private firms. Thus the longer the term of the contract, providing that the contractors live up to their obligations, the better off the government may be. Second, longer contracts may encourage contractors to make long-term commitments to improve the physical outlay and the services provided in the institutions for the general benefit of correction. Third, long-term arrangements may also help to avoid major public concern and negative media attention arising from frequent changes of private contractors.

With all these factors in mind, the government should not allow its quest for long-term consistency "to overshadow the emphasis on competition among private providers that underlies the industry's claims of greater efficiency" (Ring, 1987, p. 44). On the other hand, as seen, there are questions regarding the actual competitiveness of the private prison market.[3]

Although private companies have a major interest in a long-term contract, they do realize that at this stage many states have statutory restrictions on the length of contracts that can be signed with them. Most contracts are currently limited to only one year or a few years at the most.[4] As pointed out earlier, the short period of contracts may have a negative effect on the private companies because it creates a degree of uncertainty regarding the continuity of the business, and this uncertainty may interfere with long-term planning, program development, and other aspects or organizational functioning.

Another major issue centers around the problem of termination of contracts. In the course of the operation of the facility, situations may arise in which the early termination of the contract seems to be unavoidable. Therefore introduction of a clause allowing for the termination is important.[5] There are strong recommendations for the inclusions of a termination, or an escape, clause in every private correctional contract to ensure that the state's ability to terminate the contract for a justified cause is being protected (see McAfee, 1987). The reasons for termination have to be defined and clearly stated because the government does not have carte blanche to break a contract at will. At least two general reasons for termination of the contract are agreed on: the failure of the contractor to meet the minimum standards and conditions of incarceration specified in the contract, and a failure to meet other contract provisions when such failure seriously affects the operation of the facility (Ring, 1987, p. 47).

To prepare the contractor for the new situation that evolves with the termination, usually a 90-day notification is stipulated in the contract. For example, contracts of the California Department of Corrections with private contractors include a detailed list of conditions that may result in the termination of the contracts. The short version of these conditions is listed in the *Financial Management Handbook for Private Return-to-Custody Facilities* (State of California, 1985). First, the segment on termination states that either party can cancel the contract by giving a prior written notice according to the specifications of the contract. In addition, it lists four conditions under which the Department of Corrections may immediately terminate the contract:

1. Nonperformance by contractor
2. Noncompliance with audit findings
3. Replacement of key personnel with a person or persons who are inimical to the best interests of the state
4. Conflict of interest

Further, when the contractor fails to perform according to the covenants contained in the manner and at the time described in the contract, any costs incurred by the State for termination and recontracting shall be deducted from any amount due the contractor under this agreement. (State of California, 1985, p. 2)

Suggestions for additional conditions under which the government agency may terminate the contract are "contractor default, the filing of a petition in bankruptcy, reorganization, or liquidation, unavailability of funds, or convenience" (Robbins, 1989, p. 729). This last reason, convenience, is referred to as the escape clause (McAfee, 1987); it is undefined on purpose and is meant to provide flexibility for the government.

This contract model does have a certain amount of protection for the private contractor against arbitrary cancellation by the government by stating that if the cancellation did not emanate from the fault of the contractor, the costs accrued due to the termination may be reimbursed by the state according to the specification of the contract. Although the California model also provides an opportunity for the private contractor to terminate a contract under certain conditions, it is clearly written for the benefit and protection of government agencies. Its major protective value, however, hinges on the availability of a pool of suitable private contractors that can take over the operation of the facility on relatively short notice (90 days) or on the government's ability to take back the management of the facility. As was stated before, one of the major concerns of the critics of prison privatization is that there will be only a limited number of contractors from which a choice to switch can be made, and the government, by relying on the private sector, will not have the capability and the willingness to retake the operation of the prison.[6] Inclusion of a termination clause creates the formal protection for the government agency in the case of under par performance or nonperformance by the contracting company. However, in reality the termination of the contract may be quite complex and painful. "Even the opening up to rebidding of an existing contract can prove traumatic if the contract involves heavy capital commitments, considerable staff, and a significant number of prisoners" (Keating, 1990, p. 142).

The discussion to analyze the nature of contracts and their termination leads to one of the major issues of correctional privatization, namely, the monitoring of contracts.

Issues of Monitoring Private Facilities

The monitoring of prisons, whether they are public or private, is crucial. Prisons are not institutions visible to the public eye. Since the beginning of the 19th century, the introduction of incarceration as the major punishment for serious crimes replaced physical punishment. This has changed the maximum visibility of the physical punishments, which usually were executed in public mainly for deterrent purposes, to an invisible process administered in total institutions behind walls (e.g., Foucault, 1977). Thus one problem of incarceration is the lack of visibility of punishment that has contributed to a lack of public concern with prisons. A related problem is that prisons deal with people whom large segments of society would like to forget. Prisoners are usually "wicked" people who most law-abiding citizens would prefer not to think about or would like to see pay for their crimes under harsh conditions in the prison. This nature of the prison population makes monitoring important because it is the government's responsibility to look out for people who are placed under its care, and as shown, the government cannot get rid of its legal liability for them.

The other aspect of monitoring is connected with the contractual relationship between the government and the private contractors. The function of monitoring is to ensure that the private operator is in compliance with the provisions of the contract. This is a major issue in the current context of privatization in which the contractors are almost invariably corporations because "corporations have become powerful, autonomous institutions, largely independent of external influence of control" (Mizruchi, 1982, p. 15).

The maintenance of meaningful supervision and monitoring of private correctional facilities require the establishment of an efficient mechanism. The extra cost involved in rigorous monitoring may influence the cost effectiveness of privatization, an issue that will be dealt with later. Oversight must be especially strict because the usual control mechanism of the free marketplace (supply and demand), suggested by the proponents of classical economy, may have only a limited relevance in the prison business. Therefore, as noted, there is a general opinion that a clearly written and detailed contract is a key element in the success of correctional privatization (McAfee, 1987; Mullen et al., 1985; Robbins, 1989; Woolley, 1985).

The government needs to provide a special mechanism for the monitoring of private prison operations (Logan, 1990). The monitoring must encompass all levels and all kinds of prison operations. It has to focus not only on the fiscal aspects but also on the quality of services, programs, staff-inmate relations, and so forth.

There is a need for multiple measures to oversee the operation of privately administered prisons. The mixture of approaches should include traditional contract and performance monitoring. The contract itself must commit the signing parties to effective monitoring of the many problems with prison overseeing (Keating, 1990). Many recommend the stationing of state Department of Corrections staff members on the premises of privately operated facilities on a permanent basis (e.g., Ring, 1987).

Several alternative monitoring systems may be implemented by government agencies. One method is having a full-time contract monitor at the privately operated facility who will have access to all areas of the institution and to the staff and inmates at all times. All the books, records, and reports should be available to the monitor. In larger facilities there may be a need for more than one full-time monitor. This method may be costly but seems to be the most effective in ensuring that the contractor will comply with the terms stipulated in the contract (Robbins, 1989). This kind of monitoring is in effect in California's privately operated CCFs. In some of them, a lieutenant, four sergeants, and several parole officers are stationed on the premises. The corrections personnel is in charge of the institutional monitoring and disciplinary hearings, whereas the parole agents are involved mainly with the discharge procedures. Although this method is probably fairly efficient, it may create some problems (Sechrest & Shichor, 1993a, 1993b). First, it can add substantially to the cost of privatization and has to be included in any cost analysis. Second, it may blur the chain of command in an institution because in many cases the director or manager heading the private operation will have to clear policies and particular actions with lower level (e.g., sergeant) government officers. Third, it may affect personnel morale because it increases the contact between government workers who are paid higher salaries and receive more benefits and the employees of a private facility who are paid less and have little benefits. Finally, there may be attempts from the private management to co-opt the monitors in various ways, which is a widespread problem of government monitoring (Matthews, 1989; Merlo, 1992).

A less effective alternative is to establish periodic inspections of the institution by designated officials (Robbins, 1989). This method can detect deviations from the contract clauses only post factum, that is, after they have occurred, whereas the on-site monitoring system can in many cases prevent them before they take place. Nevertheless, if for any reason the placing of on-site monitoring is not feasible, the inspection method will impose restrictions on the private contractors and will keep them accountable. This method is less costly for the government than the on-site method. To increase the effectiveness of this kind of monitoring, it is essential that the inspections will be frequent and unannounced to make sure that the private operators will not manipulate the process (Ring, 1987).

As a supplemental way of monitoring, open public access to the private facility has been proposed. Because there is no constitutional guarantee of public access to prisons, it should be included as a provision in the contract. This provision, especially with respect to the media, can offer an additional opportunity for monitoring without financial cost to government agencies. If this is included in the contract, it will provide an avenue for the inmates to alert the public and the media to problems that may prevail in the institution. However, as noted, this practice can be only supplementary to a more structured government monitoring system and cannot be a substitute for it. It should be pointed out that public access as a monitoring device of correctional facilities can be effective not only in private institutions but in publicly managed facilities as well. Nevertheless, the likelihood that this method will be very effective is limited because of the previously mentioned general lack of public interest in prison conditions.

Finally, it is suggested that sanctions for abuses to control the private firms should be implemented. These sanctions should be in the form of fines to reduce the potential profit from the violations, and they may serve as an incentive for the private firm to follow the contract. If the violations continue to occur then the agency should have "contractual remedies to cure the breach" (Robbins, 1989, p. 727). But, again, implementation of this kind of contract clauses is more complex than it appears.

Another issue related to monitoring is connected with the major characteristics of private prison operations. There is a concern that the private prison's "inaccessibility to the public and its typical arrangement in monopolistic form, will, in combination with the profit motive, cause the firm's interest to diverge from its duty to implement societal preferences" (Gentry, 1986, p. 356). One problem, according to this claim, lies in the fact that the purchaser of the services (the state) is unable to observe the usage of the service. This issue was mentioned earlier when it was pointed out that the buyers and the consumers/clients of private corrections are not identical. In this situation there are ample opportunities for the supplier to provide less to the consumer than was purchased by the buyer without experiencing any major sanctions. Thus the management of private facilities might exploit this potential for abuse more than the managers of state-run prisons because there are more constraints on the ways that managers of public prisons can gain personally from this kind of violation. For example, private contractors in the prison business may increase their profits not only from cutting waste (Joel, 1993) but also from cutting corners by purchasing lower quality food, paying lower salaries, providing less or no fringe benefits, and so forth.

Another concern also mentioned earlier is that the private prison field may become a "very entrenched industry" (Gentry, 1986, p. 357). This means that there is a good possibility that there will not be enough suitable firms available in the private prison business to maintain a real, competitive market and the ability of government to replace a firm that will not live up to its contractual obligations may become a hard undertaking.

With regard to the actual oversight of private institutions, Gentry (1986) points out that the problem lies in the fact that the government has to monitor a function that society trusted government to perform, but instead this function was delegated to an entity (the private company) that, generally, society does not trust. This statement seems to be too general; there should be proof that society does not trust private entities. In fact, it seems that certain segments of the American public trust the private sector more than the public sector (Greenwood, 1981; Logan, 1990). Many take it as given that if the state was trusted to operate prisons, then it surely can be trusted to monitor prisons that are contracted out to private companies.

A new philosophy of government emphasizes that the government's role should be "steering," that is, policy management, which includes monitoring private contractors who are doing the "rowing," that is, service delivery (e.g., Osborne & Gaebler, 1992). Several problems may surface with this suggestion. First, budgetary confines—the government will not let the cost of private prison operation and the cost of government monitoring to exceed the original budget that was allocated for the prison operation managed by the government. Thus either the privately run prison has to cost so much less for the government that it will allow for financing of the rigorous monitoring, or the monitoring will not be carried out effectively.[7] Second, the government agency in charge of monitoring, usually the state Department of Corrections, may have a reason not to monitor the private firm closely because the same agency has selected the firm, and it will receive negative publicity if improprieties are discovered. Therefore the government agency has an interest not to raise much noise about these improprieties. Third, because there are no clear societal preferences concerning prison operations and their implementation, monitors have little incentive to demand the maintenance of prison conditions beyond legislated standards.

The effectiveness of contract monitoring could be enhanced in several ways. For example, fines and bonuses could be implemented; the assumption is that private contractors will respond to pecuniary incentives much more than public administrators would. In a for-profit corporation a fine will directly impact the profits, and it will not allow the company to reduce its services in proportion with the fine. Accordingly, "properly set fines will operate to align private interest with public duty and will create market incentives to innovate in care and rehabilitation" (Gentry, 1986, p. 361). This scheme suggests that the private firm will have an incentive to maintain adequate sanitary conditions, check inmate violence, establish effective security, and employ the best available methods of rehabilitation to prevent recidivism. Consequently, this policy will induce the company to monitor its staff and operations carefully. Firms that are more successful in avoiding fines will be in a better competitive position vis-à-vis other private correctional firms. Thus there maybe an opportunity for the improvement of the correctional system by controlling private contractors through the use of fines for violations of performance.

This contention seems to be somewhat optimistic. It assumes that all or at least the large majority of the contract violations will be detected by the government monitors and that the private companies will accept the fines without trying to refute government claims or without appealing either the accusation of wrongdoing itself or the magnitude of the fine set. Besides, if the government can insist on introducing an escape clause or termination conditions into the contract, it is likely that the private contractors will have a similar opportunity to terminate the contract, which they may do after being fined, or at least, they may use the threat of termination to put pressure on the government agency to revise itself. This may pose a problem for the continuous operation of the facility.

Gentry (1986) admits that meting out fines is an incomplete monitoring method. There is a need to take other measures as well to make monitoring more effective. A complementary measure could be to adapt a policy of public access to fill in for missing links in the fines method. The mass media, as noted, may have a central function in this policy because the use of prisons for profit is a controversial public issue; therefore it may receive attention from the media. According to this reasoning, because private correctional companies are entering a developing industry, they will seek favorable publicity, and therefore will cooperate with the media.[8] However, there is no reason to believe that after this start-up period is over, private prisons will remain more open to the public and the media than public prisons. They may be less open because private property is involved and private records are not open by law as public records are. An effective monitoring system will have to guarantee long-term access to relevant information, especially to all inmates who can be interviewed by the media at any time. Hidden abuse, not fully deterred by fines, could be discovered through such interviews. Access should be complete to all parts of the facility and to all records as well. This kind of access would also support the monitoring process by reducing the cost for public agencies because the media would participate in the process extensively. On the other hand, this policy would reveal only the more "newsworthy" violations and media representatives would have the discretion to determine what kind of violations should or should not be monitored and presented to the public.

Although this suggestion may have a great appeal, it may be more promising in theory than what it can deliver in reality. As mentioned several times, prisons by their nature are hidden places. Most people are not comfortable getting involved with them mainly because they are not closely interested in the fate of people who harmed society and injured innocent victims and also because most people are not comfortable with facing the spectacle of punishment. In addition, prison authorities, public and private alike, have a vested interest to show as little as possible of the institutions to the public because in a coercive institution, there is always the possibility of finding certain arrangements and practices that may be questionable and objectionable to some segments of the public—prisons are not pretty places. The managers may not readily cooperate with the full access policy. Although they may not object to this policy openly, they can always cite "security considerations" to limit or at least to discourage access to the facility or to some parts of it. Also, the ability to maintain a constant public and media interest in prisons is not ensured. Special occurrences such as prison riots, extreme violence, hostage taking, escapes, or inmates' deaths usually draw public and media interest, but for a limited time; to keep this interest alive for an extended period of time is a questionable proposition. A third suggestion is the monitoring of prison operation by the prisoners themselves (Gentry, 1986). According to this scheme prisoners would be able to confide their problems to the representatives of the media. Also, they would have guaranteed access to the legal system in cases in which their rights are violated. Although this recommendation is undoubtedly relevant and important, the formal opportunities for legal redress are already available. The question is whether these rights would be substantially expanded beyond the existing ones. This arrangement would also open the door for manipulation by the prisoners who could pressure prison operators by threatening to use their media access if certain requests are not fulfilled.

An underlying concern is the prevention of entrenchment of private correctional firms (Gentry, 1986). As mentioned, to be able to exercise effective monitoring, it is essential that the government not be at the mercy of only a handful of companies but that a free market situation evolve. In that case the government could switch with

relative ease from one company to another at the end of the contract
if for any reason it is not satisfied with services rendered or receives
a lower bid. The government also could break the contract without
major problems when the contractor violates the conditions laid out
in the contract. However, at the end of 1991 only 14 companies were
operating 44 correctional facilities in the United States; two of them,
CCA (14 facilities) and Wackenhut (8) operated 50% of the facilities;
five companies operated only one facility each; most of the others
operated in only one state (Thomas & Foard, 1991). This is a fairly
limited pool of contractors. It was suggested that the state should
promote competition in the private correctional field. To achieve this
situation the contract duration should not be too long, in order not
to lock out competition, but at the same time it should provide a long
enough period that it will be worthwhile for a company to make
efforts to better its performance. As an initial step, a contract period
between 2 to 4 years is suggested (Gentry, 1986). The pros and cons
of long- and short-term contracts have been argued earlier without
reaching any final conclusion about the optimal time period.

A core question regarding entrenchment focuses on the actual
ownership of the correctional facility. From the economic point of
view there are advantages in having the private firm provide its own
capital. However, the investment of the company's capital in the
prison business is dependent on the length of the contract signed
because the company needs enough time to recoup its investment. If
a long-term guarantee is not given the corporation may operate in
facilities that have alternative uses, such as warehouses, boarding
schools, and abandoned military camps, because in the case of a lost
contract, the firm will not lose a great deal of its investment.[9] To limit
the private firm's power in subsequent biddings or negotiations for
contracts and limiting the government's reliance on the private company, the state should own the specialized prison assets. This provides leverage for the public agency also in matters of controversy
emanating from monitoring. However, this arrangement may limit
certain advantages of prison privatization, namely (a) the private
company's ability to construct new prison facilities quickly and (b)
the incentive to make innovations in the design of the facility. On the
other hand, these benefits can be gained in other ways such as by
initiating a design competition that emphasizes the economical func-

tion of the facility and by using lease/purchase contracts for the construction of correctional facilities (Gentry, 1986).

Monitoring Corporations
and Enforcement of Contracts

The enforcement of stringent monitoring of privately operated facilities may raise similar problems as the regulation of private industry generally does. Regulation is vigorously objected to by the proponents of laissez-faire economics who claim that it distorts the very core of the free market system. Although contract monitoring and legal regulations are not the same, some of the problems in their implementation are similar. One of the concerns is the "revolving door" syndrome. Often, corporations promise a job for officials of the government agency that regulates them on their retirement from the agency. Although this cannot be classified as an outright bribe, it does have a resemblance to it. There are also privatized correctional facilities that are monitored by state officials who are promised a position in the corporation after their retirement, or some of their relatives are hired to work for the corporation while they are monitoring the facility.[10] Similarly, corporations are often successful in promoting a probusiness climate among the regulatory agency's personnel.[11] This may be done through the organization of seminars, dinners, and retreats arranged by the industry to familiarize the agency's personnel with the industry's orientation to the business. Moreover, a degree of intimacy may develop between the regulators and the company's personnel that they regulate (Clinard & Yeager, 1980).

The experience of government agencies with private contractors in various fields indicates that even when contracts are clearly written, there are problems with securing adherence to them. Critics of privatization of human services, which are referred to by some as "soft services . . . performed for or on people" (Nelson, 1980, p. 431), point out that there are efforts by the proprietary (for-profit) lobby to reduce the regulatory standards. In the field of corrections there are examples of these kinds of attempts. In January 1991 the second largest private correctional contractor, Wackenhut Corrections Corporations, which was contracted for the operation of the Monroe

County Jail in Florida, terminated its contract and returned the control of the jail to the county sheriff. The company had asked for $2.6 million extra for the 4-year period of the contract because it had planned to staff the facility with six guards per shift instead of the Florida state standards, which require 11 guards per shift. The corporation claimed that it was unaware of this requirement. In this case the county commissioners accepted Wackenhut's proposal for the terms of the termination, which included a $300,000 payment to the company to settle its claims over the staffing disagreement pending utility bills and transportation costs. Monroe County also agreed to pay $206,000 for equipment that the corporation had purchased for the operation of the facility (Keating, 1991).

Private corporations contracting with government agencies often know from the beginning of the negotiations that there is a good chance that they will not be able to deliver the promised products and/or services for the price indicated in their bid. They bank on the growing dependence of government agencies on their services that will make it very hard, almost impossible, to terminate the contract (Keating, 1990). Thus it is emphasized again that not only is the way the contract is written important but also that there will be other viable private prison companies available to replace the firm that is terminating the contract or being terminated by the government. The potential problem is presented vividly in the following:

> Costs will increase, according to opponents, because private operators will engage in low-balling: intentionally underestimating costs in their initial bids in the hope that the government will become dependent upon their services over time. Once this occurs, the contractor will raise his fees or allow conditions to deteriorate, gambling that the government will accept the charges rather than risk losing his services. (Ring, 1987, p. 25)

Contract violations by companies dealing with the government, in almost all facets of the economy, are a common occurrence. Various types of violations in the defense industry are well documented (Glazer & Glazer, 1989; Goodwin, 1985). For example, not long ago, Northrop Corporation pleaded guilty to 34 criminal fraud charges and was fined $17 million; in this case 141 other charges were dropped in a plea bargain agreement. One of the main charges against Northrop was the falsification of tests on the components of nuclear-armed cruise missiles (Weinstein, 1990). It can be assumed that if in the field of national defense, which is a major concern of the government and public alike, there are serious contract violations then in the provision of human services, which generally have a politically powerless and socially neglected clientele and lacks public interest, the likelihood of contract violations will be even greater.

An additional issue that should be taken into consideration is that the legal enforcement of the contract and the provision of proof that there was an intent to deceive the government is also a complex, drawn-out process requiring much time and allocation of substantial resources, especially because of the high quality of legal services that these companies have access to (Goodwin, 1985).

Another contention by critics of privatization that has to be given attention in the analysis of monitoring is that many companies will prefer signing contracts in which only the most essential services provided will be listed in detail. Anything beyond these will be considered to be an extra service charged separately, or the contract will have to be renegotiated for a higher price.

Although there is a general agreement regarding the importance of contract monitoring, its effectiveness may be hampered by the fact that the corporation's risk of being penalized, formally or informally, for contract violations is minimized by several factors, some of which were dealt with earlier. These factors include (a) reduced competition because only a handful of companies are active in a limited market; (b) the lack of the government's ability to take over the facilities from the company in violation; (c) the lack of major deterrent effects because penalties assessed against corporations are usually fines that are far below the gains derived from illegal activities or from the violation of regulations (e.g., Coleman, 1989; Fisse, 1985; Stone, 1975); (d) the shielding of top officials from individual criminal liability; because the decision making in corporations is diffused, there is an opportunity to abdicate personal responsibility (Clinard & Yeager, 1980; Kramer, 1982); (e) that corporations have access to expert legal services and, if there is a court case, they often have resources to outlast government prosecutors (see, e.g., Cullen, Maakestad, & Cavender, 1987); and (f) that because of the uniqueness of the "correctional marketplace," adverse publicity that was suggested as an option for corporate punishment (Fisse, 1985) loses its effect to a great degree.

All these factors make it feasible that under certain conditions private corporations contracted to serve government functions, including the operation of prisons, may have an incentive to carry out their state function imperfectly because their primary concern is to serve their own interest (Gentry, 1986).

One of the intriguing aspects of contract monitoring is the privatization advocates' strong belief in the power and effectiveness of monitoring. The monitoring as suggested would be a government function carried out by government agencies and their employees or by an independent private corporation that was formed to monitor privately managed correctional institutions (Keating, 1990). Mullen et al. (1985) note the problem of clarification of missions and scope of authority that may be involved between the management of the private for-profit facility and the officials in charge of the monitoring. They explain the problematic nature of this relationship in the following: "Unless care is taken to define the respective roles of public and private managers, two organizations are responsible, but neither may be clearly accountable" (Mullen et al., 1985, p. 75). As noted earlier, this situation may confuse the chain of command as well, when lower level state officials will have to approve decisions made by private managers.

Besides this problem of confusion of authorities, there is also the issue of government agency effectiveness to establish a tight monitoring system.[12] Privatization advocates who tend to criticize government agencies and their workers by claiming that one of the major problems of corrections is the ineffectiveness of public agencies, "suddenly" put a lot of faith and confidence into the monitoring ability and efficiency of the very same agencies and personnel that they criticized. The great confidence in the monitoring abilities of the "ineffective" government agencies and their much maligned public workers sounds idealistic, in fact paradoxical, and needs scrutiny in order to explore the motives and reasonings of these advocates of privatization.

Government monitoring systems may also be an object of corporate efforts to be weakened under the slogan that through their bureaucratic and rigid requirements they thwart innovation and efficiency and make the functioning of private business cumbersome. Corporations often threaten to take their business somewhere else where regulations are weaker. For example, it is shown that in the savings and loan industry "from the outset, industry members were able to manipulate state supervision and reporting requirements to their advantage" (Young, 1990, p. 8). Usually, the resources allocated for monitoring are inadequate (Calavita & Pontell, 1990), especially the number of investigators tend to be very limited. Furthermore, even in cases where violations were detected in the savings and loan industry, both the U.S. House Committee and the U.S. General Accounting Office reported a general lack of enforcement actions against violators.

It is also very likely that private corporations involved in the corrections business will try to ease some of the rules and regulations that they are required to abide by. This effort may be launched by claiming that certain clauses in the contract and some of the regulatory rules impede the efficiency of the delivery of services. Likely, there will be claims of overregulation and government officials and legislators may be lobbied by private prison companies to change some of the rules and methods of monitoring. The individual monitors themselves may be exposed to attempts of bribery in various forms, either to ease their monitoring standards or to overlook some of the violations (Merlo, 1992), and there is a real chance that they will be co-opted by the corporation in which they are going to spend considerable time (Ryan & Ward, 1989).

The establishment of private monitoring services as an alternative arrangement is problematic as well. Several recent corporate scandals, such as the savings and loan debacle, demonstrated that independent prestigious accounting firms submitted to the government auditing reports that did not indicate that the financial institutions were involved in shoddy business practices that may have jeopardized their investors. As a result, the government will have to carry a great financial burden for these business activities that were irresponsible at best and unlawful at worst. This kind of monitoring probably could become more effective if the government would hire and pay for the services of the private auditing outfit instead of the company monitored. One of the conclusions of a detailed review of all reports and professional literature on monitoring was that "all the contract efforts we examined were weak when detailing provisions for monitoring vendor performance" (Hackett et al., 1987, p. vii).

To a large extent the effectiveness of monitors "will depend upon the levels of sanctions that they can ultimately mobilize and the degree of critical autonomy that they can maintain from the organization being monitored" (Matthews, 1989, p. 4).

Considering the accumulated experience from the regulatory agencies and the historical examples of correctional privatization, it is hard to be very optimistic about the prospects of effective monitoring of private prisons.

Conclusion

The importance of a well-written contract and an effective monitoring system are emphasized by almost all advocates as well as opponents of correctional privatization. In a sense the great emphasis on the importance of the contract and even more so on the its monitoring reveals a certain degree of lack of confidence in the capabilities, motives, and ethics of private corporations. It seems that there is less than complete confidence in the performance of the private contractors. The most contradictory feature of this issue is that privatization proponents expect that the government agencies and their agents, which are constantly depicted by the very same privatization advocates as ineffective, wasteful, lacking interest in their work, and inept, will be able to do a good and effective job in monitoring the operation of private prisons. Basically, general privatization theorists see the government's role in planning, monitoring, taxing, and paying the bills (not only in corrections)—government should do the steering but private institutions should do the rowing.

> Privatization by prudent contracting permits government to provide a service but to limit itself to the roles that best suit it: articulating the demand, acting as purchasing agent, monitoring the contractor's performance, properly paying the bill, and levying fair taxes to cover the cost. (Savas, 1990, p. 13)

The problem is that following this approach, the government would diminish its enforcement power and backup capability, thus it could not effectively react if violations of contracts occur, except for changing private providers, which does not seem to be a very promising option in the prison business.

Notes

1. This arrangement demonstrates that the analogy of private corrections with the free market system is problematic. The government is the only customer, thus it can control the flow of "clients."

2. Although many recommend performance incentives for private companies, this kind of incentive is seldom suggested or implemented in the public sector. Probably, it would be useful to try to find ways to introduce the practice of positive reinforcement into public corrections as well. First, the general idea should be accepted then the various forms of implementation should be worked out. This could be in line with the ideas of Osborne and Gaebler (1992) of "reinventing government."

3. As mentioned, at the end of 1991 the Private Correctional Facility Census conducted by Thomas and Foard (1991) counted 14 for-profit companies operating correctional facilities in the United States. Five of them were operating one single facility, four were operating two facilities, and three were operating three institutions. Two companies accounted for 22 (50%) of the 44 total privately operated prisons and for 7,559 (56.6%) of the 13,348 total number of inmates placed in these facilities.

4. The California Department of Corrections' contracts for CCFs are unique in this respect because they run for 5 years. These facilities that handle mostly nonviolent parole violators and first-time inmates are operated by either private for-profit corporations or by local government entities (e.g., municipalities, police and sheriff's departments), which manage them for profit to supply work for local residents and to help the financially pressed local governments to pay their bills.

5. The historical example of California from the 1850s can serve as an important example. As seen, when the state tried to stop a deteriorating situation in San Quentin, its only prison operated by a private contractor, there was no clause for termination in the contract. The state had to pay $275,000, which was a tremendous sum at that time, to take over the prison administration (McAfee & Shichor, 1990).

6. In the case that the private company owns the facility itself, the government's hands may be tied because it cannot afford to lose the bed space (see Ethridge & Marquart, 1993).

7. For example, in Texas the contract stipulates that the cost in private prisons has to be at least 10% below the cost of state-operated prisons (Ethridge & Marquart, 1993).

8. As an example, Corrections Corporation of America (CCA) has a promotional folder containing newspaper articles dealing with CCA-operated facilities and a video presentation shown to visitors.

9. It is not unusual to find private contractors setting up correctional facilities in buildings that were used for other purposes than incarceration. For example, the facility in Eagle Mountain, operated by the Management and Training Corporation headquartered

in Utah, is located in abandoned buildings in a mining ghost town in the southern California desert.

10. A few years ago a student of mine was writing a term paper about a private correctional facility in California. During his interview with the state Department of Corrections' monitor at the facility, the official explained that he was planning to retire in a few months after 20 years of service, and a position was waiting for him at the facility that he was monitoring. His wife was already a uniformed officer at the same facility. Although it is not necessarily the situation in every case, this may serve as an illustration of the possibility for co-optation and conflict of interest.

11. Lobbying against regulations and using fear tactics of moving to other locations or closing factories because of "unreasonable" standards are well-known strategies by industry. It is known, for instance, that car makers use these tactics to alter proposed regulations on auto fuel economy and safety. Various industries threaten state governments that they will move out of state if environmental standards are not eased, and so on.

12. The comments of the representatives of the Prison Officers' Association of Great Britain on the lack of adequate monitoring in some privately operated county correctional facilities in the United States are illuminating. For example, after their visit to the Silverdale facility operated by CCA in Tennessee, they reported to a House of Commons committee that they saw evidence of cruel treatment of inmates and that in a sense the county official in charge of overseeing the contract was co-opted by CCA. The report stated that

> this official told us that . . . none of his colleagues in the County Government really knew what his role was. He also admitted to us that he often toured the country to address authorities interested in privatizing their prisons and was a keen advocate of the system. (DiIulio, 1990a, p. 232)

Although this comment is interesting and may be important, it should be considered with a certain amount of caution because the British Prison Officers' Association is an interested party in the prison privatization debate. It has a vested interest in opposing privatization.

6

Economic Issues

The major selling point of correctional privatization is the economic benefit that it can provide to the government and ultimately to the taxpayers. An advocate of private prisons states that "among claims made for the superiority of propriety prisons, the most frequent and most salient—but not necessarily the strongest—is that they will be less expensive, or at least more efficient" (Logan, 1990, p. 76). This proponent, being an academician, does not seem to be very comfortable with this economic overemphasis as the major advantage for private prisons, but this is the reality.

A clearer and more enthusiastic economic argument is given by representatives of organizations that may profit from privatization or are politically committed to it (e.g., Butler, 1985). This approach is illustrated by Mitchell (1988), who noted that privately owned and operated prisons became popular in recent years. He attributes this popularity to the recognition by government officials that contracting with private operators of prisons is cost effective without sacrificing safety and quality of service.[1]

There are two main points in these contentions: first, that the cost of operating the private prison is going to be cheaper for the authorities and the taxpayers, and second, that the quality of services provided, such as security, treatment, food, health, and education, will not be worse than in prisons managed by the public agencies.

These kinds of promises are very enticing for the public. Who would refuse to be "rich and healthy" rather than being "poor and sick"? In this vein an expert's statement is well taken: "The notion that private organizations can provide more for less is undeniably attractive, but probably unrealistic" (Mullen, 1985, p . 1).

The Cost of Corrections and
the Problems of Cost Comparisons

The calculation of correctional costs is a complicated matter.[2] The major reason that so much concern is dedicated to this issue in the preceding discussion is that, as seen, the major argument for the privatization of prisons is that it costs less money for the taxpayers.

McDonald (1990a), who tries to provide a detailed cost comparison between public and private correctional facilities, presents the financial arguments for privatization succinctly:

> Private firms are more likely to introduce sophisticated management techniques and expertise, are able to deploy their work force more productively because they are not hemmed by civil service restrictions—or by negotiated work rules, if employees are not unionized—and are able to purchase supplies and materials faster and at lower costs. In addition, if they design and build the facility, they can complete construction more quickly and at lower costs, and, more important, can design a structure that requires a smaller staff. (p. 86)

As a rebuttal to these claims a sheriff, speaking on behalf of the National Sheriff's Association, which is an interested party of opposition to privatization, stated that public facilities can be operated more cheaply than private ones because they do not have to make profits (McDonald, 1990a).

So far, there are conflicting estimates and conclusions regarding the cost comparisons of private and public facilities. Several estimates indicate that private facilities are indeed more cost effective than publicly operated ones (e.g., Logan & McGriff, 1989; McDonald, 1989); others claim that private institutions are more expensive because of the hidden costs that are hard to calculate, and there are also others who admit that the cost comparisons are inconclusive (Donahue, 1988), and if there is any difference it is not a major one (McDonald, 1994; Sechrest & Shichor, 1993b).

Why are cost comparisons so complicated? First, the cost comparison has to be made on the same kind of institutions at the same level of security in the same geographical area. This is an obvious requirement of any comparative study and evaluation. This issue gained some relevance in light of the controversy concerning the correctional facilities being privatized. Most of the experience with private involvement until recently was with community-based corrections, such as halfway houses and various treatment and diversion programs. These programs are what some refer to as the soft end of the correctional system (Ericson, McMahon, & Evans, 1987). The operation of closed medium- and maximum-security prisons is considered to be the hard end of corrections. When privatization advocates talk about cutting expenses not through a cheaper workforce but through the employment of fewer well-qualified workers, they may target more the soft-end operations, which usually have less custody and more human service components in their everyday operation. When hard-end operations are concerned, most of the day-to-day correctional efforts are centered around the provision of internal and external security. In other words the focus is on the prevention of prison riots, attacks on staff, large-scale fights and serious injuries among inmates, and escapes.[3] Thus cost and any other kind of comparison between facilities have to be conducted between similar institutions. The second reason that cost comparisons are difficult is that many hidden costs have to be taken into consideration. Cost comparisons may be hard to conduct because the direct cost of corrections in public institutions is often hard to isolate (e.g., McDonald, 1989, 1990a; Mullen, 1985). But it was also found that the cost of private facilities for the government, thought to be simple and visible, is more complex than it was assumed (e.g., Borna, 1986; Bowditch & Everett, 1987; Sechrest & Shichor, 1993a, 1993b).

McDonald (1989) lists the various expenditures that should be counted in a thorough analysis of public corrections. First, *amortizing capital expenditures*—the calculation of this item depends to a large degree on the estimate of the length of the period of the use of the facility. Second, *financing*—the purchasing of assets and goods if financed by borrowing generates the extra cost of interest that has to be calculated. Third, *expenditures by other agencies*—the direct costs that other agencies carry while servicing corrections—have to be counted. For example, doctors and other medical workers in a public prison infirmary are often paid by public health departments, some utility bills may be paid by the public works department, and teachers may be paid by school districts. Another seldom calculated expenditure is the share of facility in the administrative offices. For example, how much the facility costs in terms of the salaries of the department of corrections personnel and the maintenance of the central office, and so on. Fourth, *distinguishing costs within an agency*—this may be more of a problem in the case of jails than in the case of prisons. Sheriff's departments are fulfilling many functions, among which corrections is only one; often the costs of the separate services are not clearly tracked because there is more concern with controlling the agency's funds than the exact determination of the cost of the separate services. Finally, *expenditures from other accounts: fringe benefits and pensions*—in many jurisdictions fringe benefits and retirement funds are paid not from agency accounts but from a separate account for all government employees. Thus, in the case of publicly operated prisons many of these costs may be hidden. Some professionals estimate that public correctional costs (state and county) may be about 33% to 66% higher than are usually reported (McDonald, 1989). By all estimates if the underreporting is even close to these figures, it is very substantial.

One of the advantages usually attributed to privatization is that it reveals the true cost of services (Logan, 1990). In private institutions it is suggested that the cost to handle a particular number of inmates under specified conditions will be clearly visible (Mullen, 1985). This is important because it can provide a much clearer and more objective picture of correctional cost than public corrections does and may simplify budgeting for corrections. However, there are some hidden factors involved in this method of operations as well. Figure 6.1 details the various agency expenditures for corrections.

1. Monitoring by government agencies will be conducted by government employees. It seems that there is already enough awareness of the fact that this expense has to be calculated into the cost of private corrections (U.S. House of Representatives, 1985). In addition

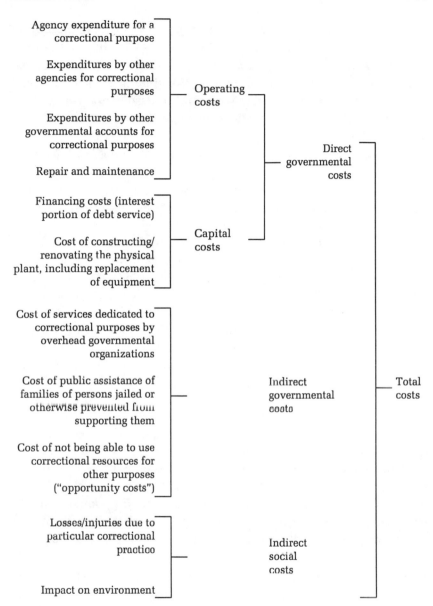

Figure 6.1. Agency Expenditure for a Correctional Purpose
SOURCE: McDonald (1989). Reprinted with permission of the author.

to this cost, the fringe benefits and retirement funds of the monitors who are usually government employees also have to be considered.[4]

2. Preparation costs of the contract, including the legal work, also should be included. In other words, the time spent by the legal personnel of the state working on the contract with the private company should be calculated as an expense accruing because of privatization.

3. Certain conjunctures for major costs may or may not occur in any particular case, but government agencies have to be ready for them (see Thomas, 1987). When they occur they may substantially influence the cost of the private facility that the government will have to cover. These include financial liabilities that the private company is responsible for but cannot cover in the case of bankruptcy. It is not only a legally complex issue; it also has organizational and operational consequences (Holley, 1988). In the first place, if the insurance contract or the performance bond of the company is not large enough to cover all the claims against the company, the state may be sued for covering the missing sums because the state has a legal liability for the institution. Although this can be a problem by itself, it is amplified by the fact that the government will have to go out again to the marketplace to search for another private contractor who is ready and able to take over the operation of the prison. The government agency has to make sure that there are arrangements for the temporary overtaking of the institution. This arrangement will involve additional costs because a backup mechanism will have to be maintained. Another potential expense involves legal costs that the government may incur for litigations that are related to the privatization of facilities. These may be a result of prisoners' and prisoner families' litigations against privately operated prisons that their insurance does not cover or litigation in contract disputes between the contracting agency and the private contractor.

4. Private corporations will continue to rely on certain public services that are financed by government agencies, especially in the case of major emergencies, such as prison riots, fires, natural disasters, public health problems, and employee strikes (Bowditch & Everett, 1987). Because the government has the ultimate responsibility to keep the prisons operating, it will have to have all the backup

services available. The cost of these services should be included in all the calculations, but currently they cannot be estimated because of the lack of benchmark data.

5. Tax benefits given to investors when a new correctional facility is built should be considered to be a cost for the government (Borna, 1986). Also, some local authorities that have economic problems, for example, high unemployment, may try to give special tax and other benefits to a corporation if it is ready to locate a facility in their jurisdiction.

6. A large portion of the medical costs, including ambulance service, is often paid by the government agencies to local health facilities and is being used by inmates of private facilities. Similarly, government medical facilities (often those in public prisons) are serving the inmates of private prisons without costing money for the private operators (Sechrest & Shichor, 1993a).

7. As a projection to the future, it can be assumed that a certain percentage of the lower level employees of private correctional corporations and their families will have to receive some public support because the private company does not provide sufficient benefits for their health care and retirement.

McDonald (1990a) sums up some of the major problems of cost comparisons:

> In theory, comparing costs should be relatively straightforward and easy to accomplish, but in practice it has been difficult. Precisely how private firms have structured their facilities and at what cost is hard to learn because the details are often guarded as proprietary information. Governments' expenditure reports are public documents, but the true costs of services are obscured by inadequate public accounting procedures, by the distribution of costs for services to more than one agency or to more than one account, and by the frequently deficient treatment of capital spending (such as failing to count the value of all physical assets used up during any year of operation). It is, therefore, surprisingly difficult to determine even so basic a cost as the average daily cost of an inmate's imprisonment. (p. 89)

Three major areas in which the cost and economic efficiency of private versus public prisons are usually examined: financing of construction, construction of facilities, and operation of facilities. The focus of this study is the private operation of correctional facilities; thus the first two areas are reviewed only briefly and the major emphasis is on the operational aspects.

Financing of Construction

The rapid and continuous growth of prison populations during the 1980s and the early 1990s made the building of new prisons and the expansion of existing facilities necessary. These undertakings are expensive. According to a 1988 Bureau of Justice publication the average construction cost per bed in a maximum-security state prison was $71,000, in a medium-security state prison the cost was $53,000, in a minimum-security state prison the cost was $30,000, and in a county jail the cost was $43,000. This cost in some states reached up to $110,000 in 1987, according to a report by the National Conference of State Legislators (Castle, 1991).

The traditional method for local and state governments to raise money for this purpose is by issuing bonds and selling them on the bond market. The issuance of bonds has to receive voters' approval. During the 1980s when the public mood was attuned toward the increased effort of the war on crime and the United States enjoyed an economic boom, the public was generally inclined to approve bond proposals for the construction of more jails and prisons. For example, in California in every election during the 1980s, propositions for the financing of jail and prison construction through bonds was approved, but in November 1990 during the economic recession, a similar proposition was defeated and in the 1992 elections was not even put on the ballot. Prison construction financing through the issuance of bonds, which is one form of borrowing, is not unlimited. Because of hard economic times during the late 1980s and the beginning of the 1990s, many states and jurisdictions have borrowed so much money that their credit ratings became lower. These government units either do not have the opportunity to raise more money through bonds even if there is a voter approval because financial institutions are not ready to take the risk, or if the money is available the interest paid on it becomes higher because of lower credit ratings.

There are many jurisdictions that have a legal debt ceiling and cannot borrow money beyond that limit. And, as was seen in the latest elections in California, there appears to be a growing resistance in the general public to the continuous borrowing and deficit spending, even if they are for specific services that the public usually favors, such as corrections.

Private corporations seem to have an answer to these problems. They promise that they can raise money through private sources such as investments, private loans, and the stock market. The most frequently suggested alternative method to traditional financing is the lease-purchase arrangement, leasing with an option of buying, which is basically purchasing real estate property through installment payments. Lease-purchase is a legal arrangement according to which the government agency is a tenant in a facility that is owned by a private company. The title of the property is held by the private company until the government agency purchases the property at the end of a certain agreed-on period (McDonald, 1990a). Because the payments under this arrangement are not considered to be debt payments but rather a part of the operating costs of a facility, the government can acquire needed capital in this way without going into further debt. This method provides the government with the opportunity of an easier termination of the lease.

Because lease purchase provides less safety for private companies than general obligation bonds, it may cost more for the government to attract money through lease bonds on which the interest is usually 0.25% to 1% higher than on general obligation bonds. Although there are some other financial aspects to this method that may be of interest for financial experts, the important issue is to understand the nature of the available private financing alternatives for prison construction. According to DeWitt (1986a) this arrangement is considered to be a lease because the agency does not receive the title to the correctional facility until all the payments are made to the entity that financed the construction. The lease-purchase is a limited obligation issue on behalf of the government; therefore interest paid to investors is tax exempt. Thus it is similar to a general obligation bond, and it is attractive for those investors who need a tax shelter.

Another benefit of this arrangement is that because the financial obligation of the government is renewable each year, the amount borrowed is usually not defined as an ongoing debt; thus it does not count against the legal debt capacity of the government. Although the lease payments are not legally considered to be debts, in reality they are. The reliance of this and other methods of creative financing may have the unwelcome effect of relaxing the government's discipline on restricting expenses (McDonald, 1990a).

Several points should be made regarding this arrangement. Because this method offers less safety for the investors than general obligation bonds, and because it is not backed by the taxing authority of the government, a higher rate of interest is paid to investors than for general loans. Lease bonds draw fixed interest rates. As a lease, payments may be terminated by the government if funds are not appropriated for this purpose. Because higher interest has to be paid for a higher risk, the cost of this financing is higher than that of the general obligation bonds. A variant of the lease-purchase arrangement is variable rate financing. In this method the interest rate changes with that of the financial market. In the short term, the interest rate is lower, but it provides a greater liquidity for investors. It is similar to the adjustable interest rates that became popular during the 1980s in the real estate market.

The repayment of debt is not covered by property tax; thus the government has to find other sources to cover the payments. Some states cover these from inmate industries (e.g., Ohio); others from criminal fines and criminal forfeitures (e.g., Kentucky, California). Obviously, it remains a question what happens if these sources of income fall short of the needed payments? How is the government agency going to find the money to pay these obligations?

A major advantage of this arrangement is the speed of the process that allows the funds to be raised much faster than conventional financing methods do. How does this new creative financing relate to privatization? The lease-purchase involves the establishment of a not-for-profit entity that acts on behalf of the government agency, which is usually the state Department of Corrections. In the case of privatization a profit-making corporation owns the facility, which was built or acquired with private investors' money.

Private financing is almost always costlier than public financing because government agencies in general can obtain lower interest loans than private companies can. In addition, lease payments for a private facility are taxable. To facilitate private financing of correctional institutions, recently, special tax benefits were available in many cases for companies raising private capital for construction. Private owners of facilities have been eligible to claim tax benefits such as depreciation and investment tax credits (DeWitt, 1986a). These tax benefits provided to private corporations and private investors should be calculated into the cost analysis of private prisons (Borna, 1986); however, because they are not visible, they often remain as a hidden government cost only. Recent federal legislation disallowed tax write-offs for accelerated appreciation of real estate, but it still allows depreciation if the facility is both owned and operated privately. Through the lease-purchase arrangement, the public entity responsible for the construction of correctional facilities may spend more money than in the traditional method. Thus the convenience of going around the voters to raise money costs extra funds for the taxpayers. But there is also a political cost in this arrangement, that is "the damage to our democratic institutions that results from lease-purchasing through the avoidance of a public vote on prison construction" (DeWitt & Binder, 1989, p. 47). DeWitt and Binder (1989) dismiss this problem as a nonissue because lease-purchase is not a debt, and the government agency has a "walk away" provision. Nevertheless, this arrangement does warrant some further consideration, if for nothing else because of the fact that various "creative financing" schemes of the 1980s, such as junk bonds, proved to be problematic not only economically but legally as well.

The option of lease-purchase, when exercised through private financing, can be seen as a necessary step to handle the contradictory problems of high crime rates and high incarceration rates that result in overcrowding, on the one hand, and the public's reluctance for spending on correction construction, on the other. Although most government officials find the public inconsistent, privatization advocates view this as voter dissatisfaction with the government's performance in constructing and operating prisons. Accordingly, it is the expression of the public's feeling that it does not get a good return on the correctional cost; therefore this attitude is rational in facing a monopolistic correctional system. "Only where competition and comparison demonstrate the true price of a product does it become irrational to demand more without being willing to pay what it takes" (Logan, 1990, p. 78).

Whether large segments of the public conduct this price analysis, or they are just tired of allocating more money for projects that are for most people invisible, or it is a part of the post-Proposition 13 tax revolt in which antigovernment feelings are so high that almost all projects needing extra money are voted down (e.g., highway funds), the fact remains that when there is a tight budget situation, correctional construction also feels the crunch (although to a lesser degree) as all other public expenditures do. It also may reflect public apathy when only a portion of the public votes on this issue, and small organized groups can influence the outcome of the vote.

In practical terms, state or local governments under court orders not to increase their existing inmate population may see no other option but that of trying to find alternatives to public funding for the expansion of their correctional system. Lease-purchase is one of the creative financing methods used increasingly to deal with this problem, and frankly, most citizens do not know and do not care that the construction financing is arranged without voter approval. On the other hand, this method has an appeal for private sector investors (Cikins, 1993).

Construction of Facilities

Another area of private involvement is the construction of correctional facilities. Private corporations claim that they can locate, finance, and build faster and cheaper correctional facilities than the government does. The largest private corporation, CCA, reports that its construction price is only 80% of the government's cost (Logan, 1990). The company, in its publication on CCA's business philosophy, states that the "careful attention to the design of a CCA facility permits considerable personnel economies" (Corrections Corporation of America, n.d., p. 1). Not only the actual cost of construction seems to favor the private sector but also the speed with which it can build. This is important because, as seen, the continuous need for additional space in the correctional system is pressing. The situation is similar in the case of renovation and expansion of existing facilities. Private corporations can do this work with their own funds or with funds that they can raise from private sources without waiting for appropriations from the legislature or government offices. According to a representative of the Federal Bureau of Prisons, it takes between 2 to 3 years to site and build a correctional facility, whereas maximum-security prisons may take as much as 5 years to be built. It also is being reported that some private contractors have designed, financed, and built a facility in 6 months (Logan, 1990).

Building-cost comparisons must be made carefully—they have to be between the construction of similar kinds of institutions, in order not to get involved in an "apples and oranges" controversy. Another issue that does not seem to be dealt with in detail is the siting of correctional facilities. It is known that facility siting often becomes a serious social and political issue impeding the swiftness of the construction process of new facilities (e.g., Farrington, 1992; Krause, 1992; Sechrest, 1992a; Shichor, 1992a). Assuming that the environmental requirements remain the same and public attitudes toward prison siting will not be substantially different when private prisons are constructed, the celerity of private construction seems to be amazing. Unless the construction takes place in localities that are actively seeking out a correctional facility because of economic depression, the siting of private facilities seems to be as troublesome and time consuming as the siting of public facilities. Either the construction will take place in economically depressed small communities where the positive economic impact (e.g., employment, procurement, local taxes) generated by the institution may be substantial, or the private companies will be ready to sign special kinds of contracts with the municipal authorities, such as readiness to close the operation if the local government demands it because of the negative impact of the facility on the community. In either case the contracting government agency has to make a decision whether the arrangement is beneficial to its purposes and will be functional for a long-term correctional facility.

A related problem concerns the actual building of the facility. Without getting into technological issues, there should be some concern regarding the quality of building. Because of the urgent need for more jail and prison space to house the rapidly growing convict population and the simultaneous need to save money, there is an increased interest in cheaper and faster methods of construction. In several states, jails and prisons were designed and built in modular design from prefabricated concrete components (DeWitt, 1986b). These methods are attractive for private correctional companies because they are in line with their promise of faster and cheaper construction.

However, there are some doubts concerning these methods of construction. Sechrest, Papas, and Price (1987), after studying this issue in detail, voiced their doubts:

> The authors are concerned about an apparent willingness to accept entrepreneurial promotions of modular, pre-manufactured, or prefabricated products for use in correctional facility construction without evidence to support their successful long-term use or their utility in meeting correctional demands. (p. 35)

These researchers underline the importance of planning a facility to meet the particular needs of an agency. They also recommend strongly the evaluation of the various new materials and designs that were used during the 1980s in the construction of correctional facilities. They especially emphasize that

> a national program of on-site post-occupancy evaluation should be created to include consideration of all types of construction, emphasizing long-term utility based on cost, time to occupancy, durability, the quality of materials, hardware, and components, and other features of use. Equally important areas for examination are staffing requirements (number and type), working conditions, inmate living conditions, security (line of sight, zones), flexibility (adaptation to new security levels), energy consumption, and such unique features as the ease of relocation of modular units. (Sechrest et al., 1987, p. 41)

The fact that private contractors will try to prove their success mainly in economic terms may lead to the use of such construction materials, methods, and facility designs that, although cheaper in the short run, will not be the most suitable and durable in the long run.

At the beginning of the prison privatization "movement" the biggest profits for the private companies were in the financing and the construction of private correctional facilities rather than in their operation (Duffy, 1984).

Facility Operation

As in the case of financing and construction, in the operation of prisons the main justification for privatization is economics. The core question in this analysis is: How can the private contractor deliver better or the same quality correctional services cheaper than government agencies can? According to the private companies, this efficiency is achieved through "the side-stepping of government bureaucracy in building and operating prisons, better staff motivation, the utilization of modern management techniques, and increased flexibility in the hiring and firing of employees" (Borna, 1986, p. 328).

These claims are not new; they were the basis for all correctional privatization throughout history (e.g., Durham, 1989; Feeley, 1991). Although it is not the intent here to go into great detail on the various ways of cost calculations, it was already pointed out that there are many complexities involved in correctional cost estimates; probably the most important is that there are many hidden costs involved, which make this task especially complex.

There are several areas in which the cost comparison between the operation of public and private institutions can be made.

Labor Cost

Corrections is a labor-intensive industry; between 60% to 80% of the correctional cost is labor related (Donahue, 1988; McDonald, 1990a). Because private corporations claim that they can operate correctional facilities at a lower cost than public agencies do and at the same time provide the same or better services, it is clear that they will have to cut their labor costs. There are several ways that this can be accomplished.

The most obvious cost-cutting practices are the following: paying lower salaries to employees, providing fewer fringe benefits for them (health insurance, sick leave, vacation time), limiting promotions, economizing on employee screening, hiring fewer employees through the reduction of staffing and the introduction of electronic surveillance systems, and providing less training. These measures may create some problems among the employees, such as low morale, lack of stability, high turnover rates, and so on.

Privatization advocates deflect the claim that labor cost cutting lowers the quality of the workforce. The means of decreasing labor costs mentioned most often by the companies are lowering the number of correctional officers through flexible staffing, using more electronic surveillance, and substituting profit-sharing plans for some of the high-cost fringe benefits (Crants, 1991; Logan, 1990). They claim that these practices would allow them to pay even higher salaries.

As an example of efficiency and cost savings, CCA reported savings in the area of security staff through efficient scheduling, facility design, and the use of electronic surveillance systems. These strategies, according to the report, led to a 60% reduction of operating costs. Basically, the report focuses on one major point, the reduction of the number of correctional officers on duty in the institution. If a building is designed in a way that it can eliminate a watch post, or if the post is eliminated by scheduling, it can reduce 5.2 guard positions for a 24-hour period, which can produce a substantial annual savings of more than $100,000 in salaries and fringe benefits (Funke, 1985). The staff reduction is viewed by private correctional companies as a variable cost that can be reduced by efficient management without sacrificing the quality of services. For example, one suggestion is the reduction of the number of guards during the night shift. This suggestion looks economically sound; however, in terms of security, it may be problematic because prison disturbances and escape attempts may occur at night. Critics of privatization, on the other hand, see payroll expenses as a fixed cost that can be reduced only at the risk of creating less safe and less humane institutions (Ring, 1987). There is also the question of how much reduction can be done not only on the basis of rationality but on the basis of set standards. Unless the private companies will be able to influence the authorities to change the standards—which is one of the concerns of some critics because they believe that by using their lobbying power, private corporations will delude the effectiveness of control institutions— the staffing standards will remain in effect. Thus private companies will not be able to reduce security staff or eliminate watch posts at will in all cases. In fact, as mentioned earlier, Wackenhut Corporation in 1991 gave up the operation of Monroe County Jail in Florida because of staffing problems. The company claimed that it was not aware of the state requirement of having 11 guards per shift, and it had submitted its original bid with the staffing of 6 guards in mind. Wackenhut requested an extra $2.6 million for 4 years to operate the jail according to the county staffing requirements.[5] The company transferred the operation to the county and the county agreed to pay $300,000 to settle claims over the staffing difference, utility bills, and transportation costs plus $206,000 for equipment purchased by the company (Keating, 1991). In short, the reduction in number of security officers has its limits and probably cannot be used as the major strategy for cost cutting unless substantial changes in the rules and regulations of the contracting agencies will be introduced. On the other hand, public agencies should be concerned more with adequate planning and with forestalling attempts of featherbedding by correctional employees' unions to streamline their operations. However, some of these unions wield so much political power that to introduce major changes into work practices is almost impossible.

Opponents of privatization admit that private companies have hired several government prison administrators having impressive credentials in corrections.[6] This is emphasized by the corporations to gain more credibility. However, the drive to cut costs on personnel may lead to much less selectivity in the hiring of lower echelon staff. As was implied before, lowering the selection criteria of workers may affect the quality of services. Similarly, a related cost-cutting measure, such as having fewer or lesser qualified professionals (e.g., resident psychiatrists or social workers) also may have an impact on the quality of services rendered by the private facility (Bendick, 1989). Supporters of privatization point out in this vein that contracting agencies have the right to determine all the training and staffing requirements; thus the private companies will have to follow the specifications. This claim is formally correct; however, it runs into the same problems of monitoring, contract termination, and regulations, namely, not having enough monitors, not finding easily available replacement, political interference, and others that were mentioned previously.

One of the core questions in the cost debate is whether the government is using the correctional budget efficiently. Government agencies and labor organizations most affected by privatization reject the claim forwarded by privatization advocates that 10% to 25% of the

operating budget of correctional agencies is wasted due to inefficiency and red tape. Privatization proponents claim that a large part
of these inefficiencies are related to the inherent lack of flexibility of
government bureaucracies. For example, the New York City Police
Department staffing system sanctioned by state law allocated an
equal number of officers to be on duty on each shift, regardless of the
differential distribution of criminal activity during the 24-hour period of the day (Savas, 1982). This is an inefficient way to use human
resources and to achieve maximum output from the officers. Government and union officials point out that even if the private companies
could reduce the cost 10% to 25%, this gain would be offset by
expenses inherently connected with privatization, such as licensing
of privately managed facilities, the need to purchase adequate liability insurance, and the expenses involved in monitoring these operations. These claims lead to the accusation that private operators can
reduce costs and increase their ability to generate profits for themselves only through exploiting inmates and their own employees.

    This point is supported to a degree by an empirical study of the
Urban Institute (Hatry et al., 1989), which compared the publicly and
privately operated correctional facilities in Kentucky and Massachusetts. According to the comparison in Kentucky, it was found that
employees in a private facility received 10 days of paid leave per year
regardless of the length of service they had in the company. On the
other hand, workers at a public facility received their vacation time
according to their seniority and it could reach up to a maximum of
21 days, more than twice that of the workers at the private facility.
Furthermore, in the private facility there was no payment for overtime, only compensatory time was given. The staff in the public
facility was entitled to 10 paid holidays per year, whereas in the
private facility they had only 7 paid holidays. In sum, the employees
in the public facility earned more annual sick and holiday leave than
employees in the privately operated facility. Public employees received 34 to 43 leave days per year, depending on their seniority,
whereas the private company employees received 22 days regardless
of the length of their service. This amounts to a difference of between
50% to 100% in paid leave. Obviously, these policies influence the
labor cost of the two facilities, although the sick leave is paid only
when it is used or payment is made for accumulated sick leave.

Privatization proponents also claim that there is a basic difference in the managerial approach between public and private organizations that has an impact on the cost of services. This has to do with the different ways that the private and public sectors are financed. Based on Drucker's (1973) thesis, in private corporations:

> Profit-and-loss incentives differ fundamentally from budget-driven bureaucratic incentives. Entrepreneurs are competitively motivated to provide maximum satisfaction at minimum cost. In contrast, bureaucrats are rewarded not so much for efficiency, but in direct proportion to the size and total budget of their agencies. (Logan, 1990, p. 84)

To stretch this approach further it can even be suggested that there are administrative incentives in public institutions to increase the cost to be able to justify larger budgets, which in turn increase the power and status of the organization and its administration. Furthermore, public institutions, to muster public and official support, have to have the ability to appeal to a broad constituency; therefore they must please large numbers of people with differing interests and must try not to alienate anyone (Logan, 1990). This may compromise their effectiveness because they cannot concentrate fully on the main task that they were assigned to do. This is a formidable argument that needs to be addressed in any discussion of the privatization debate. However, a somewhat similar argument can be forwarded in the case of private institutions as well. It very well may be that companies operating private prisons and their administrators will be so concerned with cost cutting, profit making, and satisfying their stockholders that some major goals of the institution will be neglected or overlooked. For instance, some aspects of rehabilitation that still remain a part of the functions of corrections may be affected, even more than in the public institutions; for example, psychological services may be cut or restricted unless extra monies are paid for them.

Economics of Scale

Another measure, besides the controversial method of labor cost saving, is contracting across jurisdictions. For example, city jails, county jails, and in a few cases even state prisons may rent out some of the unused cells to other jurisdictions, mainly to large metropolitan areas and highly populated states that experience serious overcrowding in their facilities. Private contractors will be able to economize by easier contracting across jurisdictions either by signing contracts with other public or private entities or using the facilities that their own company is operating in other jurisdictions (Logan, 1990). Supposedly, all parties benefit from this kind of arrangement because it helps to ease overcrowding in certain impacted facilities, and it helps to use underpopulated facilities and supports their upkeep by providing extra income for their services. Privatization proponents suggest that the contracting government agencies will benefit along with the private companies from lower fees charged, but this claim has to be substantiated. In a per diem arrangement most measures affecting cost cutting during the life of the contract primarily benefit the private company. When the renegotiation of the contract takes place, this issue may arise, but it will be taken into consideration together with a host of other factors. The arrangement of placing prisoners into facilities across jurisdictions may not always work smoothly. There may be community or government resistance to such a transfer. For example, in 1986 a private jail in Pennsylvania received 55 inmates from an overcrowded Washington, D.C. facility. The state objected and obtained a court order to transfer back the out-of-state inmates. Pennsylvania did not want to become a recipient of out-of-state prisoners. This refusal put the private jail out of business (Donahue, 1988; U.S. General Accounting Office, 1991).[7]

Another factor that may have an affect on the cost is related to the flexibility of private contractors to purchase supplies from those businesses that can offer the best prices. They can shop around for the best deal. Purchasing decisions do not have to go through bureaucratic controls as government agencies do, and private companies do not have to receive special authorizations for purchases in the case of bargain sales that may end before the bureaucratic procedures are completed. Also, they are not bound by special contracts with various suppliers, like government agencies usually are; an arrangement that in a sense provides these suppliers with a virtual monopoly to sell designated products to the government agency often for more than the market price.[8] Also, private companies can use their centralized purchasing department for buying durable and nonperishable goods nationwide in large volumes to get better prices. These measures may lead to substantial savings for the company, which may be transferred to the government agency by calculating it into the contract price, provided, obviously, that the removal of the bureaucratic controls will not affect the quality of products being purchased. However, it is not certain that these savings will be transferred to government agencies; it may largely benefit the private company itself.

Privatization advocates claim that there is also a notorious problem of waste in the public sector that relates especially to the "budget based" financing of public institutions and the lack of responsibility of public employees:

> Dereliction of duty, tardiness, absenteeism, and abuse of sick leave are probably less prevalent in private industry, where management controls are stronger.
>   Employee theft occurs in both sectors, but only in very large corporations (which are occasionally the targets of elaborate embezzlement schemes) is it as common as it is in government. Personal use of telephones and mail privileges and other types of petty pilferage are so common in government that they are hardly even perceived as theft, except for occasional abuses so flagrant as to be scandalous. (Logan, 1990, p. 85)

According to the above, budget-based financing leads to waste and abuse through the extensive spending of government agencies and units at the end of each fiscal year. It is general knowledge that surplus monies remaining in public institutions at the end of the budget year have to be spent because if a certain amount is saved, next year's budget is going to be smaller because the institution can do with less money that was allocated. Thus there is no reward for prudent money management; instead there is a penalty in the form of reduction of the next year's budget, and this creates an incentive to spend all the allocated money whether it is needed or not. Consequently, there is no incentive for cost control and cost cutting.[9] This situation is different in the private institution, in which much more effective cost control measures can be applied because every dollar saved adds to the company's profit. The question in this regard is whether budget savings in private facilities will be reflected in the cost that the government will be charged for the services, or whether it will be extra profit for the private contractor. If the latter is the case, it may prompt the contracting company to press its management and employees for further cost cutting that may affect the quality of services for the purpose of increased profits. Nevertheless, the end-of-the-year budgetary splurge of government agencies is antithetical to good management practices and seriously undermines the public image of these agencies.

Inflation

Some advocates of privatization claim that the effects of inflation are reflected more in the growth of government costs than in the general economy (e.g., Logan, 1990). Usually, an annual inflation clause is included in the contract with the private company; thus the cost is kept on the general inflation level. On the other hand, according to these advocates, the government's costs of corrections are outpacing the level of inflation. This claim is supported by quoting a study that analyzed the trend per inmate cost in South Carolina between 1974 and 1984, which indicated that inmate costs increased an annual average of 11.4%, but the Consumer Price Index rose only 7.7% annually (Logan, 1990). Although this claim may be correct, it is hard to accept an argument based on one state's figures alone, particularly when this state is among the smaller ones, having a relatively small prison population. Moreover, these figures do not indicate and analyze the various kinds of expenditures. Increases may have been due to major constructions, repairs,[10] introduction of new programs, salary increases, legislative mandates, or just bad fiscal management. Thus this kind of analysis has to be much more thorough than the comparison of gross figures from one state Department of Corrections.

Among other factors, the analysis has to take into consideration the growth in the number of inmates and the ensuing consequences of the prison population explosion, including the need to build new facilities and renovate and repair existing ones. The official statistics, for example, indicate that total state expenditures on correctional institutions in the United States increased between 1984 and 1986 by 39.5% (from $5.9 billion to $8.2 billion); out of these sums construction capital outlay-expenditures increased by 93.2% (from $695 million to $1.3 billion) (Jamieson & Flanagan, 1989).

Another issue often mentioned in the economic analysis of corrections is the comparison of privatized versus government services in fields other than corrections. The basic problem with this approach is that it usually compares "apples with oranges." Privatized garbage collections, car fleet maintenance, prison medical or food services, and others are not necessarily comparable with the operation and management of a prison. In this vein DiIulio (1988) points out that one of the assumptions on which the claim that private correctional management can outperform government run institutions is that

> there are significant differences between public and private management, that business firms are necessarily more "efficient, effective, and innovative" than government agencies, and that these advantages of private management are universal; they ascertain whether the task is picking up garbage or locking up prisoners. (p. 75)

There is a qualitative difference between the provision of human services and building and equipment maintenance. Human services deal with people's needs, their behavior, and in the case of corrections, their control. Human service organizations, including prisons, have a mandate "to improve the general well-being and functioning of people" (Hasenfeld & English, 1974, p. 1). Therefore generalizations about the cost savings and effectiveness of private firms have to be made with considerable caution.[11]

Per Diem Payments

The method of payment for the services rendered by private prisons is also an important aspect of cost calculations. The most prevalent method of payment for correctional services in a private prison, as mentioned, is a sum per inmate per day, which is usually referred to as per diem payment. This calculation includes all the expenses that the company has in running the prison (including interest payments on mortgages), divided by the number of inmates plus a certain sum per inmate for profit. This method seems to be a logical way to calculate payments. However, some critics find potential problems with this practice.

One of the major concerns voiced is that private companies will have a vested interest in keeping their prisons filled to capacity to receive maximum payments. It may lead to strong lobbying efforts in the legislatures to follow strict incapacitation-oriented penal policies (Anderson, Cavoli, & Moriarity, 1985), and to the neglect of rehabilitative programs that may advocate earlier release from confinement. It also can lead to attempts to influence the length of incarceration through the prison discipline process, which would result in the reduction of good time, thus making sure that longer periods of incarcerations will be the rule rather than the exception.

Proponents of privatization claim that these are only speculations brought up by opponents to torpedo plans for privatization. They categorically state that initial information on privatized facilities does not support these claims (Brakel, 1988; Logan, 1990). Furthermore, they point out that in the reality of the 1980s and early 1990s, there was such a high inflow of sentenced offenders to prisons that the claim that private companies would try artificially to fill up their facilities is completely speculative. It may have been true that, in those years, attempts to fill the prisons were not needed because they had more referrals than they could handle, but the question is whether that high level of incarceration is going to continue infinitely. It was pointed out earlier that there have already been indications in the early 1990s that the number of new commitments to prison was leveling off, although it is very likely that the new three-strikes crime bill will result in a further increase in the prison population.

In government contracts with private prison companies, the agencies usually have to guarantee a certain level of occupation rate, below which the per diem rates go up, in order to create a safety net for the contractor against major income losses (State of California, 1985). In the per diem arrangement, there is a built-in incentive to continue a high incarceration rate to prevent "losing money" and to "make money." Therefore, if government becomes dependent on private corporations for incarceration, it will either be compelled to keep people imprisoned who otherwise would be released or would participate in community programs or it will have to agree to price adjustments. On the other hand, if the prison population continues to grow, public institutions do not have to worry about substantial cost increases with the addition of extra offenders above a certain limit; they can add prisoners without increasing, by much, the operational cost of the facility. In fact, the addition of more inmates in government facilities reduces the per capita cost. This may add to the reasons for serious overcrowding in public prisons. On the other hand, every additional inmate in a private facility will increase the expenditure by a full per diem cost. McDonald (1989) refers to this phenomenon as the "marginal cost" because "many costs are quite fixed and vary little with changes in inmate population" (p. 20).

As an example, the first year (1984) of private operation by CCA of the Hamilton County Jail in Tennessee resulted in a $200,000 cost overrun because the county faced an unexpected explosion in the number of inmates (Tolchin, 1985). Apparently, county officials were unaccustomed to the per diem calculation of incarceration costs. They had to pay $21 to CCA for each excess inmate, whereas under the county administration it would have cost only $5.[12] Contracting should take into consideration the possibility of decline in inmate population, which may decrease the attractiveness of private prisons, on the one hand, and the diminishing fiscal advantages in certain situations of overcrowding when the "marginal cost" of corrections is low in public prisons but in private prisons the per diem cost remains constant. At the same time, the negative effects of severe overcrowding have to be kept in sight.

It is possible that costs in both kinds of facilities are quite similar. A comprehensive study conducted by the Urban Institute (Hatry et al., 1989) that compared private and public correctional facilities in Kentucky and Massachusetts concluded that "the public and private programs we studied, although differing somewhat in the way they allotted their funds, differed little in the total amount of money they required to provide service to a client" (p. 212). Although the above study plays down the cost differences between the public and private correctional facilities analyzed, it found that private facilities were costing 1% to 10% more to operate than public facilities.

Continuing their review of several public and private facilities, Hatry et al. (1989) concluded:

Based on this highly limited information, it appears that in most cases
the contractor costs were somewhat less than government-operated
facilities would have been, thereby achieving savings. Our interviews
suggest that some of the contractors were having difficulty with their
current per diems, such as in Kentucky and Pennsylvania. In both cases
the vendors had recently been asked by the government to bring down
costs to budgeted levels. Thus, there remains some question as to
whether these operations in the future will be able to maintain their
current level of quality. In these two cases, at least, these private
for-profit firms are not likely to be achieving much, if any, profit (and
may well be operating at a loss). (p. 53)

Also, the preliminary indications of the cost aspects of California
private facilities that primarily house parole violators do not show
clear evidence that these facilities run for less cost than public
facilities (Sechrest & Shichor, 1993a, 1993b; Tumulty, 1991).

The fact that some of the private facilities do not make any money
or have even operated with a loss is an intriguing and, at the same
time, disturbing fact. According to Donahue (1988) CCA lost from
1984 to 1986 an aggregate of $6.8 million, although in 1989 it reported
for the first time a net income of $1,606,040 in its annual report
(Corrections Corporation of America, 1989).[13] The question is whether
the private companies are not as cost efficient as they originally
claimed to be or if initially they were lowballing to get into the market
and to wait until the government would be so much in need of their
services that it would be ready to pay higher prices. Either way, it
seems clear that these companies will not be able or ready to operate
for a long time with losses or with very meager profits. If they cannot
increase their profits at the agreed-on cost, either they will try to raise
their prices, which will lower their cost effectiveness for the government, or they will have to close their operations, which may cause
problems for the state authorities.

Empirical Studies of Cost

A few empirical studies attempt to assess all (both the open and
the hidden) costs of operating correctional institutions. Here a brief
review focusing on the cost comparisons is presented. A more thorough

discussion of comparisons is in the following chapter, which deals with the issues of evaluation and the available studies in more detail.

One of the comparative studies of cost was conducted by Logan and McGriff (1989) in the Silverdale Detention Center in Hamilton County, Tennessee that has been operated by CCA since 1984. It is a 350-bed minimum-security work camp. The county auditor McGriff prepared a yearly analysis in which he compared the operational cost of the prison under the CCA contract with what it would cost under county management. The hidden costs taken into consideration included property and liability insurance, maintenance, garbage collection, wages of record clerks, the county hospital's expenditure on inmates care, cost of capital assets, government overhead for various support activities (e.g., financial management, data processing, accounting), personnel, and purchasing. All these expenditures were accounted as direct costs by the private company; thus for the purpose of comparison, similar costs by the county government had to be calculated.

This detailed comparison revealed, according to the authors, that being on the conservative side, the county spent between 3% to 8% less on the facility contracting out to CCA than it would have were it to resume the operation of Silverdale. McDonald (1990a), reviewing this, pointed out that this comparison obscures the fact that CCA had made several important improvements in the physical outlay of the facility and in medical and recreational services. He also suggested that correctional officers had been given more training than they would have received under the county-operated system, and also, that the institutional standards became more stringent. These factors made the cost-benefit comparison even more favorable for the private contractors's side. McDonald (1990a) concluded that the major difference in the operating costs between the private and the county management is due to the cheaper labor cost in private facilities. He estimated a real savings of 5% to 15% by private institutions.

The U.S. General Accounting Office (GAO) has reviewed the above study and expressed some reservations concerning the way it reached its conclusions. It noted that the private-public cost comparison was made by using the private company's expenditures as a basis and estimating from them how much the same services would cost under public management. According to the GAO report (1991) this method is problematic because it assumes that no unanticipated changes would occur through time, in the staffing level, in salaries, and in routine and extraordinary expenses. Any such change, should it occur, could result in different cost figures.

Another study comparing public-private costs of facility operations that the GAO reviewed was conducted by the Urban Institute (Hatry et al., 1989). This study examined three pairs of public and private correctional facilities in Kentucky and Massachusetts. The focus of the study was to assess cost, service quality, and service effectiveness between similar public and private facilities. As quoted earlier, the study concluded that the operation of private facilities cost more by 1% to 10% than similar public institutions. The report also indicated that privately run facilities provide a somewhat higher quality of services than public facilities do.

The GAO report noted that the Urban Institute's study used sound research methods to provide a reliable set of empirical data regarding the facilities. However, GAO researchers found certain limitations for the applicability of this evaluation. First, they pointed out, as they did regarding the previous study, that because of the limited scope of the evaluation, it is very hard to make generalizations. Furthermore, they questioned the comparability of the facilities that were studied. They found, for example, differences between facilities in the size of the inmate population as well as in the types of inmates in terms of "dangerousness," time served in confinement, and other background factors. There was also a difference in the unionization of employees in one of the comparisons. Thus these differences, according to the researchers, did not allow isolation of the public-private cost variable, meaning that observed variances of cost or quality of service could not be clearly attributed to the differences in private-public management. In the Kentucky comparison this problem was even more acute because there was an inclusion of some of the capital cost in the private prison calculations, but there were no similar costs included in the public prison data. This difference in cost calculation might have accounted for at least some of the 10% differential in costs between the private and the public facility in Kentucky.

One of the first privatization studies, which was not reviewed by the GAO, was that of the Florida School for Boys in Okeechobee. This 400-bed security institution was taken over in 1982 by the Eckerd

Foundation, a private not-for-profit organization. A comparison with a similar state operation could not find a substantial reduction in cost, and there were some indications of decline in quality of the program (Levinson, 1985). The significance of this study has to be evaluated with caution because it is not known how much an operation run by a not-for-profit foundation is comparable with the operation of a for-profit correctional corporation.

The GAO review does mention that correctional officials in several states made favorable statements regarding the ability of the private sector to provide additional prison capacity much quicker and cheaper than government does. Some state officials also report per diem savings through privatization. However, these reports were not documented as yet by systematic evaluation.

The empirical comparisons reviewed in this section are important in advancing a reliable database on private-public correctional costs. However, they tended to involve low security levels and small juvenile institutions and not medium-sized and large maximum-security prisons in which the flexibility to control expenses may be more constrained.

Conclusion

The major reason behind public support for the privatization of prisons is the conviction that private corporations can operate with more cost-effectiveness than can public agencies. The review of this issue has not shown overwhelming evidence that the privatization of prisons would save such a substantial amount of money for the authorities and ultimately for the taxpayers that the risks of mismanagement, lack of effective government control, increased opportunities for corruption, government dependence on private corporations, and so on could fully justify the operation of prisons by for-profit corporations. The growing emphasis on efficiency and cost-effectiveness in public administration and the continued trend toward privatization of human services (including corrections) undoubtedly will help to clarify the problems of hidden costs. These will also help to improve research capabilities and methods to conduct more reliable studies to determine the true cost of services and to compare the cost-effectiveness of the different correctional operations.

One of the fundamental questions that will remain is whether the economic factor and promised savings achieved by privatization should be the key factor in the private debate.

Notes

1. Mitchell is director of tax and budget policy for Citizens for a Sound Economy, an independent public policy organization.

2. Among the most detailed analyses of criminal costs is Wayson and Funke's (1989) publication, *What Price Justice?* published by the NIJ. Concerning correctional costs, see McDonald (1989, 1990a).

3. The prevention of escapes is especially important because each escape or publicized escape attempt raises major public concern.

4. For example, in California, facilities operated by for-profit firms and local government agencies for profit (e.g., municipalities, sheriff departments, police departments) are supervised by the Parole Division of the state Department of Corrections. Parole officers use state cars to travel to work, an expense that has to be considered as a privatization cost.

5. It is possible that Wackenhut overlooked the staffing requirements when it signed the contract with Monroe County. However, this seems unlikely because it is an established and well-known security corporation that has long-time experience with various contract works. It is more likely that at the signing of the contract the management believed that the company would be able to influence the authorities to change the staffing formulas.

6. This policy may be a mixed blessing because these administrators are coming from the same sector that is branded as inefficient, wasteful, and inept by privatization advocates.

7. As noted, the siting of new correctional facilities is often problematic. Many communities and local governments object to having a prison in their territory. Authorities often have to face the NIMBY (not in my backyard) reaction of the local population.

8. This arrangement may also breed corruption by the suppliers trying to pay off government inspectors to be able to supply goods of lower quality than is stipulated in the contract. This kind of problem was found many times with military suppliers, especially in the meat-packing industry (see Coleman, 1989). Government contracting is often vulnerable to corruption (see Benenson, 1985).

9. This is a known and a very disturbing characteristic of budget-based financing prevalent in the public sector. The changing of this practice should be a first priority of government agencies. A policy that would reward rather than punish fiscal prudence should be devised by the government authorities. Being a professor in a state university, I find the prevailing practice wasteful and an offense to the logic and intelligence of employees at all levels. The frantic, often unplanned and unneeded spending at the end of the fiscal year is an unintended but persistent negative feature of budget-based financing.

10. For example, after the major hurricane damages that occurred in Florida and Louisiana in 1992, there was a steep increase in the price of certain types of building materials nationwide. Similar increases may have happened in other instances as well.

11. In the 1970s and early 1980s, researchers were focusing on refuse collection in their evaluation of privatization, even though there was contracting in other services as well. For instance, health care services were usually not evaluated (Ascher, 1987).

12. Interestingly, the very same correctional facility that later was named Silverdale became a "showcase" institution for privatization. Most of the existing evaluation studies of private prisons either focus on or refer to this institution.

13. Neither Logan and McGriff (1989) nor McDonald (1990a) referred to the financial losses incurred by CCA during the period 1984 to 1986.

7

Quality Issues

Advocates of privatization claim that they can not only operate correctional facilities cheaper than government agencies do but also provide better quality services at the same time. The cost analysis is inherently tied with the analysis of quality of services. One of the problems in approaching this issue is that there is no clear-cut agreement about how to define and measure quality in social services (Gurin, 1989).

Definition of Quality of Services in Corrections

In the context of prisons, quality is referred to by some in terms of the quality and quantity of food, the variety of services, and the professionalism of the personnel (e.g., Logan, 1990). One major comparative study of public and private facilities, mentioned earlier, tried to operationalize quality and effectiveness by examining factors such as physical conditions of the facility, escape rates, security and control procedures, physical and mental health of the inmates, adequacy of programs for inmates (e.g., education, counseling, training, and recreation), and indicators of rehabilitation mainly in terms of reincarceration (Hatry et al., 1989). These issues are connected to cost analysis because one major way of reducing costs or increasing profits for the private company is to cut corners on these services. Logically, any corner cutting would increase the profitability of the private-enterprise prison. In fact, an extreme emphasis on cost alone may affect the quality of services. O'Hare, Leone, and Zegans (1990), who are management and public policy experts rather than criminologists, express this concern: "We are disheartened by the willingness of some to consider wholesale privatization of prison systems, especially using a single contractor, and by the relentless effort to focus on cost rather than product quality as a motivation to privatize" (p. 125).

On the other hand, they point to contract specifications as a major problem that may stifle incentives for innovations and changes that may lead to improved quality of services, even if the private contractor is motivated to do so. The specifications are written by the government bureaucracy. Because of the repeated warnings about the problems of efficient monitoring and the need to follow and control the activities of private correctional companies, there may be obstacles to allowing the introduction of new programs and methods aimed at upgrading the quality of services even if the for-profit company is interested in doing so.

DiIulio (1987) provides a framework for the analysis of quality of services in prisons that can be applied both for analytical and comparative purposes. He lists three major elements that are relevant: order, amenity, and service. *Order* is defined as "the absence of individual or group misconduct that threatens the safety of others." The concept of order is important because "in the ordered society people feel safe; traditional values are preserved; human behavior is predictable; and those who play by the rules are honored and valued members of the community" (Bartollas & Dinitz, 1989, p. 3). In other words, order means structured and stable surroundings. *Amenity* includes "anything that enhances the comfort of the inmates," such as good food, clean living quarters, ample recreation, color television, and so on. *Service* is "anything that is intended to improve the life prospects of the inmates," such as educational and remedial programs, vocational training, and counseling. Accordingly, a *good prison* is defined as "one that provides as much order, amenities, and service as possible given its human and financial resources" (DiIulio, 1987, pp. 11-12). This definition also makes a clear connection with cost-related issues because human resources are influenced by the numbers and qualifications of personnel that the facility can afford to hire and the financial resources are cost related by definition. According to the same author, although a great deal of recommendations have been made about how to improve prison conditions, there is a lack of policy-oriented knowledge in this field.

Prisons are "depressing places" as DiIulio (1987, p. 49) states. In a sense they are designed to be like that because among the various penological aims that they are supposed to fulfill (e.g., retribution, incapacitation, and rehabilitation), there is also the deterrence function that includes the notion that prison should be a place in which people will be afraid to be confined. This does not mean that all prisons are exactly the same. Some prisons are more depressing than others. Their "quality" may be different on the basis of order, amenity, and service.[1]

Order

To be able to analyze the quality of life in prisons, it is essential to operationalize this concept to go beyond impressions or organizational rhetoric and to create a more precise and reliable measurement tool that can be used for the comparison of the various correctional facilities. Order, as one major aspect of prison life, can be measured by the extent of prison violence in the institution. This would include such occurrences as assaults, homicides, rapes, and riots and the ways they are handled by the administration and staff. Research shows that, generally, prison violence is rampant, especially in maximum-security facilities where the most violent inmates are placed (Bowker, 1980; Carroll, 1974; Colvin, 1982; Irwin, 1980; Jacobs, 1977; Sheehan, 1978). In many prisons physical violence among inmates is taken as a matter of fact by inmates and staff alike. It is seen as a part of prison life (Fleisher, 1989).

Many prisoners have a long history of aggressive behavior, and a large percentage of them are in the prison because they have committed serious violent crimes. Prison life, with all the deprivations attached to it, tends to increase the frustration level of inmates and their readiness for aggression:

Inmates are likely to explode into violence or to take what they want
from other inmates with the threat of force. The world of the prison can
be anxiety-provoking even for the hardened recidivist, and inmates are
apt to count the deprivation of a sense of security as one of the most
difficult problems with which they must deal. (Sykes, 1978, p. 526)

Violent behavior in prison has both an expressive and an instrumental value. It "reinforces a convict's status and prestige and adds
macho-value to his masculine image. In turn this image is currency
with which to buy 'social space,' power, control, contraband, sex, and
so on" (Fleisher, 1989, p. 198). Thus it is not surprising that many
correctional facilities have a violent organizational climate. The
problem of personal security of inmates in general tends to vary with
the security level of prisons. It is usually less acute in minimum-
security prisons, more serious in medium-security prisons, and the
most severe in maximum-security institutions where convicts usually are imprisoned for the most serious violent crimes and are
considered too dangerous to live in society.

As is the case with most statistical information in criminology,
there are problems of definitions of the various violent acts used by
different correctional departments. There is also a variance in the
extent of reporting of violent acts because inmates may feel too
threatened to report, depending on the organizational climate of each
facility. Also, the staff and administration may have a vested interest
not to report the full extent of violence because, in the eyes of
government officials and the public, prison violence is an indicator
of inefficient or weak administration. Nevertheless, reported information may be used as a crude indicator of the general situation in a
prison. However, the statistical data can and should be supplemented
with other types of information about the state of order in the
institution; these may include other indicators that might point
indirectly to internal problems, for example, staff turnover, formal
and informal interviews with staff and inmates, opinions and impressions of disinterested observers, and so forth (DiIulio, 1987).

The concept of order in prison has an objective and a subjective
dimension: "Objectively, a prison is orderly if there is little or no overt
violence—assaults, rapes, riots, murders, and so on. Subjectively, a
prison is orderly if life behind the walls is mostly calm, stable, and
predictable" (DiIulio, 1987, p. 51).

Although theoretically it is possible that an institution will have a high level of objective order but will rank low on subjective order and vice versa, in reality the two dimensions tend to have a high positive correlation, that is, high objective and high subjective orders seem to go together, as well as low objective and low subjective orders. The impressions of disinterested observers and also information from staff and inmates usually match fairly well the statistical picture of violence in the prison. The issue of violence will be dealt with in more detail later in this chapter.

Amenity

The assessment of the quality of amenities in a prison looks straightforward, but in reality it is not a very simple matter. For example, to measure the atmosphere of learning in a remedial class is not an easy task. What is the adequate level of cleanliness in a cell block? How is good food defined? Good-quality food may be prepared in a way that some inmates would find it not very tasty or satisfying.[2] Even the number, the distribution, and the type of television sets are hard to measure in terms of quality. Above all, there is no clear consensus about what items and pieces of equipment in a prison are a luxury or a necessity. It obviously depends on who is making the definition of what is necessity and what is luxury. Such items as color televisions, weight-lifting equipment, and various sports and exercise equipment are considered to be luxury items by much of the public— they help to create a "resort" for convicted felons and serve as symbols of leniency toward criminals. Others view them as a necessity of modern living in American society, and many prison officials regard them as an important management tool to keep prisoners occupied because idleness usually breeds violence.[3] The administration and staff usually have a different view of this matter than inmates do and the general public tends to see this differently altogether. Whatever the opinion is of the public in this regard, in reality most inmates, although they come from the poorer segments of American society, do experience a decline in their material standard of living in prison (see, e.g., Irwin, 1980).

Service

As recalled, this concept includes anything that is intended to improve the life prospects of inmates. DiIulio (1987) suggests that a rough indicator of prison services can be established by the number of inmates enrolled in certain types of treatment programs. However, enrollment itself may be a misleading measure because inmates may enroll in programs to manipulate the system, in other words, just to make a positive impression on the administration and on the parole board. Besides the numbers enrolled and hours spent in these programs, other, more subjective measures such as classroom atmosphere, teacher competency, and learning achievement should be assessed as well. A somewhat similar approach used a comprehensive list of services assembled by Camp and Camp (1984) and tried to establish to what extent and degree those services were available in a facility (e.g., Sellers, 1989). Obviously, this method of quality measurement cannot assess the hidden factor of subjective effects, but it can help to quantify the availability of various services and to provide an additional dimension for evaluation of institutions and of comparison among them.

Also, accreditation by the American Correctional Association (ACA) is suggested to be an indicator of quality of service in prisons. The ACA dates back to 1870 when the National Prison Association (the ACA's predecessor) was formed by correctional professionals and became an advocate of a humane approach to corrections. The ACA is an independent association of correctional professionals. During the 1970s it promulgated a set of national standards for jails, prisons, and community corrections. The intent was to upgrade "essential services, better overall planning, joint problem identification, coordination of services, possible long-term savings, and a generally more effective criminal justice system" (Sechrest, 1976, p. 15). These standards are widely criticized by some professionals and scholars as written on the basis of unproven opinions, speculations, and principles about how to improve prisons without accumulating "knowledge" based on research as the foundation of these standards (e.g., DiIulio, 1987). Nevertheless, ACA accreditation became a certain measuring rod indicating to what degree an institution is trying to live up to minimum standards of corrections. Relatively few of the public institutions in the United States are accredited by the ACA, but contracts with private companies often include the requirement to adhere to ACA standards, although the majority of the private institutions have not received accreditation yet. Some private companies, especially CCA, emphasize that they manage their facilities according to ACA standards to gain respectability and acceptance. Although by 1990 only two of nine CCA institutions received accreditation, the others were preparing to apply for it.

Even though the adoption of ACA standards generally does not guarantee a higher quality of prison life per se, privatization advocates maintain that

> it is likely that accredited institutions, as a group, will tend to be a higher quality than most others, so accreditation is still a useful (albeit not definitive) indicator of quality. Moreover, accreditation must be renewed every three years, so the longer a facility's history of accreditation, the more reliable that is as an indicator. (Logan, 1990, p. 130)

However, between accreditations, CCA inspections and reviews are infrequent; and therefore the certificate indicates compliance with the standards only for a short time (Keating, 1990). In addition, there is also the possibility that the private correctional corporations will try to influence the ACA so that the standards will be tailored for them.

The ACA has very close business relations with private corporations that are connected with various aspects of corrections (e.g., construction, financing, security systems, and equipment), and a former president of the ACA served on the board of CCA. These interrelations between the ACA and private for-profit companies involved in corrections may raise questions regarding the objectivity and usefulness of these standards (see, e.g., Sechrest, 1992b).

Other Ways to Measure Quality

Quality of services can be viewed from a somewhat different perspective as well. This issue can be divided into (a) the services rendered to the "clients" or "users" of the institution, that is, the inmates; (b) the services rendered to the "customers" or "payers," that is, the government and ultimately the public at large. The first aspect includes such services as the physical maintenance of the facility, food and health services, individual safety, educational and vocational programs, counseling, maintenance of inmates' civil rights, maintenance of order in the facility, prevention of violence, and preparation for release. The second aspect includes incapacitation of inmates, that is, prevention of escapes, prevention of riots and hostage taking, and reduction of recidivism, in other words, security for the community. Accordingly, a well-run prison is one that keeps offenders who are harmful to the public away from other members of society and provides them with a safe and humane environment.

Quality of Services—The Inmates

The modern way of punishment became hidden from the public with the establishment of the prison (Foucault, 1977), and the general public does not show a great deal of concern and interest in what happens behind prison walls:

> Prison inmates are objects upon whom we can righteously fasten a
> mixed bag of our own unsettling emotions. They have wronged us by
> hurting or depriving innocent victims; yet they now live, we presume, in
> ease at our expense. Freudians maintain, perhaps correctly, that criminal
> offenders prototypically represent an underside of ourselves, and that
> we tend to fear and despise them as a method of trying to demonstrate
> our clear-cut distinction from them. (Geis, 1987, p. 78)

In his well-known book *The Society of Captives*, Sykes (1958) focuses on the "pains of imprisonment," referring to the deprivations that are experienced by the inmates during their imprisonment. He describes five major such pains: deprivation of liberty, deprivation of goods and services, deprivation of heterosexual relations, deprivation of autonomy, and deprivation of personal security. Some of these have particular relevance to the present discussion.

One is goods and services; this concept is similar to the amenity issue dealt with earlier. It was mentioned that for most inmates, prison life means a substantive decline in their material standard of living. They are often placed in overcrowded, barren cells or dormitories and do not have the amenities that are taken for granted by most citizens (Sykes, 1978). In this respect, then, services such as food, health, housing, and a commissary become more important and can temper to a degree the material deprivations of prisons. The evaluation of the quality of these services is probably the most straightforward; although, as was mentioned earlier, there may be some questions about them as well. The other types of deprivations mentioned above are harder to analyze.

The deprivation of autonomy is described by Sykes (1978) as related to the institutional control of inmates. There are large numbers of rules and regulations in correctional institutions that are designed to control the inmates' lives in great detail. Besides that, there are informal orders for staff to follow. Often these rules and orders do not make sense to the inmates (Hawkins, 1976); nevertheless, they are compelled to follow them. However, some of the inmates may welcome this feature of the total institution because they prefer not to make decisions on their own; this is the well-known phenomenon of "institutionalization."[4] Many of them feel that it is intolerable that every minute's activity is controlled and that they are told constantly what they should and should not do. They also feel relegated to the status of young children because of the triviality of much of the rules and believe that most regulations and orders do not serve any real purpose, except of harassment and humiliation of the inmates and the reinforcement of their dependence (Sykes, 1978). This pervasive dependency, intentional or not, is one of the major characteristics of total institutions and an indicator of the quality of life in prisons. Public and private correctional facilities may be compared on the factor of autonomy by measuring inmate and staff attitudes toward organizational rules, regulations, and their enforcement. Obviously, the comparisons should be made between institutions at the same level of security.

Another deprivation bears similarity to the order concept forwarded by DiIulio (1987). One of the major pains mentioned by Sykes is the forced association of inmates with other inmates. They have to live with other prisoners with whom they do not choose to live. Sykes (1958) points to a paradoxical situation in maximum-security prisons:

However strange it may appear that society has chosen to reduce
criminality of the offender by forcing him to associate with more than a
thousand other criminals for years on end, there is one meaning of this
involuntary union which is obvious—the individual prisoner is thrown
into prolonged intimacy with other men who in many cases have a long
history of violent, aggressive behavior. It is a situation which can be
anxiety-provoking even for the hardened recidivist. (pp. 76-77)

To underscore this situation Sykes (1958) quotes one of the inmates
in a maximum-security prison: "The worst thing about prison is you
have to live with other prisoners" (p. 77). Many inmates live in
constant fear. It is one of the ironic aspects of the correctional scene
that although inmates are locked up in prisons mainly because
society needs to protect its members from preying criminals, the
criminals themselves are not well protected in the prison. As seen,
there is widespread violence among prisoners in many prisons and
often the authorities are not able to control it. The victimization of
unseasoned, weaker, and lonely prisoners is a familiar phenomenon
(e.g., Bartollas, Miller, & Dinitz, 1976; Bowker, 1988; Lockwood,
1980).

The dangerousness of many American prisons is described vividly
in the following: "They are dangerous because the strong prey upon
the weak, partly out of habit, partly out of boredom, and largely to
establish some sense of power and importance, two qualities stripped
from them by their incarceration" (Geis, 1987, p. 77).

The violence and the victimization among prisoners are shielded
from the public by security policies that block easy communication
with the outside world, by the lack of public interest in this issue,
and by the prisoners' normative system that favors hiding criminal
acts committed by other prisoners from the authorities as well as from
the public (Bowker, 1988). Bowker differentiates among four types of
prison victimization: physical, psychological, economic, and social.

1. Physical victimization is the one most often dealt with in the
professional literature. Prison violence has several functions (Fleisher,
1989). Prisoners often attack other inmates to move up in the pecking
order of prison society because violent offenders tend to have a higher
status in the institution than nonviolent offenders do. Another reason
for attacks by prisoners against others is their need to reinforce their

own self-esteem and the feeling that they are still competent human beings in an environment that takes away their independence and autonomy through regimentation and overregulation. Also, violent attacks can serve as a defense mechanism against attacks from others. Inmates with a fighting reputation have a better chance of not being targeted by others than do inmates who appear fearful and defenseless. Violence also may release inner tensions built up during confinement. Physical violence or the threat of it can bring to the aggressive inmate items that are valuable in the prison—candies, cigarettes, drugs, and even sex—from others who are afraid of physical violence. Violent sex attacks in male prisons are usually launched not so much for satisfying sexual needs but primarily to establish dominance over others. These attacks are increasingly launched by black inmates against whites often as a racial act to demonstrate their superiority in the prison setting (see, e.g., Carroll, 1974).

2. Psychological victimization is pervasive in prisons. Much of it involves verbal manipulations to trick other inmates into providing sex, material goods, and other commodities without getting into a physical fight. Inmates also may be manipulated by changing their cells or dormitories to cause them to be socially more isolated. Prisoners who do not have a solid standing in the prison's social structure may be victimized by having rumors circulated about them that they are snitches, child molesters, or "fags," which may further erode their status among other prisoners. Rumors may be spread about unfaithfulness of one's wife or girlfriend, which tends to have a strong psychological effect on prisoners (Bowker, 1988).

3. Economic victimization can take different forms, such as loan sharking, fraudulent gambling, and theft. The most vulnerable inmates for this kind of victimization are the first-timers who lack prison experience.

4. Finally, social victimization occurs when prisoners are victimized by other inmates because they are members of an identifiable social category, for example, an ethnic or racial group, gays, and so on.

All these forms of victimization have become more widespread since the late 1960s with the emergence of prison gangs in several states. These gangs were formed on the basis of neighborhoods, race, and/or ethnicity and began to fight over the control of prisons and prisoners, especially in maximum-security institutions. Although a large part of the violence is a result of conflicts among gangs, they have terrorized many of the unaffiliated inmates as well, often coercing them to join the gangs to gain protection from other violent inmates. The appearance of gangs in a correctional institution almost invariably raises the level of violence. The members' violent backgrounds and the nature of gangs' activities such as drug trafficking, extortion, prostitution, racketeering, gambling, and even contract murders account for much of the increased level of violence (Davidson, 1974; Fong, 1990; Irwin, 1980; Jacobs, 1977). A study focusing on prison gangs found that they accounted for 50% or more of the major problems in prisons (Camp & Camp, 1985). Gangs were also making the officials' job to maintain discipline and order in the institution more difficult (Irwin, 1980; Jacobs, 1977). The presence of violent prison gangs is pervasive in many institutions and makes a major impact on the quality of life. Although there are no accounts as yet on gang activities in privately operated prisons mainly because private prisons tend to deal with lower security inmates, it is feasible that when high security level institutions are privatized, this problem will have to be faced in these facilities as well.

The reduction of the pains of punishment from the vantage point of the inmates may be considered as a major issue of quality of life. Obviously, it is important from the management's perspective as well because, as was suggested by earlier researchers (Clemmer, 1958; Sykes, 1958; Sykes & Messinger, 1960), the reactions of inmates to these deprivations can make life much harder for both the management and staff.

Studies of Service Quality in Private Prisons. There were a few attempts to study the quality of services in privatized institutions. As stated earlier, Silverdale Detention Center in Tennessee is the most researched correctional facility that was privatized and managed by CCA. An attempt to explore the quality of services in this institution was conducted by interviewing 20 inmates (out of 350), concerning various prison services and other aspects of institutional life (Brakel, 1988). This small-scale research found positive attitudes toward the quality of services in Silverdale, especially in the areas of "(a) the physical plant, (b) classification, (c) staff treatment of inmates, (d) the disciplinary system, and (e) medical services" (Brakel, 1988, p. 179).

Brakel (1988) is cautious not to make a wide-ranging generalization based on his pilot study:

> One positive experience . . . does not the case for privatization make. CCA is the leading, best-endowed company in the field. It is operating in a context of heightened public scrutiny, at a time when it hopes to convince the public—corrections bureaucrats, other law- and policymakers and executors, academics, etc.—of its capacity to do the job and at the same time to capture a sizeable share of the market. This creates the specter of halo-effect performance, an out-of-the-ordinary effort on the part of the entrepreneur to put his best foot forward. (p. 244)

This may be the reason that this particular facility became the object of research so many times. In fact, a delegation from the British Prison Officer's Association (POA) that visited Silverdale described it in their report as a showplace institution (Porter, 1990). Sources in the British press note that the first few U.S. private facilities were "show-piece institutions" (Sampson, 1992, p. 23).

Other studies found the quality of services in privatized correctional facilities generally positive. One of them focused on the programs available for the inmates. In comparing three pairs of public and private institutions, it was concluded that "private prisons provided more services at lower cost than their public counterparts" (Sellers, 1989, p. 241) and that "private facilities emphasized cost-savings without a loss in service quantity or quality" (p. 254). This research, however, was conducted on relatively small institutions; one comparison was made on institutions for juveniles, another included Silverdale, the same CCA facility that Brakel (1988) and Logan and McGriff (1987) studied before. The few available studies seem to agree that the quality of services for inmates in private institutions is either at the same level or is better than in public correctional facilities. Obviously, it will have to be seen whether this trend also will continue when larger and higher security prisons will be privatized. It is also an open question whether the above results were affected by the earlier-mentioned halo effect; in other words, the few private prisons studied, some of them several times (e.g., Silverdale), may operate at their peak efficiency because the private corporations know that they are being observed as test cases for further privatization. They are in a sense the pioneer institutions of the prison privatization movement.

On the other hand, there is room for continuous scrutiny of all penal institutions. In the case of profit-making companies the main concern is that their profit motive should not override all other considerations in the operation of a facility. There is always the possibility that the combination of the pains of imprisonment with the pursuance of profit may exacerbate an already volatile situation. Simply, every time when a private corporation can cut corners in services, whether or not it results in the decline of quality, it provides an opportunity to increase corporate profits. Although government-operated prisons are riddled with major problems of overcrowding, various kinds of abusive practices, violence, lack of effective programs, neglect, waste, and often ineptitude, at least they are not exposed to the potential problem of corporate or personal greed that privately operated prisons are.

Quality of Services—The Community at Large

A second aspect of quality of services concerns the quality of services provided by the prison to the community at large. Correctional institutions were established to a large degree to benefit society. Following the cui bono perspective to organizational analysis, prisons can be seen as commonwealth organizations that benefit the community at large by contributing to public safety (Blau & Scott, 1962). Since the decline of the idea of rehabilitation as the major goal of corrections, the emphasis of social control has shifted from the rehabilitation of the individual to the protection of the community. During the 1980s and early 1990s the major function of punishment became incapacitation, especially in the United States and England. This principle rests on the commonsense idea that "all else being equal, taking criminals off the street will at least keep them from committing more street crimes for as long as they stay behind bars" (Currie, 1985, p. 81). As seen, this penal policy has resulted in an unprecedented increase in prison population, overcrowding, and staggering correctional expenses. It has also prompted support for prison privatization in these countries.

Punishment Policies

A policy option derived from the idea of incapacitation that com-
manded widespread interest is "selective incapacitation." This sanc-
tioning alternative suggests that if there will be refined methods to
successfully identify a relatively small group of hard-core or habitual
offenders and incarcerate them for longer periods while other prisoners will serve less time, serious crime can be significantly reduced
without increasing the potential harm to society. This idea was
behind a research project by the RAND Corporation that suggested
that with proper identification of career criminals, the volume of
robbery could be reduced by 15% and at the same time prison
populations would decline by 5% (Greenwood & Abrahamse, 1982).
A well-known study suggested that the crime rate in the state of New
York could be reduced by two thirds if every offender convicted for
a serious crime would be incarcerated for 3 years (Shinnar & Shinnar,
1975). There are many methodological problems with conducting
these types of estimates. Visher (1987) provides a detailed review of
these problems. Here the focus is on the theoretical and ethical
aspects of this policy.

This penal policy seems very attractive, but it raises some basic
questions and criticisms. One of them points to the fact that it is based
on the prediction of future criminal behavior, which is in contrast
with the American concept of justice that one should be punished
only for criminal acts that he or she has committed (von Hirsch,
1985). On a more practical level, there are serious doubts about our
ability to predict future human behavior accurately (e.g., Monahan,
1981; Morris, 1974). It is a fundamental question, then, of what
amount of predictive error is acceptable, because according to this
practice, some people will be treated more harshly than their law-
breaking behavior would warrant because of a faulty prediction
("false positive"). Also, according to all probabilities, there will be
"false negatives," that is, people who are not considered to be a danger
for society will be handled more leniently than they otherwise would
be, but nevertheless they will commit serious crimes after their
release. The false positives reflect an overprediction that is often
ignored because the inmates seldom have the power to object to it
(von Hirsch, 1985). On the operational level some questions have to

be answered regarding selective incapacitation, for example, (a) how to arrive at a reliable estimation of the amount of crime reduction that can be achieved as an outcome of this sentencing policy; (b) how to enhance, refine, and increase predictive ability to identify chronic offenders;[5] and (c) how to handle the political task of convincing the community that it is all right to release early, or not to lock up at all, low-risk offenders to "reserve" the existing prison capacity for high-risk criminals.

The issue of justice is problematic. Should one be given a more severe sentence than another offender having the same criminal record and committing the same crime, just because he or she is predicted to be more dangerous? For instance, in Greenwood and Abrahamse's (1982) study, employment history was a predictor of future criminal activity. Thus the question arises whether one should be penalized for unemployment (Walker, 1989).

If selective incapacitation would be accepted as a major punishment option, it would have ramifications for private prisons. First, one of the factors used for predicting further dangerousness is whether the individual was incarcerated more than 50% of the preceding 2 years. As mentioned, there are concerns that private prisons will try to hold inmates in prison as long as they can to keep the institution filled to maximum capacity. Therefore in some cases this policy may influence future sentencing because one may be kept longer in a private than in a public prison. There are some indications that juveniles in private institutions spend more time than in public institutions (e.g., Krisberg, DeComo, & Herrera, 1992). Second, privately operated correctional institutions are generally geared toward the less serious offenders (soft-end corrections), whereas hard-end maximum-security prisons are run by government agencies (Erickson et al., 1987). Selective incapacitation would compel private prisons to deal with a growing number of high-risk, hard-core offenders to remain in business. This possibility would not be welcomed by many private correctional corporations. It is a question, then, how well a privately operated prison would provide an effective service to the community by keeping hard-core criminals away from society. Some historical precedents of private prisons' handling of dangerous offenders are not very encouraging (e.g., McAfee & Shichor, 1990; McKanna, 1987). The security questions of how well a private for-profit facility will be able to prevent hard-core offenders from escaping and to prevent large-scale prison riots are paramount concerns for the public.

Another issue related to the service to the community, although not as visibly as incapacitation, is the matter of rehabilitation. Although the emphasis on rehabilitation has declined sharply since the early 1970s, the importance of this issue cannot be discarded completely. An obvious fact is that the overwhelming majority of inmates are going to be released into the community after their incarceration, most of them sooner than later. The public's quest for some kind of rehabilitation efforts to change the behavior of offenders still exists even with the decline of official interest in this penological goal. Several studies found that the general public neither abandoned the idea that rehabilitation should be a major function of corrections nor lost belief completely in the possibility to reform offenders (Cullen, Cullen, & Wozniak, 1988; Cullen & Gilbert, 1982; Stinchcombe et al., 1980) and does not oppose rehabilitation-oriented correctional programs (e.g., Duffee & Ritti, 1977). In fact, public opinion is more favorable toward rehabilitation and less favorable toward incapacitation than policymakers believe (Gottfredson & Taylor, 1987). It seems that there are compelling reasons for the survival and revival of rehabilitation as a major penal principle and correctional practice in American society (Shichor, 1992b).

Logically, private correctional companies do not have an intrinsic interest in rehabilitation. Because private prisons make their profits on their occupancy rate, that is, per diem per capita, there is no incentive for them to institute meaningful rehabilitation programs in prison. At the extreme, one even can argue that the interest of these companies would be not to have successful rehabilitation programs at all because participation in these programs usually adds good time for prisoners and participation in them figures in parole considerations. Because, as seen, private administration has a vested interest in keeping the institution fully occupied, earlier release may result in vacancies that would financially hurt the company. Although this problem, with the rapid growth of prison population of the 1980s and early 1990s, was not realistic, if there is a leveling off in prison commitments that may change the situation.

One suggestion in this vein is to incorporate the rehabilitation factor into the private contract that rehabilitation will become a meaningful purpose for the private corporation; in other words, it should be tied to the profit motive. According to this suggestion the quality of services, in terms of rehabilitation, should be linked to the amount of profits that the company can make (Cullen, 1986). Obviously, it would have to be decided how effectiveness will be measured and determined. A clear specification of the appropriate criteria for success will be needed. For example, it should be determined how much the completion of a rehabilitation program and how much other indicators such as an available job on the outside—as a consequence of the completion of rehabilitation programs—should be considered in release or parole decisions. Whatever the suggestions are in this respect, it should be recognized that the evaluation of quality of service in the private as well as in the public sector is problematic and often elusive. It is even more so regarding the quality of correctional services as they are perceived by the community at large.

If this idea is accepted, the determination of success in rehabilitation also should be connected to the characteristics of each one of the correctional institutions operated by private corporations; it will have to be different in minimum- than in maximum-security facilities. One of the indicators could be the extent, nature, and frequency of recidivism. This point also brings up the often mentioned criticism leveled against the private correctional sector, that of "skimming" or "creaming," meaning that private firms try to handle the least troublesome offenders. The claim is that with less troublesome offenders to begin with, it is easier to produce positive results investing less efforts than with hard-core, violent criminals who are usually placed in maximum-security facilities. In addition, special kinds of offenders such as drug abusers and mentally disturbed offenders can be offered special treatment programs, which are more profitable for the private contractor than ordinary incarceration.

In the analysis of quality of services to the community at large, the various functions of correctional institutions should be considered. Correctional services have to be examined in the framework of the aims of punishment, namely, retribution, deterrence, incapacitation, and rehabilitation. As seen, since the early 1970s the aim of rehabilitation was largely abandoned. Currently, retribution, deterrence, and especially incapacitation are in the forefront of correctional interest.

Imprisonment by itself is a form of punishment. To what degree its retributive effect can be measured and used as an indicator of the quality of service rendered to the public remains to be developed. The basic social function is to spread the feeling that justice is being served. It is hard to determine whether a prisoner receives the right amount of punishment in the prison or what he or she deserves. The contention here is that justice is better served and legitimated if it is administered by the government than if it is delegated to a private profit-making company because, at least theoretically, if a private entity makes profit, it can be perceived that there was an excess over the exact cost or value of the harm caused by the offender.

Regarding deterrence, we are in a more favorable position to try to measure the impact of incarceration, particularly the effects of special deterrence. Although officially known recidivism is not very reliable, by examining the percentage of returning offenders to prisons a rough estimate of special deterrence can be inferred. Currently, between 60% to 70% of the inmates are serving time in prison for the second, third, fourth, or more times. According to these figures, the specific deterrent effect of imprisonment is questionable. One way that private enterprise could provide and improve the quality of service in this respect is by reducing recidivism among their released offenders vis-à-vis convicts who served their time in comparable public prisons. As one measure of comparison, convicts released from government-operated prisons and privately managed prisons could be followed up and their subsequent official records could be used as a surrogate indicator of special deterrence or the lack of it. Obviously, this kind of comparison will require that released offenders with similar criminal records and personal and social backgrounds will be followed up.

Incapacitation, as seen, became the prominent aim of punishment during the 1980s and early 1990s. The pursuit of this policy reflects a change in correctional ideology in which the interest from the individual offender—the focus of rehabilitation—has switched to the maintenance of public safety. According to this emphasis the major service to the community that a prison can provide is the efficient protection of society from offenders. As a very general and rough approach, incapacitation effects can be measured by the examination of official crime rates and their relation to incarceration rates. However, the distinction between private and public prison effects could be methodologically problematic.

Also, the number of actual escapes and escape attempts can serve as indicators of service quality to the community. This kind of comparisons probably will be easier to make in the future if and when more privately managed high-security correctional facilities are in operation. One of the major concerns in this vein is that privatization proponents will try to reduce the number of correctional officers to make more profits. It is an open question whether the more sophisticated technical surveillance that private companies want to employ will provide a better or at least equal quality of service in this respect as do correctional officers. This is a focal issue because escapes and inmate riots are the most visible aspects of incarceration in the public's eyes, and they can attract significant attention to the prisons and may become the major indicators of their performance.

Conclusion

A quality-of-service-related discussion was presented by Gentry (1986), who argued that "serious problems may arise in attempting to ensure the fidelity of entrepreneurial jailers to societal preferences." According to his opinion it will be very hard to make sure that "conditions in private prisons will not be worse than those prevailing in public facilities, but to harness existing private motivations to generate improvement in prison quality" (p. 354).

It is important to point out that the opposition against private prisons is not grounded in a high appreciation toward state prisons. The correctional system is a heavy fiscal burden on society, it is not effective economically, it often fails on humanitarian grounds, it is riddled with violence, and it fails to demonstrate any significant level of rehabilitation. Although there have been many attempts to improve prison conditions, they have resulted only in marginal improvements. Court orders and the threat of litigation are not enough to change the situation. One of the problems is the apparent lack of serious efforts by correctional administrators to effect change: "Administrators have little incentive to close the gap between court decrees and actual prison conditions, and no incentive at all to go beyond the narrowest reading of orders" (Gentry, 1986, p. 354). In spite of all the problems plaguing public prisons, it does not necessarily mean that privatization would substantially improve this situation. There are several considerations that cast doubt on whether private management of prisons would upgrade the quality of services for the inmates and/or for the community.

One of the problems in this regard centers around the issue of the "divergence of duty and interest" (Gentry, 1986, p. 355). As seen, advocates of prison privatization argue that private prisons will be cheaper and will run more efficiently, that is, provide better quality of service, than state or federal prisons. However, Bentham, who envisioned the panopticon under private management (cited in Mack, 1969) and wanted to be a private contractor himself, has pointed out the importance of having prison management whose duty and interest are united. In private prisons this unity does not necessarily exist. The major reason for this possible divergence between duty and interest can be traced to two characteristics of prison operation: "Its inaccessibility to the public and its typical arrangement in monopolistic form, will, in combination with the profit motive, cause the firm's interest to diverge from its duty to implement societal preferences" (Gentry, 1986, p. 356).

This implies, as stated before, that the profit motive that can lead to financial savings also may cause the private firm to sacrifice prison conditions in ways that may not happen under public management.

The issue of hidden delivery is also important. There is a strong possibility of emerging problems when the purchaser of a good is "unable to observe its consumption" (Gentry, 1986, p. 356). In such cases, the one who pays for the goods or services cannot check the quantity and evaluate the quality of the delivered product. The supplier, therefore, has the opportunity to shortchange the recipient without enduring negative consequences. Potentially, in the case of public prisons, some administrators can take advantage of the "hidden delivery" factor that opens the door for making extra money for themselves; this opportunity may lead to corruption. However, in a prison-for-profit, the question is not only how to curb individual corruption but how to control the whole organizational atmosphere that is geared toward profit making rather than toward public service. It is likely that there will be more constraints over administrators to make personal gains in private prisons than in public institutions because of the private management's concern with profit (thus individual corruption will be curbed), but there will also be more attempts for cutting corners because the company benefits directly from "every dime not spent" (Gentry, 1986, p. 351). Therefore there is a much stronger incentive for private companies to save costs, not for the public's benefit, but for their own profit. Many of these practices are such that it is hard to pin them down, especially if they are done in small increments that make them hardly visible and noticeable. Monitoring operations, as was seen before, can be complex and expensive and not completely comprehensive. Usually, monitoring expenditures will have a budget limit unrelated to the quality of services rendered by the private contractor (Gentry, 1986). Wecht (1987) summarizes these problems in the following:

> Process rights and service delivery are expensive, and a cost-conscious manager in the employ of a for-profit firm will have an interest in limiting both. The courts' unwillingness to impose procedural checks on prison officials' decisions regarding discipline, parole, good time, inmate transfer, and eligibility for rehabilitative programs may lead to abuses by private contractors seeking to increase profits and cut costs by lengthening sentences, lumping offenders in distant, multistate facilities, and limiting services provided to inmates. Reductions in the quality of health care, educational and vocational opportunities and food services are more probable immediate responses, because they impinge less directly on liberty interests and thus are less likely to give rise to litigation. Both sorts of abuse can be expected, however, especially after the initial "honeymoon" period—in which a private contractor will seek to demonstrate its intention to meet, and perhaps even surpass its contractual standards—has passed. (p. 830)

Notes

1. More recently, Logan (1991) evaluated the quality of prisons according to their adherence to the principle of retribution. He proposed that the punishment should be proportionate to the seriousness of the crime and the evaluation should focus on the prison's main mandate, that is, confinement model, which centers around processes and adherence to standards (e.g., prisoners' rights) rather than abstract goals such as rehabilitation and deterrence. Logan (1991) used eight dimensions for the evaluation of the quality of prisons: security, safety, order, care, activity, justice, conditions, and

management. The dimensions seem to overlap to a degree with the quality indicators suggested by DiIulio (1987): order, amenity, and service, which are applied in the analysis conducted in this chapter.

2. Some of the spontaneous prison riots are triggered by food that is found not to be satisfactory by some inmates. Sometimes disturbances occur because certain prisoner groups claim that there is not enough ethnic food served.

3. Many prison administrators and staff consider weight lifting and other sports equipment to be very important in their institution because they provide an outlet for the physical energy of prisoners who according to their average age are in the peak of their physical power and development. On the other hand, there are politicians who want to outlaw weight lifting in prison in order not to build up the physical power of inmates because it may make them more violent after release.

4. *Institutionalization* refers to the dependence of an individual on an institution, not only physically but also psychologically, for making decisions for them. In many organizational settings, particularly in total institutions, the individual is being told what to do, and the daily timetable is tight; therefore personal decision making is minimized.

5. Blumstein (1983) points to the need for continued research in the development of tests, evaluation, and implementation programs to improve our predictive capacity. He also tempers expectations by stating that the implementation of this policy "will make marginal rather than profound changes in the crime-control effectiveness of the criminal justice system" (p. 100).

8

Management and Personnel Issues

The management and staff have a major impact on the operation of a correctional facility, including the legal, economic, and quality of service aspects.

Correctional Personnel

Previous discussions concerned the size and quality of personnel and their relationship to the cost-effectiveness and quality of prisons. The correctional enterprise is a labor-intensive "industry." Therefore the staff-inmate ratio and the training and preparation of the staff have an important role in determining the cost of institutionalization and the quality of life in prison.

The major function of the staff in influencing the quality of life in prisons is in the area of maintaining order in the facility. The concept of order maintenance is not limited to its narrow meaning of physical control, but has a wider implication embracing the more complex aspects of personal relationship between correctional officers and inmates.

It is increasingly recognized, however, that the guards' tasks are more complex than previously understood and that they often reach well

189

beyond the limits of formal assignments. It is also more apparent that the
motivations and perceptions of the individual officer play an important
part in determining "what he (or she) does," extending officer activities
into areas formally outside his (or her) domain. This aspect of the
correctional officer's duties has been labeled "providing human
services." (Lombardo, 1988, p. 287)

If this description of the role of correctional officers is generally
correct and accepted, then the staff-inmate ratio should be considered
to be an important factor in the maintenance of order in correctional
institutions. Besides the major concern of physical security, there are
also social and psychological factors of alleviation or amplification
of violence, tension, and stress that are pervasive in prisons. Similarly, the professional training and the general personality characteristics of the staff are considered to be important in providing a
better atmosphere in the facility. These factors contribute not only to
the maintenance of order in the institution but also to the quality of
services. Well-trained, better educated, psychologically screened personnel are likely to provide more meaningful services.

Private corporations claim that they can deliver the same or better
correctional services at a lower cost than governmental agencies do.
Because labor is the major expense in corrections, lower cost implies
that private firms will be able to reduce their labor cost in one or more
of the following ways: (a) cutting salaries or the pay scale of employees (Johnson & Ross, 1990; Patrick, 1986); (b) providing less or no
fringe benefits and pension funds (Johnson & Ross, 1990; Patrick,
1986); (c) economizing on the screening procedures of employees; (d)
hiring fewer employees; (e) hiring less qualified employees; (f) providing less training; or (g) a combination of any of the above (Shichor,
1993).

Many private and public prison guards are recruited from the
unskilled labor force; however, in private facilities a large number of
them work only on a part-time basis (Weiss, 1989). In some private
prisons quite a few retired state correctional officers and retired
military personnel are working to supplement their public pensions
(Sechrest & Shichor, 1993a). Another likely pool of private correctional employees is the personnel of private security companies.
Comparing this possible source of employees with public prison

guards, Donahue (1988) found that public employees were more likely to be high school graduates, full-time workers, and in the prime working age than the pool of private security employees. There is also the question of quality of the workforce. Often, individuals who wanted to be law enforcement agents but for various reasons were not hired by police or sheriff's departments become private security officers. Generally, private security companies have a higher turnover rate than public agencies do, mainly because they pay less and provide very few fringe benefits in comparison with public agencies. Using information from the 1970s, Lipson (1975) concluded that private security firms did not have minimum standards, neither for physical or mental fitness nor for educational and literacy levels. Also, the job training of the officers was limited. Similar trends in the British private security industry, including low standards, little training, and high turnover of employees, were found. Private security companies also were trying to cut corners in their contracts to make profits (South, 1988). A similar situation was found in a privately operated work furlough facility in California. The private company that operated that facility and several other community corrections and INS detention facilities required no formal training from its line employees and paid minimum starting wages to new correctional workers (Shichor & Sechrest, 1992). Some private companies leave several positions vacant to save money on salaries (see Lampkin, 1991). Obviously, it is not necessarily the case with every private contractor, but there is a pattern of lower pay, less benefits, and lower staffing formulas (whenever the contract allows it) in comparison to public prisons.

Correctional Management and Personnel Salaries, Training, and Quality of Services

Critics of privatization are concerned that paying lower salaries to correctional employees, whose income is not very lucrative to begin with, may result in the reduction of the quality of lower echelon employees in private prisons. As noted, in the 1985 Senate subcommittee meeting that dealt with prison privatization, the representative of

the Sheriffs' Association (an interested party against prison privatization) voiced the opinion that any cost cutting by the private sector
will be done to increase the profits of private contractors (U.S. Senate,
1985). He was convinced that the first step to control cost will aim to
cut the wages of correctional personnel because that is the largest
item in the expense category. At the time of the hearings, in May 1985,
the average salary of a correctional officer in the United States was
$10,780. This was on the low end of the average pay scale of American
workers. The question raised was: How can reliable and well-trained
correctional officers with an average high school educational level be
hired by a private company for an even lower salary? How many
well-qualified people will be ready to apply for a correctional position
for less money and/or for considerably lower fringe benefits (i.e.,
health insurance, job security, pension plan, and paid vacation)?
Advocates of privatization single out these fringe benefits, particularly public employees' pensions, as a major expense of corrections
(Logan, 1990).

Another major source for potential cost cutting may be the reduction of the level of training required for correctional officers. Reports
from several private companies, especially from CCA, the largest,
show that staff in private corporations receive at least the same
amount of training as staff in most government facilities do, and in
some cases even more (Logan, 1990). However, some investigators
disagree; for example, Bendick (1989) claims that CCA employees
receive only 160 hours of training, whereas federal jail employees
receive 240 hours. It is suggested that contracts with private companies should require that correctional officers employed by a private
company have at least the same amount of training as their counterparts in public facilities receive. In fact, this requirement can be
standardized by adopting the ACA standards. However, the training
requirements are not always spelled out clearly in the contract. For
instance, the California Department of Corrections' (1987) contract
for the management of "return to custody"[1] facilities for parole violators
in Mesa Verde included the following clause:

> The contractor, in concert with CDC, will develop and implement a
> training program for staff which focuses on the knowledge and skills
> necessary for effective management of residents and supervision of

resident activities. Training will consist of a minimum of 40 hours per year per staff member. Areas such as Searches, Drug Detection, Discretionary Decision Making and CPR, etc., will be scheduled for all staff. Coordination of training to be done with Regional Reentry Staff.

The most interesting feature of this clause is that the sentence requiring 40 hours of training per year per staff member was stroked out by pencil. Whether this was a unique measure just for this particular contract or reflected a general policy change has to be clarified. Nevertheless, this kind of lack of specification can open the door to reduced training requirements for staff in private institutions. If the private company tries to reduce staff training to increase its profits, it could become a public relations problem not only for the company but also for the correctional authorities.

In an attempt to provide a different perspective on employee training, the president of CCA, D. R. Crants (1991), claims that the private sector can be more efficient in training expenses; because state laws require between 160 to 320 hours of paid training before correctional officers start supervising inmates, the high turnover rate of these employees (40%-50%) causes large losses. He blames "the public sector low quality training" as being partly responsible for the high turnover rates. On the other hand, according to Crants (1991), CCA officers undergo rigorous testing when hired and extended on-the-job training, which help to weed out employees who would quit their job fast; thus, in this way, CCA is able to maintain a lower turnover rate. Crants (1991) supplies neither the number of hours required for formal training, if any, nor any comparative figures of turnover rates between public and private prison personnel.

Private corporations deny that their cost cutting would focus on lower employee salaries or shortened training periods for correctional officers. On the contrary, they claim that higher quality, better trained, and better paid officers are essential for the provision of higher quality services. One possibility is to provide the same or higher level of service that is being given by government agencies, with substantially fewer officers in private facilities. Thus a major source of cost cutting would stem from the fact that fewer staff members will be on the payroll. One way to accomplish this is to increase mechanized surveillance technology as a substitute for correctional officers. Another is to make staffing more flexible, for example, to have fewer officers during shifts when inmates are locked up. The introduction of staffing changes, however, may run into problems because many of the staffing formulas are considered to be ironclad rules by departments of corrections.

Advocates of privatization claim that effective personnel management can cut operational costs without cutting salaries. "Adequate and appropriate staffing, better working conditions, and more efficient procedures improve productivity and morale, decrease absenteeism and turnover and reduce expensive reliance on overtime" (Logan, 1990, p. 81).

Providing that private corporations would be able to institute more economically efficient staffing policies, the question of how these would affect correctional staff has to be taken into consideration, especially in higher security level institutions.

Critics of privatization present a different picture than the CCA executives and other proponents of private institutions do. Alan M. Schuman, Director of the Social Service Division in the Superior Court of the District of Columbia, states that

> privately financed institutions can cut costs by paying lower salaries and can reduce costs even further by providing no or minimum pension and fringe benefit packages. However, lower salaries could attract less qualified staff who would require extensive high quality training, and this would offset some of the cost savings. My personal observation has been that privately funded agencies offer lower salaries and have very high staff turnover rates. In fact, many of the best qualified private sector staff eventually apply for public sector probation positions that offer more job security and higher salaries. The high turnover rate must impact the quality of services that are provided; a factor that should be considered in any cost analysis formula. (1989, p. 32)

Problems of Staff Turnover

The high turnover rate also may be a result of the pressures of the everyday work with a generally hostile and manipulative "clientele" and monotonous routines that usually lead to a high staff burnout rate. Beyond that, in private institutions high turnover is also likely to be influenced by lower salary and benefits. This would especially be the case with a large number of correctional officers who choose to work for the correctional system because of job security and "decent" benefits. Even though the salaries in public institutions have been raised during the past 10 to 15 years, they are still considered to be low. It is still difficult to recruit well-qualified personnel who would consider corrections as a career. One proponent of privatization states that "under government personnel practices, there are few incentives for any but the least able people to make a career of correctional work" (Greenwood, 1981, p. 7). The question is how private companies, paying less money, with more limited fringe benefits, will be able to attract a better and stable workforce. Many guards are pushed into their job by circumstances such as unemployment and injury in a previous job.[2] For most custodial officers, their position is a dead-end job. There is only a limited opportunity to be promoted to a higher rank in the custodial staff and only a very few can move into administrative positions.

Research studies also indicate that first-line work with inmates, especially in high-security prisons, is psychologically very demanding. Correctional officers work in a coercive organization and constantly exercise coercive power (Hepburn, 1989). Their fundamental task is primarily to enforce institutional rules and custody. They work in an environment fraught with tension and uncertainty. To a degree, they are isolated from their surroundings (Crouch, 1986). It is often said that not only are the inmates incarcerated but the guards are as well (Lombardo, 1981). They also feel that the public does not appreciate them and their work and that many people even despise them (Jacobs & Zimmer, 1983). Line officers' morale is usually low due to a large degree of fear and uncertainty that emanates from the "structured conflict" relationship between guards and inmates (Jacobs & Kraft, 1983). This relationship reflects the reality that prisoners are in prison against their will and do not have an interest in the goals of the institution or the welfare of the guards. Inmates challenge a guard's authority constantly; thus correctional officers have to deal effectively with a hostile clientele without becoming overly abusive. Several researchers mention the problem of loss of guards' power in recent years (e.g., Crouch, 1986; Irwin, 1980), partially because of increased public criticism by activist groups, media reporting, and court intervention. Because of court interventions, reduced support is given to guards by the prison administration. Many are frustrated by their perception that there is an increased emphasis on prisoners' rights in the criminal justice system, which limits their authority over the inmates. They express a general feeling of powerlessness (Fox, 1982; Lombardo, 1981) and feel pressure from the administration and from inmates as well. Another source of uncertainty is danger. Most prisons have a great number of violent inmates who, under the conditions of incarceration and the constant interaction with other violent offenders, usually create a violent organizational climate. Correctional officers feel that they may be attacked at any time, and inside the prison they are unarmed and vastly outnumbered. In fact, actual assaults on guards is on the rise (Crouch, 1986; Hepburn, 1989). Correctional officers' uncertainty also is increased by their role ambiguity (Cressey, 1965; R. Johnson, 1987). Guards are often expected to fulfill treatment and custodial roles simultaneously. Generally, they are

> expected to exercise professional judgment and flexibility in performing their job, yet they are subject to disciplinary actions if they violate, or permit the prisoners to violate the many official rules and procedures of the prison. (Hepburn, 1989, p. 193)

Another major issue in this vein is related to the dependency that guards have in their relations to inmates. To be able to do their job satisfactorily, they need a certain degree of cooperation from the prisoners because if there is a constant conflict in the blocks or cottages in which they work, they will be judged by their superiors as unable to manage inmates and will be evaluated accordingly. Thus their authority is compromised. In extreme situations they may be even fired from their jobs. The prisoners understand the situation well and often take advantage of it.

Sykes (1958) goes so far as claiming that inmates run many prisons because of the "corruption of authority" (p. 58). According to his research the guards

> are under strong pressure to compromise with their captives, for it is a paradox that they can insure their dominance only by allowing it to be

corrupted. Only by tolerating violations of "minor" rules and regulations can the guard secure compliance to the "major" areas of the custodial regime.[3] (Sykes, 1958, p. 58)

The low social status of the job coupled with the relatively low salary limits social participation in the community. This situation is reinforced by the work schedule; that is, working in various shifts often disrupts family and social life. Also, the use of force in controlling inmates can become a routine behavior among correctional officers (e.g., Crouch, 1986), and this pattern may spill over to their family life as well (i.e., problems of domestic violence). These working conditions together with the almost permanent feeling of danger from inmates who may attack or take hostage officers who do not carry weapons in the prison (Jacobs & Crotty, 1983) create a stressful occupational environment, may generate cynicism among the guards (Poole & Regoli, 1981), and result in job dissatisfaction and alienation among many officers (Toch & Klofas, 1982). All these factors contribute to a high turnover rate, about 28% nationwide, and to a high rate of absenteeism among custodial officers.

Unionization

Correctional officers in the public sector are organized in unions. The unionization came in part as a response to the above-described problems of the correctional officer's job and the prison conditions, but it was also a part of the general trend toward public employee unionization (Hawkins & Alpert, 1989). Although unionization has helped to secure for the correctional officers their due process rights vis-à-vis the prison administration, it also had some less welcome effects, such as featherbedding, increased bureaucratization, decreased administrative flexibility, and restriction of public access.[4] Many of these unions became strong political interest groups. For instance, in California, the California Correctional Peace Officers Association is one of the major contributors to state political campaigns.

Private prison companies and privatization proponents try to diffuse the concerns regarding cost savings achieved through wage cutting, reduction of fringe benefits, and paid leaves. Understandably, they object to staff unionization, whereas correctional employee unions oppose privatization for obvious reasons. Privatization advocates claim that prison employee opposition is rooted in the unions' fears that jobs are threatened, and even more significantly, they are afraid of losing their political power (Logan, 1990). Undoubtedly, that is an important argument. Some unions became powerful and were successful in negotiating work contracts that put financial and bureaucratic burdens on the system. The only major legal limitation that most of these unions have is that they do not have the right to strike. For the critics of privatization, objection to unions serves as proof of the intentions of private companies to do their cost cutting at the expense of their employees.

Dissatisfaction with low pay and difficult working conditions may lead to employee strikes in private prisons, if and when employees unionize, although private correctional corporations make every effort not to employ unionized workers and not to let their workforce join any unions. There also may be employee refusals to work with certain kinds of inmates (e.g., AIDS patients). It is pointed out that "being in the private sector, employees will have the legal right to organize a union and conduct slow downs with potential strikes as an end result" (Novey, 1985, p. 5). If this problem arises, government authorities may have to intervene by staffing the facility until the strike is over or the company is able to hire strikebreakers, who probably will be less qualified than the striking workers and will not have even the minimal training that the permanent correctional officers have. If the correctional personnel in private prisons will not be able to unionize, as is the case currently, employees will be laid off or fired early. The question could be raised, then, whether the government should work with companies that make their profits because their workers do not have civil service or union protection. Some critics refer to this policy as a form of union busting (see Geis, 1987). Avid supporters of privatization, on the other hand, go out of their way to attack public workers' unions by accusing them of involvement in various kinds of corruption (see Logan, 1990). Because the government has the ultimate liability for the fate of the prisoners, any problems emanating from labor disputes, such as violence or abuse of inmates by inexperienced personnel, still will be the government's responsibility.

To alleviate this situation, some private companies, like the CCA, provide a stock option plan for key employees on authorization by the board of directors, which may be beneficial in retaining employees mainly in the administrative branch, but this usually does not include the custodial personnel. There is also an employee stock ownership plan whereby each employee who completes 1,000 hours of service in a year is eligible for membership (Corrections Corporation of America, 1989). This program may offer some counterbalance against the low level of fringe benefits in the private institutions and also provides a basis for incentives for better performance in order to receive more contracts. However, it is questionable that this kind of program would provide immediate money helping correctional officers to "pay the bills."

Management

The study of correctional management is one of the relatively neglected areas of correctional research.[5] There are some who maintain that quality of life in prisons and jails depends to a large degree on the quality of management (e.g., Irwin, 1980; Jacobs, 1977; Street, Vinter, & Perrow, 1966). Thus the issue of management in private prisons is an area that has to be a major concern for policymakers and for everyone who has a genuine interest in corrections (DiIulio, 1988). It is suggested that the negligence of the study of prison administration may be due to the sociological approach dealing with this subject because in the past the study of correctional institutions was mainly the domain of sociologists. According to this claim the sociological approach viewed prison management as an

> attempt to manipulate inmate society. Inmates must be coaxed, not coerced. Paramilitary features of prison management should be kept to a minimum. The symbols and substance of formal controls—weapons and badges for officers, restrictions on inmate movement—should be reduced or abolished. (DiIulio, 1987, p. 19)

DiIulio (1991) also blames, besides the scholarly prejudice of sociologists, prison activists who have an ideological bias against prisons, correctional practitioners who blame prison conditions for correctional problems, and funding agencies that are not very interested in management problems for the neglect of prison management studies.

There are clear differences in the ways that various prisons are managed, especially as far as the enforcement of institutional rules are concerned. This is particularly important in maximum-security facilities where the most violent offenders are being kept, and generally the most serious violations occur. Tight control, although often considered to be antithetical to rehabilitation or even to humane conditions of incarceration, may enhance the general level of security in the prison, thus contributing to one aspect of better quality of life in the prison, namely, the maintenance of order.

Correctional Philosophy

The way a prison is run is influenced by the correctional philosophy held by its management. DiIulio distinguishes between three major management models based on three different correctional philosophies: the *control model*, the *responsibility model*, and the *consensual model*. The control model, which was prevalent in the Texas correctional system, emphasized inmate obedience, work, and education. It was organized along paramilitary lines and was characterized by

> strict enforcement of discipline and a daily routine in which the inmates had virtually no say. All inmates would wear regulation white uniforms. All would have short-cropped hair. All would shave and bathe regularly. All who were illiterate would, like it or not, go to school at least one day each week. All would work in the fields for their first six months. All would address the officers as "boss" or "sir," and so on. Prisoners had certain minimal rights, but beyond that everything was to be earned as a privilege that could be taken away by the authority without any extraordinary hearing process. (DiIulio, 1987, p. 175)

The authorities did not expect that this correctional regimen would result in rehabilitation directly. However, it was hoped that some inmates would get used to law-abiding behavior through the coerced adherence to prescribed rules and would be able to function in the community after release without getting into trouble. But this model of correctional regime has contributed to the institutionalization of inmates, which is basically a psychological dependence on the institution. Through the strict institutional control, this policy has allowed very few opportunities for inmates to make their own choices and has made it easy to get used to the fact that others will make decisions for them. The control model may have had positive effects on curbing violence in the prison, but it was antithetical to the preparation of inmates for life outside the prison walls because it considerably reduced decision making and the ability to make choices, which are the hallmarks of a modern, complex society. Another controversial feature of this model was the "building tender" system (BT), using inmates, usually seasoned and violent ones, to control other inmates (DiIulio, 1987). This policy was challenged and ruled unlawful by the well-known *Ruiz v. Estelle* decision (see, e.g., Crouch & Marquart, 1990; Martin & Ekland-Olson, 1987).[6]

The responsibility model was represented by the Michigan correctional system. This model de-emphasized paramilitary prison operations and emphasized inmate classification and elaborate grievance procedures. It saw incapacitation as the main purpose of incarceration. The only expectation from the inmates was that they refrain from violence, but they could, if they so desired, participate in treatment programs and work opportunities available in the institution. There was also a concern for rehabilitation whereby prison officials had argued that various services, especially education and work programs, would lead to a reduction in recidivism. The responsibility model allowed for a certain degree of participation by inmates in institutional decision making with the intention to limit their dependency on the institution. This model embraced the theoretical thesis that "if inmates are allowed to participate in decision making, they will tend to act more responsibly toward themselves, others, and the prison society" (Murton, 1979, p. 24). The administration encouraged the education of inmates about their rights and gave them the opportunity to use the grievance system when they felt that their rights were violated by the staff. There was little emphasis on dress code and grooming standards and on regimentation in general.

The consensual model was followed in California. Like in Michigan, criminal behavior was seen as stemming from complex and deep psychological, social, and economic reasons, and not only from the individual's decision to violate the law, as it was seen in Texas. The California approach to prison management was a middle ground between the Texas and the Michigan management ideas in terms of methods of control over inmates. The institutional atmosphere in terms of discipline and the extent of inmate participation in decision making varied among prisons.

Correctional Leadership

Another major factor in prison management is the individual leadership of top echelon correctional officials. The role of top prison officials and their influence in the operation of prisons is also neglected because correctional managers work in a bureaucratic environment in which they are subject to a variety of legal and administrative constraints and exposed to a great deal of political pressures from office holders, legislators, and pressure groups (DiIulio, 1987). They are often political appointees, and therefore it is assumed that they have little to say about broader philosophical and policy issues in corrections. However, because prisons are hidden from the public's eyes and are not high on the public agenda, the individual wardens have more influence to direct and control the institutions than was believed. It is important to remember that policies are made at the top level of the organization, even though many outside factors may have an impact on them (Duffee, 1980). Therefore the top executives' personal correctional philosophy and agenda have to be taken into consideration because they may have a major impact on what is going on in the prisons and can influence the social climate of the institution.

The importance of managerial leadership in correctional organizations was emphasized by Street et al. (1966):

> At least three crucial dimensions of executive leadership shape the organization. First, the executive formulates specific goals and basic policies that give meaning and direction to the enterprise. . . . Second, the executive is the key link between the organization and its environment. . . . Third, the executive establishes the structure of roles and responsibilities within the organization that enables it to pursue its goals. (p. 45)

Jacobs (1983), referring to his major case study of the Stateville Penitentiary, Illinois's largest maximum-security prison, underscores the role of individual wardens and their impact on the life in the prison:

> In 1970 the Stateville warden who had risen through the ranks, and who had shared a background and ideology identical to the rank and file, was replaced by a young college-educated professional oriented toward treatment. The new warden's first expressions of empathy with the plight of the prisoners convinced the wards that he was "for the cons." The subsequent estrangement of the rank and file from the growing number of professional administrators resulted in a deterioration of the prison's ability to provide food, showers, clothing, mail, and other basic services. Ultimately, the breakdown of administration led to more and more violence and a "crisis in control." (p. 22)

The growing correctional bureaucracy, the increased legislative concern with correctional issues, the expanding rights of prisoners, the readiness of the courts to intervene in corrections, the unionization of correctional employees, and the technological developments that allowed the mass media to report news close to their occurrence have considerably curtailed the personal impact of correctional leaders. Nevertheless, their influence on the everyday life of prisons cannot be dismissed lightly. Although there is criticism of DiIulio's typology of prison management models (e.g., Klofas, 1987), his work does indicate a strong connection between prison management and the quality of life in prisons.

The analysis of management, and, indirectly, the quality-of-life issue, cannot be divorced from the nature of the organization that is being dealt with. As mentioned, privately operated correctional facilities tend to be small, usually 500 inmates or less, minimum-security, or in a few cases, medium-security institutions. This character of private facilities allows for management policies that are closer to the responsibility model than to the control model. It also may lead to less regimentation, and among others, to the reduction of custodial personnel and increased flexibility in changing staffing schedules and formulas. The analysis also highlights the pivotal role of prison wardens and administrators in determining the organizational atmosphere and influencing the quality of services in the institutions. The concept of "organizational climate" can be applied as an analytic tool to study certain dimensions of organizations in general. This concept refers to

> a relatively enduring quality of the internal environment of an organization that (a) is experienced by its members, (b) influences their behavior, and (c) can be described in terms of the values of a particular set of characteristics (or attributes) of the organization. (Tagiuri, 1968, p. 27)

Organizational climate is the "total effect of living and working within an organization" (Duffee, 1980, p. 126). Thus, among others, this concept includes the incorporation of formal authority into the organization.

Leadership styles have been found to be important in determining organizational climate and the motivation and performance of employees:

> Distinct organizational climates can be created by varying leadership styles. . . . Once created, these climates seem to have significant, often dramatic, effects on motivation, and correspondingly on performance and job satisfaction. . . . Organizational climates may effect changes in seemingly stable personality traits.[7] (Litwin, 1968, p. 189)

In the post-World War II period many management methods and techniques used in the private sector were adopted into the correctional field. Nevertheless, critics of the correctional enterprise claim that these efforts had only limited impact on public corrections because of the confines of government bureaucracy and ineptness and also because most administrators advanced to management positions through the ranks without experience in private management. Indeed, one of the interesting features of the current privatization trend is that almost all the private prison wardens and some of the administrators came from the "not very successful" public correctional system without having any background in the private sector.[8] According to private prison critics, several of these administrators followed managerial policies and practices that raised questions of whether they are appropriate for a humane correctional institution. These questions were raised particularly in the case of a former vice president and board member of the largest private correctional corporation, CCA, and the head of another private corporation, Buckingham Security Limited. The former CCA board member was the commissioner of corrections in Arkansas at the time when the U.S. Supreme Court found the entire correctional system in that state unconstitutional (McShane & Williams, 1989). In the well-known *Hutto v. Finney* (1978) case, the U.S. Supreme Court upheld a lower court's decision that keeping inmates in Arkansas's segregation cells for more than 30 days was a cruel and unusual punishment (Clear & Cole, 1989). The U.S. Supreme Court declared that in the Arkansas correctional system, officials were making profit from the inmates' work on prison farms. Prison conditions were harsh, and the prisoners had to work for 10 hours a day with only one day off a week; often they were not provided with adequate clothing. The court found the prison completely unsuitable for a free society (Becker & Stanley, 1985).

Similarly, the president of Buckingham Security, who was the warden of three different federal prisons, had legal problems. He was found guilty of inflicting cruel and unusual punishment on two inmates in Lewisburg Penitentiary (Becker & Stanley, 1985). There were also reports that in the mid-1980s, Buckingham Security, one of the pioneers among the private prison companies, proposed to build a correctional facility near Pittsburgh but it was revealed later that the suggested location for the facility was a toxic waste site that the company purchased for one dollar (American Bar Association, 1986; Donahue, 1988; Robbins, 1986). In Texas several correctional managers who were fired or resigned amid allegations of brutality and civil rights violations of inmates have found new careers in private correctional corporations (McShane & Williams, 1989). There are additional instances in which the backgrounds and previous records of the private entrepreneurs can be legitimately questioned. Some of these cases are mentioned in a *Wall Street Journal* article in which, among others, the vice president of Private Prisons of America Ltd. was found to have an unsuccessful management record with juvenile facilities, a bankruptcy filing in 1989, and a conviction for receiving stolen property in 1965 (Mason, 1991). Although these cases do not necessarily indicate that people with questionable backgrounds will be the dominant figures in this industry, the cases do raise reasonable concerns, regarding the correctional leadership and the screening methods of private prison companies, that have to be taken into consideration in charting long-term correctional policies.

Logan (1990) rigorously attacks these claims and characterizes them as mudslinging. For example, he points out that in the case of the head of Buckingham Security:

> The U.S. District Court, in its review of the case, found that no one was beaten or terrorized or offensively touched, that escorting and restraining the prisoners had involved only "privileged contact," and that all of Warden Fenton's actions had been reasonable except for one. The action found by the court to be "not reasonable" (but also "not extreme and outrageous") was the decision to keep one plaintiff's handcuffs on while he was in his cell for three days. (Logan, 1990, pp. 126-127)

As noted, Logan (1990, p. 125) dismisses this case as an example of "mud slinging" by "the ACLU and some other critics" but this "allegation" emerges several times in the literature and is repeated by reputable scholars such as Ira P. Robbins; Bernard T. Welsh, Professor of Law and Justice, American University; John D. Donahue, Assistant Professor, John F. Kennedy School of Government, Harvard University; and the American Bar Association, Section of Criminal Justice. Although professional reputations, scholarly achievements, and prestigious institutional affiliations are not necessarily proofs of complete factual accuracy, they do lend some credence to this information. The vehement defense of private companies and their executives and the branding of their critics as mudslingers do not promote an objective and useful analysis of this issue.[9]

Without expanding the argument of whether these cases were such that they could reflect in a negative way, in general, on the private administration of prisons, they do indicate that many of the administrators and the higher echelon professional staff of private prison corporations will come from the public prison system, at least at the early stages of privatization. There are several issues in this connection. First, private companies will leave the training and the initial experience period for the development of managerial skills to the public correctional system. This strategy may be a wise one on their part because it can be cost-effective for the corporations, saving training expenses and avoiding potential "trial and error" problems. Second, advocates of prison privatization are usually very critical of public system bureaucracy and the lack of innovation of the public sector, but they expect that administrators and officials who "learn the ropes" and receive their professional socialization in the criticized public system will become effective private administrators just by transferring to a private company. Third, these administrators are expected to be innovative but to keep in mind the importance of cost savings for the company. In fact, there is a good chance that a large part of the innovative energy will have to be channeled into the cost-cutting and profit-making aspects of corrections, paradoxically by administrators with a background in the much maligned public correctional system that is considered to be wasteful, inefficient, and inept.

The question may boil down to whether the executives of private corporations will have the ability to create opportunities for correctional innovations and to motivate line administrators (i.e., wardens) who were socialized into the public system (which according to the proponents of privatization is lacking incentives for innovation) to introduce new management ideas, and all this with profit making in mind. There is a likelihood that the correctional creativity and innovation on the managerial level primarily will be channeled into cost saving and profit making partly because these aspects of corrections lend themselves to quantification and documentation, whereas other aspects, such as quality, are much harder to assess.

The general trend in American business is to have top executives with financial backgrounds rather than with technological or professional backgrounds heading corporations. This trend emphasizes the primacy of economic considerations over professional or technological ones, especially in publicly traded corporations where the managers have to satisfy the short-term profit expectations of the shareholders. These considerations may have a major impact on the management of private prisons as well.

Some additional factors raise concerns regarding corporate managers of private institutions. Managers in corporations seem to have a very wide range of discretion; in effect, they have more actual power than the legal owners—the shareholders—have (e.g., Ermann & Lundman, 1982). Therefore they may be freer to resort to unethical or deviant practices to manage an organization. As Clinard (1983) has shown, corporate managers with financial backgrounds more readily cut corners to achieve performance goals than do technologically oriented managers. Also, corporations tend to shield their top managers from personal liability by delegation of responsibility to various departments and middle-range managers (e.g., Braithwaite, 1989a; Conklin, 1977; Vaughan, 1980), who are judged by how close they come to their set target of profits (Gross, 1980). The risk of penalty for corporate executives who violate rules is relatively minor (Clinard & Yeager, 1980), a fact that is likely to mitigate the preventive effects of deterrence that otherwise may well be strong in the case of corporate violations because of their rational nature (Braithwaite & Geis, 1982).

Conclusion

In summary, although advocates of privatization argue that the flexibility and relatively little bureaucratization that characterize private institutions will create more incentives for improvement and efficiency on the managerial and staff levels, there are other factors that may have less positive or outright negative effects on the operation of private facilities. There are major concerns that the generally low salary range and meager fringe benefits offered by private prison companies will negatively affect the quality of staff that they will be able to hire. These conditions also may lead to a higher than usual rate of staff turnover, which has implications for stability and order in correctional facilities.

Furthermore, there are some questions regarding the management and leadership of private companies and the facilities they operate. The fact that chief executives with business backgrounds run at least some of the corporations indicates the emphasis on profit making, which in some cases may be counterproductive in a correctional organization. On the facility level, wardens, superintendents, and other higher ranking administrators are the "products" of the public correctional system, some of them with questionable records. It becomes an open question whether this leadership will be effective in achieving a better quality of service for a lower cost, which are the main promises of privatization.

Notes

1. Originally, return-to-custody facilities operated by private companies were established in California to manage parolees during a period of increased number of parole revocations (State of California, 1990). As prison overcrowding increased, the Department of Corrections began using them for the housing of first commitments as well, and the name was changed to Community Correctional Facilities (CCFs) to reflect the changing role of these facilities. Currently, there are CCFs that are operated by private firms and others that are managed by cities and counties through contract with the California Department of Corrections (see Sechrest & Shichor, 1993b).

2. The job market has a major impact on the availability of qualified correctional personnel. The supply and demand clearly works, at least on the correctional officer's level; that is, during economic hard times the supply of qualified candidates for correctional positions is much higher than during an economic boom.

3. Several empirical studies on correctional institutions tend to confirm the relevance of the "corruption of authority" thesis for the understanding of prison life (see, e.g., Glaser & Fry, 1987; Hewitt, Poole, & Regoli, 1984).

4. In California, outside evaluators of public correctional programs have a hard time getting approval for interviewing correctional personnel or asking them to fill out survey questionnaires. Every research instrument has to be screened and approved by union representatives. The California Correctional Peace Officers Association is one of the most politically powerful labor organizations in the state.

5. For general discussions and analyses of correctional management, see Bartollas and Miller (1978), Duffee (1980), DiIulio (1987), and England (1990).

6. During the 1960s and 1970s the control model came under fire. Severe and inhumane practices in Arkansas, including whippings and the trusty system (similar to BT), were challenged in the courts, which ordered sweeping improvements in the prison (*Jackson v. Bishop*, 1968; *Holt v. Sarver*, 1970). Also, the conditions of solitary confinement in several control-model prison systems were changed by court orders, like in Tennessee and in Arkansas (*Hutto v. Finney*, 1978).

7. For an exploration of the concept of social climate in correctional institutions, see Duffee (1980), Moos (1968), and Street et al. (1966).

8. According to CCA's 1989 annual report, all the wardens that are listed were either wardens or high-ranking prisons officers (deputy warden, captain, etc.) in public facilities.

9. It seems to be perfectly acceptable by privatization proponents to degrade public employees, calling them lazy, inefficient, unmotivated, and so on, but the mentioning of the case of a private correctional corporate executive who while in public employ prompted a U.S. District Court review and condemnation is found to be "mud slinging." This approach does not indicate much objectivity in dealing with the problems of public administration and privatization of prisons.

9

Empirical Evaluations of
Private Correctional Facilities

This chapter focuses on studies conducted to evaluate privately operated correctional facilities. Almost all the available studies compared the private versus public facilities on correctional cost and quality. The chapter, besides reviewing these evaluations, also analyses the various problems (methodological, administrative, etc.) involved in conducting these kinds of studies.

There are relatively few available empirical evaluations of privately operated correctional facilities. Some of them include not only adult confinement facilities (prisons, jails, etc.), but juvenile secure facilities as well. Whether adult and juvenile facilities are comparable remains a question, but because there is a paucity of well-designed empirical studies of private prisons available, it was decided to include rigorous empirical evaluations of secure juvenile facilities as well.

Logan and McGriff's Study of Silverdale

Logan and McGriff (1989) compared the cost of operating the Hamilton County facility (Silverdale) in Tennessee by CCA versus what the cost would have been had the operation remained in the public domain. This study showed that there was an annual savings of at least 4% to 8% (but more realistically 5% to 15%) in comparison to the estimated cost of county management (McDonald, 1990a). The authors do point out that these results may vary in different correctional systems. They also suggest that the prison services are better under private management because there are now two full-time managers in the county, instead of one, who are performing three functions: that of the warden, the superintendent, and the monitor. The authors claim that the county has gained correctional experience because the new warden is a person with a considerable record in public corrections, whereas the previous warden had no prior background in corrections. In addition, the county jail now benefits from the experience and expertise of the private corporation's officers who oversee the operation of more than a dozen private facilities around the country. As argued, it is not clear why high-ranking prison officials hired away from the much-criticized public sector would necessarily enhance the quality of services in private institutions. Similarly, the fact that top corporate officers of CCA were overseeing the operation of the facility does not automatically add to the quality of services. Their involvement may be as much, if not more, directed toward increasing the profitability of the operation than toward improving the quality of services. One of the authors, McGriff, was the county assessor of Hamilton County, thus he was familiar with the accounting practices of the various county agencies. However, cost calculations based on somewhat hypothetical assumptions and projections should be handled cautiously. Also, as seen, contracts of private operations may have some hidden costs for the government agencies. These were not considered at all, whereas there was an elaborated discussion about the hidden costs of public corrections. Furthermore, any possible improvements in government management were not taken into account.

Brakel's Evaluation of Silverdale

Another evaluation of Silverdale was intended to study the quality of services as they are seen from the inmates' perspective (Brakel,

1988). The study surveyed 20 inmates in detail concerning the conditions of confinement, the nature and quality of available programs and services, due process procedures, and relations with the outside. Generally, the answers were more positive (157) than mixed or ambivalent (67) or negative (96) assessments. Positive ratings by the inmates were given for physical improvement, upkeep, cleanliness, staff competence, work assignments, chaplain and counselor services, requests and grievances, correspondence, telephone, and outside contacts. Mixed ratings were in the areas of safety and security, classification, medical care, food, education, discipline, and legal access. Negative ratings were mainly in the areas of recreational programs and facilities and release procedures. Release decisions and good time credits were handled by the county superintendent of corrections, and it was not the responsibility of CCA. Probably, it should have been mentioned that private operators do have an impact on these procedures through the everyday running of the operation as it was discussed earlier.

Six inmates were able to compare the current conditions in Silverdale with the previous conditions in the same institution when it was operated by the county. Out of 28 comparisons (before-after) provided by these inmates, 24 were favorable to the conditions in the private CCA-operated facility versus 4 who favored the county administration. Although these comparisons are interesting, this kind of methodology poses problems of validity and reliability because of the after-the-fact questioning.[1]

Brakel (1988), in analyzing the free comments made by a few respondents at the end of the questionnaire and his own impressions before the survey was conducted, concluded that "the inmates could not care less about who runs the prison, by what political mandate or on what contractual terms. Their paramount interest is much simpler: decent conditions and decent treatment" (p. 240). He also presented some inmate comments that are generally favorable of the private management, but criticized one of the negative statements that was put quite articulately, in which the profit motive of the company was singled out as the first priority of the facility and rehabilitation was claimed to be the last priority. This particular inmate also criticized the quality of food as poor because of corner cutting by the company. Brakel (1988) dismissed this criticism by commenting that

though the inmate is a pretty good writer, the ultimate judgement must
be that he is not credible. The charges he levels do not stand up against
the evidence, as it has been developed throughout this article via the
statements of other inmates, the statements of the staff, analysis of
documented information, and observations. This is prisoner rhetoric
mixed with anti-privatization propaganda that the inmate thinks an
investigator will want to hear. (p. 241)

This seems to be a strong statement for an objective evaluation
study. The evaluation had some methodological problems. First, the
analysis of comments is based only on a few cases that may or may
not represent the opinions of the general population of inmates.
According to the author the questionnaires were mailed to the chaplain, who distributed them to inmates. This procedure was "random
in all respects except that they were known by him to be reasonably
articulate" (Brakel, 1988, p. 181). This sampling procedure should
have warned the author to be very cautious in arriving at his conclusions because they were based on the personal selection of the
chaplain. There are many prisoners who easily can be judged as not
being very articulate, therefore they would have been excluded from
this study. Second, using Brakel's dismissal of the above-mentioned
negative comment, it can be argued that inmates who made favorable
comments regarding the CCA administration did so because they
thought that researchers would like to hear answers supporting
privatization. It is notable that, although this study is quoted in a
book written by a social scientist with a long record of empirical
research (Logan, 1990), no methodological problems of this evaluation are mentioned.

In the same study, there were a number of inmates who could make
external comparisons with the conditions prevailing at the county
jail in downtown Chattanooga or with those at the state prison in
Nashville. From 102 after-the-fact comparisons, 66 were favorable for
Silverdale, 10 for Chattanooga County Jail, and 26 for the state
penitentiary in Nashville. These answers suggest that the quality of
services is better in Silverdale. Although this may be so, it was not
shown whether the other two facilities were holding the same kind
of inmates as Silverdale was. For example, it is possible that the
security levels were different. In the case of the county jail, it was not
mentioned whether the jail contained mostly detainees or convicted

inmates. A state penitentiary usually has inmates with longer sentences who have committed more serious crimes than inmates held in a county penal farm such as Silverdale. This may make generalizations problematic. Finally, Silverdale may be a showcase facility, meaning that conditions may be different there than in other institutions because the company wants to prove the advantages of privatization. As seen, several different evaluation studies have focused on this institution, for example, Logan and McGriff (1989), Brakel (1988), and Sellers (1989). It seems to be one of the most researched facilities in the United States.

It is noteworthy that these evaluation studies of Silverdale fail to mention either that the facility in its first year of operation had a $200,000 cost overrun (Tolchin, 1985) or that in 1986 there was a riot in this facility. In the riot situation inmates demanded better food, more adequate recreation, and generally better treatment. A police SWAT team had to be called in to restore order (DiIulio, 1990b).

Sellers's Study of Three Pairs of Institutions

Another comparative study of private and public correctional facilities was conducted by Sellers (1989). He compared three private facilities—(a) Weaversville Intensive Treatment Unit, Northhampton, Pennsylvania, operated by Radio Corporation of America (RCA); (b) Silverdale Detention Center, Chattanooga, Tennessee, operated by CCA; and (c) Butler County Prison, Butler, Pennsylvania, operated by Buckingham Securities—with three public prisons: (a) Pennsylvania Department of Public Welfare's North Central Secure Treatment Unit, Danville, Pennsylvania; (b) Warren County Correctional Center, New Jersey; and (c) Salem County Prison, New Jersey. The author, according to his own account, tried to find comparable facilities. The comparisons were made through on-site visits lasting 3 days in each facility, touring the facility, and conducting structured interviews with "principal personnel" (i.e., various administrators), corrections officers, and other staff members. Inmates were not mentioned; it is assumed that they were not interviewed.

First, Sellers compared the information collected from Weaversville Intensive Treatment Unit with that of the North Central Secure

Treatment Unit, both maximum-security juvenile detention centers in Pennsylvania housing a small number of inmates, 26 and 28 respectively. It was found that the per diem weighted (the weighting procedure takes into account the number of services available) cost of $91 in the private facility was substantially lower than the $136/$141 per diem in the public facility, whereas the services available were about the same. Admittedly, the quality of services was not measured, only their quantity.

The second comparison was between the privately operated Butler County Prison, used to detain short-term county inmates and overflow inmates (felons) from state and federal institutions, and the publicly administered maximum-security Salem County Prison, which detained county inmates and overflow state inmates. Butler had a capacity of 106 beds with the occupancy of 96; Salem had a capacity of 95 with an occupancy of 184. Sellers (1989) found Butler to be a well-kept facility, whereas Salem was poorly maintained and grossly overcrowded. Butler had 18 programs, a guard/inmate ratio of 1:4.2, and an administration/inmate ratio of 1:10. Salem had 14 programs, a guard/inmate ratio of 1:4.6, and an administration/inmate ratio of 1:23. It is not clear who is included in the "administration" category, and what their functions are. The actual per diem in Butler was $28.52 and the weighted per diem was $28.52, whereas in Salem these figures were $25.11 and $32.29, respectively. This means that the actual cost was lower in the public facility than in the private facility. Only the weighting procedure hiked up the cost in Salem, and it remains a question how much of the extra services that Butler had were vital for the inmates or for running the facility.

The third comparison was between the privately operated Silverdale facility and the publicly managed Warren County facility in New Jersey. Silverdale had 375 inmates although its official capacity was 350, whereas Warren, a new high-tech facility opened in 1986, had an official capacity of 87, but it already had an occupancy of 109. The major difference between the institutions was that although both were rated structurally as maximum-security facilities, the guard/inmate ratio in Silverdale was 1:6.25, whereas in Warren it was 1:2. At the same time, the administrator/inmate ratio in both facilities was 1:19. Silverdale had 18 services; Warren had 16. The actual per diem in Silverdale was $19 and in Warren County $43; the weighted per diem was $19 versus $48, respectively. These figures showed the largest cost difference so far between private and public institutions and, apparently, reflected the difference in the guard/inmate ratio between the two institutions and the presence of 4 nurses for 109 (1:27.5 ratio) inmates in Warren versus the 3 nurses for 375 (1:125 ratio) inmates in Silverdale. The reasons for and the effects of these differential staffing patterns were not mentioned.

In his discussion, Sellers (1989) stated that the main motive for prison privatization is monetary. He recognized that private companies may deliberately submit low bids to obtain contracts (lowballing) to have "a foot in the door" of the correctional "business" and later raise the costs. However, he seemed to accept the private firms' claims that competition will force private contractors to keep costs down in an increasingly competitive marketplace. This is an assumption that has to be substantiated in the future. As noted, so far the facts do not confirm the existence of a thriving and competitive private correctional marketplace (Thomas & Foard, 1991). Another positive effect of prison privatization, according to Sellers (1989), is the increase in options and alternatives for the public sector, an effect that also may lead to net widening. It also allows the criminal justice system to evaluate itself by constant comparisons and by ongoing monitoring. In addition, there is a potential to introduce to the public prisons new methods of operation that have been proven to be useful in privately managed prisons.

Although Sellers's (1989) study contributed to the small number of empirical evaluations, it does have some additional research problems. The most notable one is that the "quality" of institutions was equated with the number of services reported. It is also noteworthy that in the few evaluation studies of private facilities conducted so far, as seen, the Silverdale Detention Center seems to have a central importance, being the most evaluated facility (Brakel, 1988; Logan & McGriff, 1989; Sellers, 1989). This raises questions regarding the reliability and validity of generalizations derived from these studies.

The Urban Institute's Comparative Study

Another comparison between private and public correctional facilities was conducted by the researchers of the Urban Institute

(Hatry et al., 1989). This study compared one private and one public facility in Kentucky and one private and one public facility in Massachusetts. There was an attempt to compare institutions that have similar inmate populations and security levels in the same state, trying to control for the social, political, and economic environment. In Kentucky, the Marion Adjustment Center (MAC), a privately operated minimum-security institution, was compared with the Blackburn Correctional Complex (BCC), a minimum-security facility operated by the state. MAC was under private contract since 1986, had a capacity of 200 beds, and the contractor was the U.S. Corrections Corporation. It was described as being "between a privately run half-way house and a state minimum security prison" (Hatry et al., 1989, p. 1). BCC is a minimum-security facility; it does not even have a perimeter fence. The population in BCC was larger than MAC's; it had a capacity of 353 beds. The race distribution was roughly the same in the two institutions, but in MAC there were fewer violent offenders and more property offenders than in BCC; also, the population of MAC was somewhat younger than that of BCC. In addition, the median sentence length in BCC (10 years) was 3 years longer than that of MAC (7 years). These figures indicate that the private facility had a less seasoned offender population in general that committed less serious offenses than the population of the public facility.

The institutions were compared by two research staff members through ratings on a specially constructed Visual Inspection Checklist. Both institutions were scored "good" or "excellent" in all categories. The rated characteristics were physical plant, institutional climate, staff-inmate interaction, and quality of life. The raters did not find any substantial differences between the two institutions. The other sources of information for the purposes of comparison were (a) survey of the correctional personnel, (b) survey of the inmates, (c) in-depth interviews with the wardens, (d) data from inmate files, and (e) central office statistics.

The MAC-BCC comparison project concluded that, on the program side, the private facility generally scored higher than did the public facility in the delivery of quality programs and in the provision of basic inmate services; however, there were some areas in which the publicly operated facility was rated higher, for example, in food services. In terms of cost the picture was less clear cut. The per diem

expense of the private facility was 10% higher than the BCC; however, if the construction cost of the facility would have been included,
then the public facility's cost would be 28% higher.

Logan's Study of Female Prisons

Few evaluation studies are conducted on female prisons, and
hardly anything is written on the privatization of female facilities.
Logan (1991), in a project sponsored by the National Institute of Justice,
compared the quality of incarceration in three multiple-security-level
women's prisons: a privately operated female prison in New Mexico,
the same prison a year earlier when it was operated by the state, and
a federal prison for women.

The "quality" was measured along eight dimensions: security,
safety, order, care (mostly medical), activity, justice, living conditions, and management. The comparison concluded that the private
prison outperformed the state and federal institutions in six dimensions and that only the dimension of care was better in the public
prison, but in the dimension of justice, the federal prison matched
the quality of the private institutions. The findings are sensitive to
the data on which the measure of quality is determined. Using only
inmate surveys, the state-operated prison outscored the private prison
on all quality dimensions except in the activity category (e.g., education and work programs). However, "the inmate's marginally more
negative evaluation of the private prison was outweighed by the far
more positive comparisons based on the staff surveys and the institutional records data" (Thomas & Logan, 1991, p. 24).

In the executive summary of the report, Logan (1991) combined all
the three-way comparisons among private, state, and federal prisons
of staff and inmate surveys and institutional data. This method
yielded 595 pairwise comparisons among the three prisons, covering
the eight indicators mentioned above. A Prison Quality Index was
calculated for each institution, based on the above comparisons; this
index was as follows: Favorable Differences + (Similarities +2)/Total
Comparisons (Logan, 1991, p. 5). The summary of these comparisons
(the combined figures of the three sources of information) showed
that the private prison received more favorable evaluations than the

state and federal prisons in six of eight dimensions. On the dimension of care the state outscored the private institution, and on the justice dimension the federal and state prisons had equal scores. However, when the data sources were examined separately, it was found that although the staff survey and official records showed a higher quality of confinement in the private prison, in the inmate survey the state prison outscored the private one. These figures show a divergent pattern of opinions between the inmate and staff groups. The official-records data tend to support the private prison, according to Logan (1991), although it is problematic to arrive at strong conclusions on the basis of grievance records, significant incident and discipline logs, health clinic reports, inmate work and education records, and staff personnel records. Some of these records may extend them-selves to various interpretations and may reflect the policies and practices of the prison administration and staff rather than anything else.

In the conclusion of the report, Logan (1991) emphasized that in all three institutions the quality was high. He found that by contract-ing with a private firm, New Mexico raised the quality of its women's prison. This conclusion may be correct; however, it is not clearly seen from the executive summary of the report. Although this study examines a wide range of factors that seem to be relevant for the quality of life in the institution, it also raises some questions of methodology and interpretation. First, the use of the Prison Quality Index seems problematic. In combining the staff and inmate survey data with the records data, the various perspectives about the prison are blurred and the results do not easily lend themselves to interpre-tation.' Whose quality ratings, the staff's or the inmates', are more valid and useful in terms of policy making, introduction of changes, and so on? How objective are prison official records? When staff and inmate surveys were analyzed separately, as soon, the picture turned out to be much more ambiguous and the interpretation of overall quality became tenuous, relying to a large degree on subjective attitudes, opinions, and judgments.

The evaluation also found that the per diem cost per inmate in the private facility was $69.75 in its first year of operation. That shows a 12.8% savings in comparison to the $80 cost of the public prison during its last year of operation (Thomas & Logan, 1991).

The Texas State Auditor's Report

Thomas and Logan (1991) refer to a 1991 report by the Texas State Auditor's office on four 500-bed prisons that are contracted out to two private corporations, CCA and the Wackenhut Corrections Corporation. The auditor's report indicated that the two private companies operate the prisons 10% to 15% cheaper than what it would cost the state Department of Corrections to run them.

On the basis of their reviews, Thomas and Logan (1991) conclude that the available research to date "is sufficient to support a reasonable expectation of low costs and high quality as a consequence of contracting" (p. 28).

However, at the beginning of operation (September-December, 1989), there were problems with these facilities. The Texas Board of Criminal Justice released a monitoring report criticizing CCA and Wackenhut for (a) inadequate health services, (b) insufficient programs, (c) abusive treatment of inmates by inexperienced guards, (d) filling positions slowly or not at all, (e) lack of educational programs for Spanish-speaking prisoners, (f) minimal participation in substance abuse programs, and (g) absence of self-monitoring (Ethridge & Marquart, 1993). By mid-1990, another audit reported that most of the specific contract violations were corrected, and by fall 1991 almost all noncompliances were corrected.

A report by the Texas Sunset Advisory Commission to the Texas legislature that convened in January 1991 compared the cost and quality of privately operated facilities with similar services operated by the Texas Department of Criminal Justice (TDCJ). It stated:

1. As of August 31, 1990, the private prisons were operating at close to 10% below the cost of a hypothetical equivalent unit run by the state.
2. The TDCJ does not have a state-run equivalent of a private prison unit. Therefore, no conclusions could be drawn as to whether the private prisons currently provide services that are equal to or higher in quality than the state's (Ethridge & Marquart, 1993, p. 43).

On the basis of these findings and the reports of the monitors, state officials renewed the contracts with the two companies for 2 years.

This study did not report whether the monitoring and the frequent reports to the legislature were included in the cost estimates. It also pointed to the problem of reliable evaluation and comparison with state facilities because the study was based on "hypothetical equivalent" state operations. Ethridge and Marquart (1993) conclude: "it is not yet known whether privatization is the panacea for state prison systems. It is still too early to tell whether privatization is a remedy or just another correctional fad" (p. 45).

Sechrest and Shichor's Evaluation of California's CCFs

Sechrest and Shichor (1993a, 1993b) compared public and private CCFs in California. The CCF title may be somewhat misleading because these are residential facilities handling parole violators, first prison commitments, and in one institution civil commitments (mainly drug related). Another unique feature of these facilities is that they are under contract with the Parole Division of the California Department of Corrections (CDC), and that the public facilities are operated by municipal governments or police and sheriff's departments for profit. The authors refer to these facilities as "public proprietary" facilities.

The preliminary evaluation revealed some problems endemic to most such attempts, namely, that the data available do not satisfy all the needs for a reliable comparison. For example, overhead figures (e.g., how much money from the cost figures goes for company headquarters or municipal administration) were not kept uniformly, there were hidden costs of medical treatment in the various facilities (some cases were treated in prison hospitals at the expense of the CDC), and there were no figures of CDC legal costs of the contract preparation. The preliminary cost comparison based on the available data from the CDC indicated that the per diem cost in 1991 to 1992 in the public proprietary CCF was $50.08 and in the "private proprietary" CCF was $54.49. These figures were favorable in comparison to the cost of state-operated prisons in California, which on average had a $59.04 per diem cost, including all the institutions and all security levels. On the basis of this comparison, the authors came to the conclusion that according to all indications there are no substantial cost differences between the publicly and privately operated CCFs.

In regard to quality, three CCFs were compared: (a) a facility operated by a police department in a small town near Bakersfield, (b) a facility handling civil commitments (drug abuse offenders) managed by a small municipality in the Mojave desert, and (c) a private proprietary institution in the California desert not far from Indio. Inmate responses to a questionnaire concerning items of order, amenity, and service indicated that, by far, the highest level of satisfaction was expressed in all three dimensions by the inmates at the publicly operated facility for civil commitments. These results may be influenced by the special type of inmate population at this institution. Comparison between the other two facilities seems to be more appropriate because of the similarity of the inmate groups. The results were mixed—on the order dimension the private proprietary inmates were more positive, whereas on the service dimension the public proprietary answers scored higher. In the amenity category there were four indicators; on two items inmates from the public proprietary facility gave more positive answers, whereas on the other two the private proprietary inmates did so.

This preliminary evaluation did not show any major differences in quality between CCFs operated for profit by private corporations or by public agencies.

Evaluations of Juvenile Institutions

Recent privatization literature includes empirical comparisons and evaluations of secure juvenile correctional facilities as well. Although evaluations of any confinement facilities are important, the issues involved in the operation of youth programs may not be exactly the same as in adult prison management. The Urban Institute project justified this comparison by stating that Massachusetts contracts out for most of its juvenile secure treatment programs. Nine of 13 such programs that house 10% to 15% of the most violent and troubled juvenile offenders in the state are operated by private not-for-profit organizations. An additional question is whether the not-for-profit private sector and the for-profit (proprietary) private sector can be considered similar in the analysis or whether by dealing with privatization through the not-for-profit sector an additional variable is brought into the analysis that may confound the issues. Furthermore, these facilities handled very small numbers of delinquents, which set them apart even more from the adult prisons that we have been dealing with so far. Thus, although evaluations of small juvenile institutions are reviewed here briefly, any implications from these studies for adult corrections will have to be viewed with caution.

The Urban Institute Study
of Juvenile Institutions

The Urban Institute study also compared two pairs of (public-private) carefully matched small (15-16 beds) juvenile secure treatment programs. The facilities were not identical; although their programs and the composition of the offenders in terms of age, gender, type of offense, sentences, and household income were fairly similar, there were a few exceptions. For example, there was a difference in the racial composition of the two programs. Public programs housed a significantly higher percentage of black juveniles than did private programs. The researchers attributed this difference to geographic factors rather than to any selection bias. There were no significant age differences; the average age of the juveniles was between 15 and 17 years. Regarding the average time spent in the programs, the differences between the public and private facilities were in the range of 10%. In the private programs, the average time spent was 9.8 and 9.4 months, respectively, whereas in the public programs the figures were 8.9 and 8.6 months. This pattern lends some credence to the claim that private institutions may try to keep inmates for longer periods than public institutions to maintain high occupancy rates.

The evaluation also revealed that staff members in the public programs were significantly older than in the private programs and had longer tenure in their employment. There was no evidence of creaming (accepting less problematic offenders) by the private programs. The majority of inmates in all programs came from families with an annual income of less than $10,000.

The study found that the per diem cost per capita of the programs was similar (public, $197, vs. private, $199). Concerning quality of services, it was concluded that (a) "staff and record data indicate, overall, that the service delivery environment is better in private programs as compared to public ones, in terms of conditions of confinement, internal security and control, and management and staffing" (Hatry et al., 1989, p. 218); and (b) the residents' data consistently favored private programs; however, the differences were significant only in the area of internal security and control. These findings show a better private performance in service delivery than public performance. More specific findings indicated that staff members in private programs were more enthusiastic about their work— this may be attributed to their generally younger age and their shorter length of service. It is feasible that in private programs, when the enthusiasm is gone and/or burnout sets in, many staff members quit because of the lack of job security, low salary, and lack of fringe benefits. There also may be a higher turnover in private programs because the management is interested in having more entry-level employees in order to pay lower wages. These practices may result in a situation in which a high percentage of staff members in private programs are in the early, enthusiastic phase of their job, whereas in public programs they are older, more seasoned, and probably more alienated—a phenomenon not unusual among corrections workers (e.g., Poole & Regoli, 1981). It is a question whether it is better for an institution to have enthusiastic young personnel showing high turnover, or an older, seasoned, and more cynical but stable workforce.

Staff in private facilities rated the program's quality higher. This may partially be related to the differences in staff backgrounds. A higher proportion of staff in private programs felt that more counseling and education leading to high school diplomas or GEDs (general equivalency diplomas) are important than in public programs. These attitudes can be interpreted as a strong commitment toward rehabilitation and to the younger age and enthusiasm of the private facilities' staff. There were no differences among the residents' positive evaluation of the programs in both kinds of facilities.

A 15-month follow-up on revocations and recommitments showed no statistical differences. Private staff reported more flexibility and opportunity for participation in decision making than did public program staff. Management turnover rates were similar in public and private facilities. Staff in public programs were more likely to file grievances against management, which may indicate less harmonious staff-management relations or that public staff members had more job security, were probably unionized, and, therefore were less concerned with the negative consequences that may result from these grievances. There were no differences in the number of grievances filed by residents against public or private staff.

The researchers concluded their study by stating, "Overall, differences observed consistently favored private providers. However, no significant differences were found with respect to cost and short-term recidivism" (Hatry et al., 1989, p. 221).[2]

The researchers reached the conclusion that this evaluation will provide generalizable results across juvenile residential programs. But it is questionable how much the results from small juvenile facilities housing 15 to 30 residents are transferable to the study of large, high-security adult prisons.

The Okeechobee Evaluation Study

A more relevant evaluation study, from the point of view of size and organizational structure, was conducted at the Florida School for Boys in Okeechobee. This was a 400-plus-bed, secure facility for adjudicated delinquents, which until 1982 was under the jurisdiction of the Florida Department of Health and Rehabilitative Services. In 1982 the state transferred this facility to the private, not-for-profit Eckerd Foundation. This organization had been involved in the past in conducting summer wilderness camps for emotionally disturbed "predelinquent" youth. The following review of this evaluation is mainly for illustrative purposes because this not-for-profit organization is not representative of the for-profit private corporations involved in the operations of prisons. As Levinson (1985) pointed out, "the Foundation's motives were not profit-oriented, but rather to seek a better way for working with delinquent individuals" (p. 77). Another caveat is that this study also focuses on juvenile facilities, whereas our major interest is the operation of adult prisons. Even though it was a secure facility, handling juveniles who are considered to be more or less serious offenders, this facility was not an adult prison, and as noted, the management and staff were not employees of the state Department of Corrections, and management policies and rules were not determined by that department, either before or after privatization. However, because relatively few rigorous privatization studies are available and this study was conducted in a professional manner, it is worthwhile to review the results, which may point to some issues that are also relevant in the for-profit privatization of adult facilities.

The cost and quality of services of Okeechobee were compared with the Arthur G. Dozier School for Boys, Florida's only other all-male training school for juvenile delinquents. The major findings of the comparison were the following. First, institutional adjustment data showed no real differences between the wards of the two institutions. Thus the program delivered by the Eckerd Foundation was equal in quality to the state program. Second, staff morale data indicated that (a) a higher percentage of the Dozier staff responded to the questions than did the Okeechobee staff, and (b) "Dozier appears to be a 'happier' place to work than Okeechobee" (Levinson, 1985, p. 79). Third, Okeechobee's cost increase under Eckerd was somewhat less than the cost increase in Dozier (3% vs. 4%), but there was no dramatic decrease of cost as was anticipated (a 5%-10% reduction was apparently promised). Fourth, based on observation data: (a) Dozier appeared orderly and well maintained, Okeechobee appeared to be the opposite; (b) in Dozier the staff was stable, in Okeechobee there was a high staff turnover; (c) in Dozier the staff seemed to be in control, in Okeechobee the staff "appeared to be barely hanging on" (Levinson, 1985, p. 82); and (d) after 2 years of operation, Okeechobee management and staff were still trying to put the program in place—there was more flexibility in the operation, but it was still not stable and was still trying to "find itself."

The study concluded that the Eckerd Foundation's management neither achieved a substantial reduction in costs nor raised significantly the quality of service and that the two programs were, on an overall level, comparable. Basically, "this example of the private sector in corrections reveals no strong support for this management alternative" (Levinson, 1985, p. 82). One interesting aspect of this evaluation was the great amount of attention given to it by some advocates of privatization. This may have been because (a) the evaluation had more negative findings about the privately operated institution than about the state-operated facility, and (b) it was conducted by the ACA, whose correctional standards are being used by private corporations as an indicator of quality. One critic suggested that the cost comparison presented in the evaluation should have been interpreted differently; if the trend in cost during the first year of private operation would have continued, the Eckerd Foundation's goal of lowering the costs of running the facility by 5% would have become a reality. Illustrating this claim is the following statement:

> In 1981, Okeechobee's client/staff ratio (1.7) was higher than Dozier's (1.6). It is thus reasonable to assume that the state would have upgraded the staff at Okeechobee at least as much as it did Dozier, at a comparable percentage increase in cost. (Logan, 1990, p. 91)

Whether this assumption should make a difference is hard to determine, but it sounds somewhat speculative. This study has drawn a great deal of attention and has influenced authorities in Alabama not to privatize a secure state facility for juveniles because it was felt that the cost would increase rather than decrease under private operation (Hackett et al., 1987).

Proponents of privatization have contested some of the findings of this study and have tried to point out methodological shortcomings. Logan (1990) dedicated six pages in his book to criticizing this evaluation. The great effort to contradict the findings of an evaluation conducted by the ACA (an organization that is, by all means, not a foe of privatization) just because it does not support the claims of the proponents, may do more harm than bring benefits to the cause of privatization.

Problems of Evaluation

It is clear that there is a need for more empirical evaluations to assess the effects of the privatization of prisons. However, there are some questions concerning certain obstacles associated with privatization that may complicate the evaluation process. Durham (1988) mentions five major potential hazards in this context, some of which are probably more serious than others. These are (a) anticipating the future, (b) in-process monitoring, (c) the need for expertise, (d) evaluation versus monitoring, and (e) political urgency.

Anticipating the Future. Durham claims that evaluation designs are based on assumptions about what is going to happen during the evaluation period. However, it is hard to project forward in the case of private prisons because of the paucity of benchmark data. If the concern is only with the "anticipation of the future" during the evaluation itself, this concern seems to be overstated, as some aspects of evaluation can focus on short-term results to provide an immediate picture of cost, staff and inmate attitudes, programs, and so forth. These may be helpful in providing early feedback and in making changes, if needed. These efforts will have to be repeated to assess the continuous operation of the facility, but that is the case with other programs as well.

In-Process Monitoring. The problems of monitoring have been dealt with previously. In evaluations it is important to make sure that certain procedures are followed because otherwise the results will not be applicable for assessing the real quality and effectiveness of a program. Effective monitoring and evaluation will need ongoing data collection by the staff, which obviously costs money, and it may become problematic because it is unlikely that it will be a high priority for the contractor, and staff time will be allocated reluctantly, if at all. Either this task will have to be written into the contract and will have to be monitored for accuracy and objectivity, or it will have to be funded by the government and public employees will have to collect the in-process data of the prison's operation. Whichever option is going to be applied, the evaluation will add to the cost of facility operation.

The Need for Expertise. It is important that the evaluation be designed by independent researchers who do not have a vested interest either pro or con in the privatization debate and who are not paid by private companies. A government-sponsored report has pointed out that there is little evidence of the participation of experts in the design and monitoring of private prison evaluations (Council of State Governments and the Urban Institute, 1987). For the sake of objectivity, it should be stated that efforts to evaluate the operation of public prisons do not seem to be much more thorough or successful than the evaluation of private institutions. The major interest in conducting rigorous evaluations is the government's; interest because it is the one who pays the bills, and as seen, it has the final liability for corrections. Durham (1988) makes the point that

given the already extant common perception that private industry can
do the work of government cheaper, what incentive is there for private
companies to expend resources on evaluations that can at best merely
confirm popular perceptions and that can at worst cast doubt upon a
primary basis of private sector appeal. (p. 67)

This reflects on the sociopolitical climate of the 1980s. The private
sector was put on a pedestal; therefore positive evaluation results
would add only a small increment of prestige and benefits to the
contractors. Thus an evaluation may have only diminishing positive
returns for private companies, but it carries the risk of criticism, loss
of reputation, more government inquiries, more regulations, and
could cost more money.

Evaluation Versus Monitoring. Evaluation should not be confused
with monitoring. Monitoring is aimed at ensuring that the provisions
of the contract are followed by the private company, whereas evaluation is directed toward the outcomes of the operation. This difference is mainly one of process versus results. Budget allocations for
monitoring are often mistakenly thought of as having included impact evaluation; this point should be clarified and the budget should
include monies for evaluation.

Political Urgency. The political context in which the evaluation is
designed should be taken into consideration. The unprecedented
growth of inmate populations, the ensuing overcrowding in prisons
during the 1980s, and the high costs of prison construction and
operation have put strong public pressure on legislators and public
officials to devise and implement alternatives to traditional prisons
to alleviate the situation. One of the most attractive "solutions" to
these major problems is the entrance of the private sector into the
construction and operation of prisons. Once this decision is made,
there is pressure to pursue it vigorously. Thus there is no major public
and government interest in spending time to devise an elaborate
preprogram evaluation scheme that may delay construction and/or
operation of a facility by a private company. In a sociopolitical
context in which rapid solutions are needed, outcome evaluations are
too far away in the future. Authorities do not have the time nor the

willingness to wait months or even years to receive data about the performance of the privately operated institutions, especially when the reversal of the privatization policy may be problematic.

In sum, effective evaluation needs the cooperation of evaluators, private operators, and government officials to make sure that the required procedures are followed, in other words, that systematic data collection is undertaken, provisions to oversee the correctness of data are ensured, and easy access for evaluators are provided. As seen, private companies may not be interested in cooperating fully with these efforts, and government agencies under pressure to alleviate everyday correctional problems may put a low priority on pressuring the private companies on this issue. These concerns are not shared by everybody interested in privatization; for example, there are claims that the evaluation of private prisons is not much different from that of other prisons (e.g., Roberts & Powers, 1985). This opinion may reflect on the general problems of evaluation of correctional institutions, regardless of whether they are run by the government or by private companies.

Conclusion

Many issues involved in the evaluation of social programs are not directly connected with the content of the program itself. For instance, most attempts to solve social problems are political in nature; therefore many political considerations are built into them (e.g., Weiss, 1973). The basic fact is that evaluators need the cooperation of those whose programs are evaluated and who are very often not interested in, or even hostile to, the evaluation itself. Many program administrators, in the public as well as in the private sector, feel that independent evaluators are there to look for trouble in the programs, whereas the possible gains from a positive evaluation are limited. This may be even more so in the case of privately run programs (e.g., private prisons) in which substantial monetary interests are involved because there are potentially serious economic consequences of negative evaluation results. Thus, clearly, there are more risks for the private operators to lose than chances to gain from a rigorous evaluation and therefore it is plausible that they may have a negative attitude toward this process from its inception. If this is the case, then the likelihood for large-scale cooperation with the evaluators is not highly feasible. The objection may not be expressed openly, but obstacles can be placed in the path of the evaluators.

Generally, the existing evaluation studies seem to show a somewhat lower cost and higher quality of services in private facilities, although these findings, as seen, are not universal. Among the various problems of these studies, it was found that, first, there was a major interest in evaluating the Silverdale facility. The obvious question is why? What is the reason for the popularity of this facility for evaluators? Even taking into consideration that there are only a few available private facilities for research, the focus on one institution seems to be unusual. Is it possible that this facility is unique? Is it a showcase institution? Is the management particularly inviting for evaluators? Are the inmates selected on a particular basis? All these and other questions may be asked with regard to these comparative evaluations. The focus on this institution may create a halo effect that leads to generalizations from one facility to all private-sector corrections facilities. Second, some of the studies focused on facilities that were not mainline prisons, such as juvenile institutions, small facilities, facilities for special inmate populations (e.g., civil commitments), and so forth. Findings from these studies are not necessarily applicable for "regular" adult prisons. Third, in some cases the evaluators cannot be considered as more or less neutral researchers, but as active supporters (e.g., Logan, Brakel) or critics (e.g., Shichor) of prison privatization.

The U.S. General Accounting Office's conclusion that, so far, empirical studies in toto have not shown a clear advantage of private prisons over publicly operated prisons and, therefore, a clear-cut recommendation favoring them cannot be made (U.S. General Accounting Office, 1991) is well taken and speaks for itself.

Notes

1. Problems of validity focus on questions of *what* is being measured and whether we measure what we think we are measuring, whereas reliability focuses on the

consistency of answers, that is, whether a person will give the same answer on the same question at different times.

2. It is worthwhile to mention, without trying to arrive at far-reaching conclusions, that in private juvenile institutions the average stay in 1987 was 317 days, whereas in public institutions it was only 225 days. This is a 41% difference (Thornberry, Tolnay, Flanagan, & Glynn, 1991). Granting that some aspects of juvenile institutionalization are different than adult incarceration, still these figures indicate such a difference between the private and public sector that it should be investigated when prison privatization is seriously considered.

10

Further Considerations

Several issues should be given some further consideration in dealing with private prisons. One of them is corporate involvement in the financing, building, and operation of private prisons.

Corporate Involvement in Private Prisons

One of the unique features of the correctional privatization that picked up momentum during the 1980s is that it usually involves corporations whose stocks are publicly traded, meaning that their economic performance is constantly in sight of the stockholders and that they have to live up to the investors' expectations.

Many consider private corporations to be more efficient than government agencies because they are driven by the profit motive, thus they have a strong incentive to do better and to be more flexible and less encumbered by restrictions and bureaucratic procedures than the much maligned public sector. Thus it is almost taken for granted that the private sector will provide public services cheaper and better than public agencies do, and it will be more flexible and therefore easier to add services and answer new demands (Savas, 1982). Some advocates of privatization see the core of the problem in the monopoly that the public sector usually enjoys in the delivery of public services. One of them states:

> I advocate prudent privatization, not willy-nilly privatization. I have worked with many cities and governments in designing systems that will reap the benefits of competition and not simply trade government monopoly for a private one; I do not think the people will be served well under either monopoly. (Savas, 1985, p. 23)

Basic to this argument are the principles of the classical liberal economy focusing on the free enterprise system, free competition, and profit maximization. The major goal of corporations according to the classical model is the maximization of profit (e.g., Garsombke & Garsombke, 1987). Although there are claims that corporations seek a "satisfactory" level of profits rather than "maximization" of profits (e.g., Stone, 1975), the definition of what is satisfactory remains in the hands of the management who take into consideration the expectations of shareholders. Because corporations are formally rational, the congruence between their procedures and their substantive goals is closer than that of most other social groups (Sutton & Wild, 1978). This means that profit making can be rigorously and systematically pursued by private corporations. Chief executives may demand profitability from midlevel managers, who will sometimes violate rules or even laws to fulfill the profit goals set from above. Because of deliberate corporate decentralization of decision making, the top executives may avoid liability for wrongdoing (Hagan, 1994; Pearce & Tombs, 1992; Stone, 1975). In terms of corporate priorities, profitability tends to rank the highest, whereas public responsibility is much lower on the list (Conklin, 1977). This ranking sends a message to the firm's employees. The profit motive in corporate America became so prevalent that it was often used to justify questionable business practices, especially through the embracing and the promotion of the "caveat emptor" doctrine (Hamilton, 1931; Shichor, 1989).

One way that corporations can increase their profits is by limiting competition (see Vaughan, 1980). Although formally they support free markets and free competition, in reality large corporations tend to engage in various strategies to limit competition to reduce uncertainty in the marketplace (Sutherland, 1956; Thompson, 1967). In several major industries, such as car manufacturing, oil, airplanes, and defense, a handful of large corporations dominate the market. In this situation certain kinds of accommodations and market sharing among these companies are likely to develop (Moore, 1962). Thus symbiosis among corporations rather than a genuine competition becomes the reality (Blau & Scott, 1962). This development also may lead to antitrust violation and price fixing (Geis, 1967). There are indications of reduced competition in privatized public services as well (Starr, 1987). As seen, a survey of private corporations contracting for the management of prisons report that two major companies account for 50% of private prison contracts (Thomas & Foard, 1991). In an emerging field of enterprise, such as private corrections, the oligopolistic trend is even more problematic because a few dominant corporations may influence the standards for the evolving industry.[1]

The pursuance of profit by corporations has other ramifications as well. Managers, by setting performance standards often tied to income goals, can "indirectly [initiate] deviate actions by establishing particular norms, rewards, and punishments for people occupying lower level positions" (Ermann & Lundman, 1982, p. 7). In this way a crimogenic organizational atmosphere (Leonard & Weber, 1970) could develop, which in a private prison may be furthered by lower echelon employees, mainly guards who are dependent on the management because of lack of job security.

Corporate Involvement in Privatization: Political and Ethical Issues

There are also concerns regarding the political influence of corporations moving into the prison business. Large corporate interests are involved in lobbying (see Mayer, 1980) and often organize in political action committees (PACs) through which they can make substantial contributions to political candidates with the intent to influence legislation favorable to the PAC's contributors. Corporate America considers business PACs as a relatively new and effective instrument to influence the political process (Fraser/Associates, 1980).

It is feasible that correctional corporations will form their own PACs and/or will organize other lobbying efforts. The development of PACs since the 1970s has demonstrated the growing influence of corporations in America. A major aim of this political involvement has been the neutralization of "government regulation of business practices and to obtain government assistance for business activities" (Ryan, Swanson, & Buchholz, 1987, p. 105). Conceivably, private corrections PACs will seek to influence issues that are of importance to the industry. At the same time, they also may collaborate with other PACs to form a political force in contributing to "candidates whose ideology is perceived as compatible with free enterprise values and business positions on public policy issues" (Ryan et al., 1987, p. 119).[2] This kind of activity will confirm the contention that privatization of human services, including corrections, is basically a political act aimed at diminishing the social role of government (Kamerman & Kahn, 1989).

There are already indications of lobbying activities by private correctional interests. For example, in Texas when the legislation in 1987 was convened to deal with the surging prison population, and a bill was introduced to allow for contracting with private companies to ease the situation, "representatives from private corrections firms and financial institutions, as well as city and county officials besieged the capitol" (Ethridge & Marquart, 1993, p. 38).

Generally, corporate involvement in correctional privatization amplifies the political influence of the private sector on correctional policy making. Through political lobbying, PACs, campaign contributions, and the provision of perks to politicians (as industrial and business corporations do), corporations are likely to continue to support and even accelerate incapacitation-oriented legislation and policies by which more people will spend longer periods of time in correctional institutions. Conversely, this trend may diminish the emphasis on alternative programs and will result in the pursuance of the "Hilton Inn mentality," that is, trying to maintain high occupancy rates for profit purposes. As a rebuttal to these claims, Savas (1987) points out that prison officials and correctional officers' unions have similar reasons to lobby for higher levels of incarceration.

There is also a concern that by using their political clout, corporations will be able to "cream the crop," meaning that they will be able either (a) to handle inmates classified as lower security risks, allowing the firms to hire fewer custody personnel and operate without major disturbances thus avoiding adverse public reaction, and/or (b) to manage institutions with a specified clientele such as drug addicts or psychologically problematic offenders because higher profits can be made when specific services are provided. In this situation, the most violent inmates and career criminals would have to be handled by public institutions, whereas the private companies could be demonstrating a better performance record achieved by handling less problematic inmates on top of their greater profits.

There is also the problem of using legal procedures against correctional companies in disputes between the government and the contractor. Corporations can usually afford high-quality legal services, and their resources for long-term litigations may be greater than those of local governments.[3] They often have their own legal department or have lawyers on retainer. Also, the risk of penalties for corporate wrongdoings is minimized because, usually, the corporations are punished rather than the decisionmakers. In general, punishments are monetary and are not in proportion to the gains derived from the unlawful practices. Because of the uniqueness of the "correctional marketplace," adverse publicity, which is suggested as an important option for corporate punishment (Fisse, 1985), will be minimized as a deterrent because the market is restricted to government agencies.

The fact that corporations may violate legal or moral codes is underscored by the extensive professional literature on corporate ethics (e.g., Anderson, 1989; Bradshaw & Vogel, 1981; Donaldson, 1982). It is recognized that large corporations often do not act according to the highest moral and ethical standards or even according to the letter of the law. This reality can be particularly disturbing in the provision of human services when the recipients of these services are politically powerless and do not command much public concern (see Shichor, 1993).

The credibility of corporations was hurt especially after the savings and loan crisis, the bankruptcy of large insurance companies (e.g., Executive Life), banking scandals (e.g., BBI), the cost overruns on government contracts, and corruption of inspectors and contract monitors. Regarding corrections in the early 1980s, E. F. Hutton, a major brokerage firm, intended to move into the private prison market. Meanwhile, this company was found to be using about $10 billion of clients' money without interest through check kiting, and it had to pay $2 million in fines. Shortly after, E. F. Hutton merged with another brokerage firm, Shearson and Lehman, which was connected with American Express. These possibilities underline not only the problem of stability and continuity of private enterprise in the correctional business but also raises questions concerning the ethical principles and modus operandi of corporations that want a piece of the human services business. Sagarin and Maghan (1985) commented on the E. F. Hutton case: "It is only an added irony that E. F. Hutton itself became involved in one of the largest white collar frauds in American history. Is this the company to which we are going to turn over the prisons?" (p. E4).

"The Criminal Justice-Industrial Complex"

Corporate involvement in crime control is seen by some as part of the evolving "criminal justice-industrial complex's" interference with the state's functioning (Maghan, 1991; Quinney, 1977). It is similar to the emergence of the "social-industrial complex" (O'Connor, 1973), which is basically an involvement of the private industry in "the planning, production and operation of state programs" (Quinney, 1977, p. 117).[4] Recently, it was argued that there is a criminal justice-industrial complex that has an interest in the continuation of high incarceration rates. The suggested participants of this complex are (a) private corporations that profit from imprisonment policies, (b) government agencies that formulate criminal justice policies, and (c) professional organizations involved in corrections (Lilly & Knepper, 1992). According to Sparks (1994):

> Many of the companies most keenly interested in prison privatization
> are defence contractors experiencing a "negative peace dividend," whose
> lobbying skills and ties to government are already strong and whom
> governments may experience a strong political pressure to assist. (p. 25)

It is claimed that the criminal justice-industrial complex is responsible to a large degree for U.S. correctional policy. The major characteristics of this complex are identified in the following:

(I) The participants in the corrections subgovernment share a close working relationship supported by the flow of information, influence, and money. (II) There is a distinct overlap between the interests of for-profit companies, professional organizations, and the interests of Federal agencies that is maintained by the flow of influence and personnel. (III) The corrections-commercial complex operates without public scrutiny and exercises enormous influence over corrections policy. (IV) This complex shows signs of becoming a fixture within the national policy area of punishing lawbreakers; the participants define their activities as being in the public interest. (Lilly & Knepper, 1992, p. 175)

This complex is becoming international and multinational; a few countries already have privately operated facilities, and several others are interested in establishing private prisons (e.g., the United Kingdom, Australia, New Zealand, and Canada). Some of these facilities are run by the same companies that operate in the United States. They enter into joint ventures in which corporations from different countries cooperate to further the business of corrections. For example, foreign business groups invested in CCA stocks, CCA joined a British consortium to build and manage prisons in Britain, and so on. This international business activity does not focus only on the prison "market," in fact, it is only a relatively small portion of it. There is major activity in electronic monitoring; many companies in this field are defense contractors who can supply the sophisticated electronic surveillance systems, that were developed for military purposes, for monitoring offenders. The same companies are also likely to enter the facility building market, where they can use their surveillance systems and communication equipment (Lilly & Knepper, 1992). They need to expand continuously to survive (Christie, 1993), and there is a good probability that they will use their political influence to increase and expand social control policies.

Private security firms that have already made inroads into the prisoner transportation and escort business will continue to penetrate this industry, and in the past few years some probation departments in the United States started to privatize as well. The major professional organization dealing with corrections, the ACA, is heavily influenced by the private correctional industry. Its catalogue and its professional journal *Corrections Today* carry hundreds of advertisements of companies producing correctional equipment and offering various correctional services. ACA conventions have many correctional industry exhibitors; some of them sponsor cocktail parties and lavish receptions for the attending correctional professionals (Sechrest, 1992b). It seems that there are strong financial connections between the ACA and the criminal justice-industrial complex.

The ties between private industry and the ACA may have something to do with the accreditation process in corrections as the correctional standards were written by ACA personnel. Accreditation of correctional institutions is supposed to be a step toward improving prison conditions by following the development of operational standards with an external evaluation process (Sechrest, 1976). Critics claim that the standards are not stringent enough and therefore the accreditation process has lost credibility (Gettinger, 1982). Another problem is that "reviews occur infrequently, and certification documents compliance with standards for only a brief period" (Keating, 1990, p. 147).

As seen, private correctional corporations use ACA accreditation as a vehicle to gain credibility and legitimation. For example, CCA emphasizes that several of its facilities already have received accreditation and the others are preparing to apply for it. The close connection between the ACA and the private correctional industry does raise questions regarding the influence of this industry on the standards. The fact that the ACA president from 1984 to 1986, T. Don Hutto (former commissioner of corrections in Arkansas and Virginia), was a cofounder of CCA just prior to his presidency of ACA reinforces the impression that a powerful and influential criminal justice-industrial complex, having strong interlocking directories, is developing. This kind of interrelationship may lead to co-optation, a concept that refers to "a firm's appointment of an outside director who is employed by a vertically interdependent organization. By creating the appearance of shared decision making, the focal organization neutralizes the firms it has coopted" (Pennings, 1980, p. 23).

To what extent this criminal justice-industrial complex will try to succeed to co-opt government officials and the leadership of professional organizations that have influence on correctional policies is not clear, but the possibilities do exist. A vivid example of this possibility was revealed in 1985 when CCA bid for the management of Tennessee's entire prison system for the next 99 years. Among the stockholders of CCA were Governor Alexander's wife and the Speaker of the House of Tennessee, who at the time was a leading candidate for governor. They sold their shares in the company to avoid conflict of interest. However, other major political figures remained involved with CCA; the state insurance commissioner was a stockholder and CCA president Tom Beasley was a former head of the state Republican party and had close ties to the Alexander administration (Vise, 1985). Similarly, two Hamilton County, Tennessee commissioners who voted to renew the CCA contract of operating the country workhouse in 1986 had private business contracts with CCA (Morgan, 1986). Although some supporters of privatization view the involvement of prominent state figures in CCA as an enhancement of the firm's credibility (Folz & Scheb, 1989), the privatization trend opens up ample possibilities for the emergence of conflict of interest problems and increases the possibilities for corruption. In general, governmental contracting is vulnerable to corruption (Benenson, 1985).

Public Sector-Private Sector Comparisons

There was already a discussion earlier in this book about the public and private sectors. Here new angles and a more focused summary of this issue are presented.

In any analysis of the advantages and disadvantages of private sector involvement in the provision of human services such as welfare, elderly care (Mendelson, 1974) and corrections, there is a need to consider what the major problems are with public sector operations. Why can they so easily be criticized and targeted for privatization? Is it only because there is a generally negative public attitude toward the public sector and civil service, or are these criticisms more substantive and well based?

At least partially, the American tradition that favors independence, small government, and free competition furthers a negative attitude toward the public sector and a generally favorable opinion toward the private sector. Public administration, which did not have a strong following in the United States to start with, came under strong attack during the Reagan administration (see Lane & Wolf, 1990). There is

a widely held opinion that private sector management is more efficient than public sector management (Chandler, 1986) and that
private sector workers work harder, are more efficient, and do a better
quality job than public sector workers do.

There are several differences between the private and public sectors in general that may buttress the negative attitudes toward the
public sector.

1. The private sector is profit oriented; therefore it tends to hire
only people who are needed and productive. Those who do not
perform satisfactorily may be fired. Similarly, changes in the economy or technology may lead to large-scale layoffs. The public sector
lacks the profit incentive to keep personnel costs down. Government
agencies are often seen as the natural source of employment for those
who are not employable by the private sector; they are considered to
be the providers of vocational training for these groups (Johnson &
Ross, 1990). The use of seniority for promotion in civil service may
lead to mediocrity. There are few monetary rewards for achievement.
All these lead to a lack of incentives to improve services (Chandler,
1986).[5]

2. The private sector is competitive; the public sector tends to operate
as a monopoly. Competitiveness presses corporations to be cost
conscious. Public services that are monopolies have a "captive audi-
ence"; they don't have to worry about the clients going to another
firm. Governments usually can raise taxes or borrow money if their
operating cost increases (Chandler, 1986). Private firms are limited
in their ability to borrow.

3. The public sector is labor intensive, using many people for its
work, whereas the private sector tries to use more technology and is
quicker to adopt new inventions and new administrative practices.

4. There are higher expectations of ethical standards from public
than from private sector workers. Public workers who provide service
to the citizenry are expected to be ethical, whereas private employees'
actions may be seen as a business practice and are judged accordingly.[6] One reason for these different patterns of expectations is that
public sector employees, especially those who wear uniforms, represent and symbolize the government. The public feels that these

workers are in its employ; therefore they have to be ethical and loyal to the citizens whom they are supposed to serve.[7] In addition, public workers' activities are generally more visible than those of private sector employees; public records tend to be open (excluding security-related documents), whereas private records are usually closed. Because of that, mistakes and misdeeds of the public sector get into the open much more easily than those of the private sector.

5. Managers in the private sector usually have greater freedom in personnel matters than public managers do. It is harder to hire and fire people in the public sector, where workers are usually unionized. These factors tie the hands of public management in attempting to get rid of ineffective, unproductive, and often even rule-violating employees.[8] However, this generalization should not be overdrawn. Some public employees do not have job protection; on the other hand, there is increasing concern with job protection in the private sector, for example, there are now laws against age, sex, and racial discrimination. Furthermore, public employees are restricted in their political activities, are subject to a code of ethics and residency requirements, are restricted in certain associations and in ownership of certain interests, and some of them have dress codes and uniforms (Chandler, 1986).

6. Authority is more structured in the private than in the public sector. In a corporation it is clear who the boss is. In government organizations, authority may be more dispersed. Employees may be held responsible both to their superiors and to the legislature. There may be a conflict when public employees have to follow a policy that is opposed by the political leadership. This may become especially problematic for public administrators if they are political appointees—which is often the case in the higher echelons of state departments of corrections and the wardenship of some prisons. Somewhat similar problems may emerge in private correctional facilities when the manager may have a problem with following legal guidelines, codes of professional ethics, company directives, and the instructions of on-site government monitors.

7. The leaders of the executive branch of government are politicians or political appointees having relatively short tenures; the top executives in the private sector are more experienced managers.[9]

8. Private sector personnel usually have a single purpose to serve, whereas public sector workers may serve multiple purposes. Private employees work for their companies to generate profit; that is their primary responsibility. Government employment may be used to reduce unemployment, to stimulate economy by increasing consumer spending, to reward political supporters, or to disguise unemployment.

According to this analysis, it seems that efficiency is not a major variable in the measurement of public sector job performance. This contributes to the general perception that the private sector is superior to the public sector in personnel administration. The term *bureaucrat* became a watchword that represented society's negative attitude toward public sector employees. Even though there is some research available that refutes the "inferiority" of public sector employees (e.g., Goodsell, 1983), it is not able to debunk the "myth of private sector superiority" (Chandler, 1986).

Another public-private divergence pertains to the budgeting practices that were mentioned earlier. Public agencies tend to be budget driven, that is, their administrators are rewarded according to the size of their budget rather than for efficiency.[10] Private corporations are based on profit-and-loss incentives (Drucker, 1973; Logan, 1990).

The claim that the availability of the privatization option puts pressure on public agencies to perform better because it provides competition and breaks their monopoly may be valid to a degree. Osborne and Gaebler (1992) show that public agencies in several service areas may compete successfully with private companies. Thus in some cases the introduction of competition can improve public services. It would certainly be worthwhile to explore this proposition in more detail. The fact that public human service organizations do not lend themselves easily to privatization because of their organizational goals, incentive structure, raw materials (human beings) that interact with the production process, intangible services, and so on has to be given serious consideration (Hasenfeld, 1983; Schiflett & Zey, 1990). There also should be more emphasis on finding ways to improve public management and services to perform better and to project a more favorable image, but to change the American ethos of a negative attitude toward government agencies and their employees may prove to be a difficult undertaking. In the public's eyes, civil service employment is often associated with jobs that were artificially created for people who could not find regular employment. This perception is related to the New Deal strategy, which attempted to fight poverty by creating "public service" jobs for the unemployed to put them to work on various government projects (Dye, 1978). Opponents of public service job programs have argued that the government should seek to create productive employment in the private sector rather than generate "make work" government jobs. However, it is often forgotten that the government is expected to take care of those who cannot find employment. The critics also fail to mention that during the 1980s and early 1990s the private sector in the United States created more low-paying service jobs than economically productive ones, while hundreds of thousands of manufacturing jobs were eliminated.

Because large segments of the public view government jobs as inefficient, often unneeded, and camouflage for "hidden unemployment," these jobs are seen as wasteful. In addition, critics point to the fringe benefits, especially pension programs of public employees, as excessive. Critics resent the job security of these employees, which, according to them, promotes ineffectiveness and idleness among workers who know that it is hard to fire them. Also, public employees' unions are seen as too influential in trying to maintain the status quo, contributing to the lack of efficiency by featherbedding and by opposing measures aimed at increasing productivity and cost cutting. On the other hand, public employees and their organizations are aware of the negative attitudes toward them and are suspicious of any new ideas or suggestions aimed at altering their work routine or working conditions, and they fight any changes.

To what degree these negative perceptions are valid is hard to tell. The question of how to motivate workers who have very few positive incentives for good performance and do not have to worry about losing their jobs is a relevant and important problem. It seems that in spite of the new attempts, until now it has been hard for the public sector to find meaningful incentives that would lead to better performance by public employees. This may be even harder in the violent and hostile atmosphere of prisons.

The Public Image of Prisons

Publicly administered prisons often show a poor record, in terms of violence, riots, waste, and in some cases even abuse of prisoners. Along with the lure of cost savings, this record contributes greatly to the public's readiness to support private prisons.

It should be recognized that prisons have a difficult job to do. They deal with hostile and often violent inmates, most of whom have long histories of involvement with the juvenile and adult criminal justice systems. Since the 1960s this population has included an increasingly large percentage of minorities (Carroll, 1988). This development amplified prison problems by the infusion of ethnic and racial strifes. This situation was exacerbated by the emergence of violent prison gangs in the correctional systems of several states, such as Illinois, Texas, and California (e.g., Camp & Camp, 1985; Davidson, 1974; Jacobs, 1977). These gangs are based on racial, ethnic, and geographic lines and vie for control over the inmate population and the prison trade. Some of them, such as the Mexican Mafia and the Aryan Brotherhood, also have extensive organizations outside the prison that are involved in criminal activities such as the drug trade, extortion, and racketeering. Gang confrontations in the institutions add a great deal of anxiety to the already violent atmosphere of prison life. The situation became even more critical during the 1980s when the unprecedented increase in the prison population that led to overcrowding also resulted in growing levels of violence and tension and contributed to the decline of rehabilitation programs. Often, the public image of prison administrators and prison personnel became negative; they were seen as inept, abusive, wasteful, and even overpaid. Some of the inherent problems of the correctional staff are built into the organizational nature of prisons themselves. Prisons are total organizations in which all aspects of life are conducted in the same place and under the same single authority; inmates' activities are carried on in the immediate company of a large group of other prisoners; the activities are tightly scheduled, with one activity leading into the next; and they are imposed from above by officials. The contents of the various activities are brought together into a single rational plan purportedly designed to fulfill the official aims of the institution (Goffman, 1961).

Some additional features of prisons also have an impact on the relationship between prisoners and their guards. First is the existence of a clear-cut division between employees and inmates, that is, the lowest level worker is in a superior status above all inmates. Second, prison is a coercive organization, that is, the compliance with organizational rules is maintained by coercive methods (Etzioni, 1961). It is also known that the performance of prisons to a large degree depends on the maintenance of satisfactory relationships and a degree of cooperation between its clients and its staff (e.g., Montilla, 1978). This situation often leads to the "corruption of authority" in which prison staff have to compromise with the inmates to maintain order in the prison (Sykes, 1958).

The dependence on the clients for maintaining performance standards and the simultaneous reliance on coercive compliance create many potential conflicts between the staff and the inmates. Sociological studies of maximum-security institutions have demonstrated a generally hostile relationship between inmates and staff and the oppositional/negative nature of the relationship between the prison subculture and the prison administration (e.g., Clemmer, 1958; Schrag, 1961; Sykes & Messinger, 1960). The high rate of returning prisoners does not indicate that prisons are successful either in deterring further crime or in rehabilitating convicted offenders. Publicity about prisons tends to be negative because it usually appears in the headlines only when something goes wrong, such as a violent outbreak, hostage taking, corruption, claims of staff brutality, or use of deadly force. The negative image of prison staff is reinforced by the low educational and skill levels required for staff positions and the generally low social status accorded to this occupation. Conrad (1984) captured this situation when he claimed that the constituency for corrections is narrow and seldom influential.

Often, the problems of inefficient management, violence, lack of rehabilitation, physical deterioration, poorly prepared food, and guards that do not handle prisoners well in overcrowded facilities, coupled with increasing costs, give a general picture of lack of order, waste, brutality, and mismanagement of public prisons. Facing these perceptions and images, the public reaction is often that "the situation cannot become worse," "let's try something else, we don't have anything to lose." These attitudes provide fertile ground for the promoters of private prisons who, besides emphasizing cost cutting, promise to create better quality prisons. No doubt that the major selling point is the promise of lower cost to the taxpayers because only a small segment of the public is really concerned with what is going on in the prisons; the negative image of public agencies and public employees also contributes to the readiness to support private prisons.

Changing Criminal Justice and Corrections

The privatization debate in a sense diverts attention from the need for the development of viable crime prevention policies. It continues to deal with the symptoms and not with the causes of crime. And it impedes the development of alternatives to the prevailing punishment policies.

Surprisingly little attention is being paid to the failure of criminal justice policies of the 1980s and early 1990s. The simple fact is that in spite of the tremendous increase in criminal justice expenditures and the unprecedented growth of the prison population, crime rates did not show any major change as a result of the "get tough" approach. The fear of crime did not dissipate, and the large majority of Americans are still afraid to walk their cities' streets after dark and in many cities even during daylight. America remains the most violent modern society and has overtaken South Africa and the Soviet Union (before its breakup) as the country with the highest incarceration rate in the Western world.[11] The United States, which carries the banner of freedom all over the world, cannot provide the basic freedom for its citizens to walk, and lately even to drive, the streets of its cities and to be free from the omnipresent fear of crime. The failure of criminal justice policies ranks with the savings and loan debacle and the Iran-Contra affair in its magnitude and inaptitude. Relating to this failure, Reiman (1979) raised the question some time ago:

> How are we to comprehend this monstrous failure? It appears that our government is failing to fulfill the most fundamental task of governance: keeping our streets and homes safe, ensuring us of what the Founding Fathers called "domestic tranquility," providing us with the minimal

requirement of civilized society. . . . How are we to understand this
failure? (p. 13)

Similarly, Garland (1990), referring to the British scene, found contemporary punishment policies to be "irrational," "dysfunctional,"
and counterproductive.

The privatization policy continues to promote the failed crime
control approach of the preceding years. It subscribes to the idea that
incarceration can win the "war" against crime (Rogers, 1989) and that
the major task is to make this policy cheaper and more flexible. As
seen, this policy helps to expand the net of social control (Feeley,
1991) and to increase the number of people under direct surveillance.

No doubt that there is a need for measures to protect society, for
example, by police protection and various means of crime prevention
such as "target hardening" (making physical or technical changes that
discourage crime such as better lighting in parking lots), alarm
systems, and so on. But these policies are for the short run. For the
long run, however, there is also a need to learn about causal factors
that contribute to the high crime rates and are embedded in the social
fabric of American society and culture (see, e.g., Messner & Rosenfeld,
1994). Some of these probably can be addressed through social
policies and programs, an area that was neglected during the 1980s.
The causal factors may be related to many facets of social life in a
complex society, such as the opportunity structure, the welfare
system, the educational system, socioeconomic inequality, political
patronage, immigration policies, urban policies, gun control policies,
employment policies, housing policies, health care, child care, fed-
eral-state relations, work relations, race relations, community relations, family relations, and to cultural factors such as the prolifera-
tion of guns, media violence, and many others. Granted, social and
cultural factors are very hard to change, take a long time, and can be
bogged down in a political system that includes thousands of interest
groups, but some changes, at least, have to be attempted. The belief
that the public good can be achieved best by every individual pursuing his or her personal interest, while the government regulates the
individual pursuance of happiness with the invisible hand in a way
that hundreds of millions of people's interests will not seriously
collide, seems to be utopian. The attitude prevalent in the 1980s—

that the government does not solve problems but is the problem itself—did not work very well and furthered individual and social excesses, such as the social climate of greed, Wall Street scandals, junk bond financing of takeovers, and the savings and loan debacle costing hundreds of billions of dollars, and it contributed to the increase of the national debt to $4 trillion. This approach made the United States the largest international debtor, and it led to an economic recession unparalleled since the Great Depression. It also resulted in millions of unemployed, hundreds of thousands of homeless, and in the highest bankruptcy rate of individuals and businesses. There was also a contradiction in the invisible hand policy of government control because of the great increase of government intervention in areas that served the ideological and political interests of a conservative administration, such as reproductive choice, sex education, and so forth. The 1992 election results were to a large part the repudiation of these policies and a search for major changes in social policies and in the social climate.

As a part of these changes, probably, we can try to devise some neoprogressive crime control and penal approaches. The progressive movement at the beginning of the 20th century saw crime as a predominantly urban problem and tried to improve ghetto conditions such as public health, landlord-tenant laws, public housing, and criminal justice procedures—including individualized justice, probation, indeterminate sentencing, and rehabilitation (Clear & Cole, 1990). "The mood of progressivism was a sense that American institutions had to be changed to adapt to the demands of a growing urban-industrial society" (Walker, 1980, p. 127). It was also an expression of optimism in the vitality of American society in overcoming these problems. The crime control policies of the 1970s and 1980s, on the other hand, reflected what Empey (1982) called a "brutal pessimism," that people are inherently wicked and the only way to deal with them is to try to restrain them.

The neoconservative trend in criminology has replaced the liberal optimism of the 1950s and 1960s, which believed that progress will prevail and that people can be changed for the better (see Shichor, 1992b). This "new" approach put the emphasis on certain aspects of individual offenders such as their biological and psychological characteristics, including intellectual ability (e.g., Wilson & Herrnstein,

1985), and their self-seeking decision to commit crimes (e.g., Cornish & Clarke, 1986; Gottfredson & Hirschi, 1990). Simultaneously, the attention on social arrangements and conditions in the causal analysis of crime was reduced. Also, more liberal individual aspects, such as rehabilitation, were largely abandoned.

For meaningful changes to occur, there is a need to alter theoretical as well as practical approaches to crime policies and corrections. The adoption of a neoprogressive perspective with the modifications needed for the 1990s and for the 21st century could possibly be the guiding principle for changes in crime policy and would probably preclude, among many others, the continued flirtation with punishment administered by for-profit corporations. Braithwaite's (1989b) observation is relevant in this vein: "A culture impregnated with high moral expectations of its citizens, publicly expressed, will deliver superior crime control compared with a culture which sees control as achievable by inflicting pain on its bad apples" (p. 10). The idea of the privatization of prisons diverts the attention and creative thinking in the United States, Britain, and other Western countries from seeking alternatives to large-scale incarceration, a focus that many believe should be taken (e.g., Porter, 1990; Vass, 1990).

On the other hand, no one would seriously argue that there is not a need to make substantial changes in the operation of public prisons. As mentioned, in general, public prisons and public correctional personnel cannot be seen as very efficient and successful in providing a safe and humane prison environment.[12] Correspondingly, their image in the public is far from positive. Although the generally negative American attitude toward public institutions and their employees undoubtedly contributes to this unflattering image, at least some part of it is well earned by the institutions, by their management, and by their staff. Improvements of management and operations are badly needed not only in the prisons but also in the departments of corrections themselves. Also, the cooperation of employee unions will be crucial to make sure that a correctional job will not be the last resort of workers who cannot find or cannot hold a position in the private sector. Over the long run these changes will enhance the public image of correctional workers.

There are signs that many public executives and political leaders recognize that government policies and practices have to be drastically changed to create more efficient operations and to provide better quality services. It seems to be clear that when reinventing government, we need to be able to tackle the problems of a complex, highly technological, multicultural society (Osborne & Gaebler, 1992) and to improve the image of the public sector.

Recently, Governor Pete Wilson of California, the very same conservative politician who promoted the three-strikes law for felons and the one-strike law for sex offenders, espoused this approach and proposed changes in public management that may have implications for corrections as well (Weintraub, 1993). One of the major features of this proposal is the decentralization of administration. Administrators would receive a free hand to run their departments with only minimal interference from legislators and top officials, and they would be held more accountable for their performance than they currently are. How this proposal would be operationalized in corrections is not yet clear because, characteristically, the emphasis on the economic issues of administration prevails. Nevertheless, these changes may prove to be applicable for the operation of prisons. One major innovation would be the introduction of new ways of budgeting for government agencies, away from "rule-driven" budgeting, which requires agencies to justify every element in their budget every year. This system discourages innovation, maintains obsolete programs, lacks flexibility, and encourages waste because if the budgeting money is not spent by the end of the fiscal year, the agency loses the saved money and will get less for the next year (e.g., Osborne & Gaebler, 1992). The new ideas include, for example, the introduction of "mission-driven" budgets, which free the agencies from the strict rules of itemized expenditures and allow them to spend the money according to their needs and to keep savings for later expenditures.[13] Osborne and Gaebler (1992) also suggest "results-oriented" budgeting, according to which an agency is allocated money for its performance, and "customer-driven" budgeting, which puts the money into the customers' hands and forces the service providers to earn their money by pleasing their customers. It is not clear how these later forms of budgeting would be used in public corrections, but they are certainly worth a review because it is obvious that correctional agencies and institutions need to introduce major changes to improve their operation, to reduce violence, to hire better trained and qualified personnel, to reduce waste, and to become more flexible.

All these do not mean that, so far, public bureaucracies are completely stagnant and no changes are taking place in their operations; however, further more concentrated efforts are needed.

Attempts at Change in Public Agencies

The fact that there are attempts to increase personal performance through furthering the "culture of self-interest" (Lane & Wolf, 1990, p. 106) among public service workers has received relatively little attention in the public. These attempts were adopted from the private sector and were based on the idea that "people work most effectively when there is a reasonable balance of effort and rewards. This concept requires explicit performance criteria, to which people will respond, given an appropriate set of incentives" (Lane & Wolf, 1990, p. 107).

This trend resulted in the adoption of the management by objectives (MBO) system, performance evaluations, and even merit pay. These methods, although fitting the business world—the amount of sales by salesmen and departments or production by divisions can be easily quantified and measured—were more difficult and less successful when applied to the public sector.

However, Osborne and Gaebler (1992) do report more recent and more successful attempts for running a "results-oriented government." They especially focus on the total quality management (TQM) method:

> Total Quality Management stands the traditional organizational chart on its head: it says that the customers are the most important people for an organization; those who serve customers directly are next; and management is there to serve those who serve customers. (Osborne & Gaebler, 1992, p. 172)

They cite some encouraging examples in which, according to customer-based information (surveys, follow-ups, etc.), there was a higher level customer (i.e., taxpayer) satisfaction achieved than before.[14] However, they have not mentioned experiences with prisons and prison management. There are obvious problems with this kind of model because of the organizational characteristics of prisons and the problems of defining who is the customer in a prison.

Measurement of individual performance in prisons is hard to define because of the multiple functions of prisons and because a large number of prison employees are correctional officers (guards), a task that does not lend itself to easy evaluation, especially by the "customers." This problem is felt less in private prisons because performance in some instances can be measured by economic standards, that is, by profit making, cost cutting, and money savings, although the economic standard is less applicable for individual guards.

A continuous effort to introduce new and more effective methods of operation and more flexibility (lessening bureaucracy) into public corrections with the cooperation of the unions would help greatly to alleviate some, but by no means all, the problems of public prisons.

Some Final Thoughts

As was claimed earlier, punishment—the deliberate infliction of pain and suffering by representatives of society in the name of society—is a moral issue. It involves values and judgments concerning what is right and what is wrong. Judgments made regarding punishment and related issues also are influenced by ideological orientations. In the debate about privatization the main bulk of arguments and justifications have been utilitarian and pragmatic.

The pragmatic approach is well presented in the following:

> The very difficult set of social policy issues raised by the privatization debate ought to be resolved by moving in whichever direction has a reasonable likelihood of yielding the more efficient and effective means of improving the quality of correctional services. . . . To favor traditional means of providing correctional services merely as a consequence of habit or from a preference for symbolic representations of the power of the State is just as absurd as to favor privatization merely because of some abstract value one might impute to profit motives. The option to be favored is the option that proves its ability to get done the job at hand. That option is not necessarily the option which wears a department of corrections badge on its state-issued shirt. (Thomas & Hanson, 1989, p. 962)

The overemphasis on pragmatic considerations in this debate and the brushing off of moral and theoretical considerations is disturbing. But as it was shown throughout this book, even on the pragmatic level, private prisons do not show sufficient major advantages to outweigh the concerns that they may raise.

The few empirical evaluation studies, which have their own research problems, do not show substantial economic savings. Even McDonald (1994), who writes extensively about prison expenditures and seems to be favorable toward privatization, states that

> further experience with private imprisonment services and systematic studies of those experiences will probably show that there is no inherent superiority of contracting, in terms of cost-effectiveness, but that certain privately operated facilities may be more cost-effective than the available public alternatives. (p. 41)

Also, studies concerning the quality of services are not showing an overwhelming superiority of privatized prisons in comparison with public prisons. The greatest potential advantage of private involvement is in the financing and building of prisons, which can help to ease overcrowding. This issue probably will be even more pressing with the three-strikes penal policies spreading all over the United States. These policies also will increase the demand for more private prisons, which because of the supply and demand situation, may become more entrenched and probably more expensive. Thus, although the privatization of prisons may show some benefits in economic terms, it also may pose some considerable problems, including, among others, government dependence on private corporations for prison services, increased opportunities for conflict of interest and corruption, the maintenance of efficient and cost-effective monitoring, legal and economic liabilities for the government, creaming, lowballing, and dealing with showcase operations.

Philosophical, Moral, and Ethical Considerations

Justification of private prisons based on the libertarian sociopolitical philosophy as it is forwarded by Logan in the last chapter of *Private Prisons: Cons and Pros* (1990) is at least grounded on principles,

rather than on the pragmatic, mainly economic and operational arguments that dominate the discourse on this issue. Although I disagree
with the libertarian approach to government and authority, I do
believe that it is important to take philosophical, ethical, and moral
considerations into account when penal policies are determined.

I have tried to deal with most of the issues concerning the privatization of prisons in this book, but here in the concluding chapter I
would like to concentrate on a few focal points of criticism that were
mentioned in the previous elaborations.

Punishment is the consequence of the violation of criminal law;
generally the violation is considered to be against the state. It is an
accepted principle in every modern society that punishment should
be inflicted by a state authority (e.g., Murphy & Coleman, 1984).
Punishment is a state function par excellence, therefore it is questionable whether it should be administered by a private entity. This
issue is rooted in the fundamental question of what type of state or
government authority should be delegated and to what extent. There
is already a great deal of private intrusion into the penal process—private entrepreneurs such as bailbondsmen may determine who will be
detained in jail and who will be released after arrest; often private
entrepreneurs and companies prepare probation reports (e.g., Greenwood & Turner, 1993; Kulis, 1983); an increasing number of private
organizations operate juvenile institutions; private corporations run
many community-based programs; electronic surveillance is often
carried out by private firms; private vendors provide a host of services
such as food, health, education, and laundry in many prisons; and as
the main topic of this book indicates, there are a growing number of
attempts for the privatization of entire prison operations. Where
should the line be drawn in penal privatization? How far can the
"steering-rowing" allegory be stretched?[15] Many who object to prison
privatization, including myself, claim that the operation of entire
prisons that handle the most serious offenders should not be delegated to private entities. This opinion was reinforced in the analysis
of the Federal Bureau of Prisons (BOP) experience with privatization.
It was found that private companies operated mainly community-
based facilities and juvenile institutions. Bronick (1989) arrives at the
conclusion that "it is arguable whether the flexibility gain and cost
benefits identified in this paper would extend also to contractual

management of more 'mainstream' facilities" (p. 26). He describes the inmates who could be served in private confinement facilities: "It is those subpopulations that do not require stringent security or elaborate programs, such as geriatric and nonambulatory inmates, short-term deportable aliens, and some short-term minimum security sentenced offenders" (Bronick, 1989, p. 26).

This conclusion supports the claim of some critics that private companies will cream the crop and will deal with offenders who are easier to manage rather than with "the real McCoy."

A related issue that was also mentioned earlier is concerned with the symbolism involved in punishment and its relevance to privatization. The ABA's (1986) report states that "when it enters a judgment of conviction and imposes a sentence a court exercises its authority, both actually and symbolically" (p. 12). The report continues and poses a question:

> Does it weaken that authority, however—as well as the integrity of a system of justice—when an inmate looks at his keeper's uniform and, instead of encountering an emblem that reads "Federal Bureau of Prisons" or "State Department of Corrections" he faces one that says: "Acme Corrections Company"? (American Bar Association, 1986, p. 12)

DiIulio (1990b) reinforces the importance of symbolism in criminal justice. He points out in his review of Logan's (1990) book that the traditional symbolism of the Anglo-American criminal justice agencies, such as uniforms, badges, robes of the judge, and the state patch on the correctional officer's uniform, emphasizes the idea that criminal justice is an inherently public function. This point of view is expressed succinctly by McClintock (1980):

> The prison service is part of the State bureaucracy and the prison staff, as servants of the State, exercise power in a highly concentrated and intimate form over those citizens who have forfeited their liberty so as to become citizens. The executive side of imprisonment consequently plays a part in the very important balance between freedom and authority, which is fundamental to modern societies. Prison affairs are therefore part of the political process and cannot be divorced from the theory of State. (p. 127)

DiIulio (1990b) illustrates the argument concerning the meaning of symbolism in criminal justice by a hypothetical scenario in which a

Medal of Honor is being awarded to a citizen for his contribution to society, and the elaborate ceremony is organized by a private company that can do it cheaper and more effectively than a government agency. Would it make a difference if the award presenter would have on his lapel a pin indicating that he is an employee of a private company rather than a government official? Very likely it would. Nalla and Newman (1990), in their book on private security, show that citizens relate differently to private security personnel than they do to police officers. They indicate one of the major differences in the following: "Public police in general and in theory are visible and accountable to the public for their actions. Records must be open to public scrutiny. . . . Private police are not accountable and open to public scrutiny" (Nalla & Newman, 1990, p. 39).

Advocates of privatization claim that inmates could not care less about this symbolism (e.g., Logan, 1990), they care only about decent living conditions in a relatively secure environment. Nevertheless, symbols do represent concepts and ideas. There are some who see in symbols the basis of human behavior and in the use of symbols the source of all civilizations (e.g., White, 1949). Parsons (1951) claims that symbolization is "the necessary condition for the emergence of culture" (p. 10). Symbols express and influence collective meanings and social reality (Gurvitch, 1942). The swastika in Nazi Germany was not an abstract creation, it indicated the Aryan roots of the German people. Americans do pledge allegiance to the flag of the United States. Thus symbols of public authority do convey the message that society through its official representatives exercises its authority to punish those who violated its laws. In this respect it makes a difference whether the officer wears the badge of the state or of a private corporation.

As I mentioned, on the symbolic nonutilitarian level, it can be found morally troubling that corporations will try to make a profit on the punishment of people (which is a deliberate cause of suffering by representatives of society). It seems to send the same message to the public that was widespread in the United States during the Reagan era, that "greed is beautiful." I disagree with DiIulio (1990a) on this point, as he maintains that the profit motive of private corporations should not be considered as a central moral issue in the prison privatization debate. I do believe that it can affect the operation of correctional facilities, and at least as important, that it will become a symbolic statement of the American value system. It is questionable whether the government should create opportunities for private entities to make profits on the administration of severe punishments that entails the deprivation of liberty and "represents gravely serious assaults on the fundamental rights of persons" (Murphy & Coleman, 1984, p. 113).

Interestingly, even the new approach to administration that tries to make government more flexible and effective does not focus on the privatization of prisons as a relevant issue. Osborne and Gaebler (1992) mention only that when Tennessee decided to build three new prisons, it let a private firm operate one and the state operate the other two, to see who would do it more cheaply. This was brought up in the context of public versus private competition, in a single sentence. In another comment, these authors note that often when government contracts with a private company "to pick up garbage or run a prison, for example, they wind up turning it over to a private monopoly, and both the cost and the inefficiency grow worse!" (Osborne & Gaebler, 1992, p. 47). These comments do not indicate that serious consideration was given in this highly praised work to private prisons. The implication of the new trend in public policy that tries to revitalize and reinvent government for prisons (Lane & Wolf, 1990; Osborne & Gaebler, 1992) is, rather, to improve the public operation of prisons than to privatize them.

The attempts to blur the differences between the public and private spheres are problematic. There are differences between public agencies and private for-profit corporations in the nature of the social functions they can carry out (see Schiflett & Zey, 1990). The fact that private corporations do a good job of picking up garbage and maintaining public buildings does not necessarily make them experts in handling prisoners. As was explored before, the blurring between public and private domains is a general trend among privatization advocates. However, there are some major differences between these tasks: "Everybody agrees on the need to pick up the garbage—all of it—but not everybody agrees on the multiple and competing public goals involved in corrections" (DiIulio, 1990b, p. 68).

Finally, in a modern complex society the model of a minimal state is not very realistic. The state has to fulfill many functions that private entities are not meant to fulfill and are not expected and not requested to do.[16] Or if they are expected to provide some services, it is only on a voluntary basis. There should be a "visible hand" that governs and gives direction. One of the major challenges that government has to meet is to become more efficient, to be able to motivate public workers and raise the level of public service to bring new ideas to the sphere of public service (Walzer, 1985, p. 12) by steering or by rowing or by doing both. Punishment in general, and incarceration in particular, have to be substantially improved, not only for the sake of better service but also to keep the profit motive away from the administration of justice, where it might create a conflict of interests between the public good and the private greed. The major challenge is to reinvent corrections as a public service and not as a private business.

Notes

1. The corporate context of the private prison industry has not been explored in detail. This issue may draw more attention in the future to better understand the various aspects of privatized corrections. There are already initial attempts to take into consideration the fact that contemporary privatization is being done by corporations (see, e.g., Lilly, 1991; Lilly & Knepper, 1991, 1992; Shichor, 1993).

2. It should be mentioned that not only private corporations organize themselves into PACs but also labor unions and other interest groups such as professional organizations (e.g., AMA, ABA). Furthermore, employee organizations are involved in this kind of political activity as well. For example, the California Correctional Peace Officers Association (CCPOA) is a major contributor to various statewide political campaigns.

3. The intricacies and sophistication of legal work of white-collar cases are analyzed by Mann in his book *Defending White-Collar Crime: A Portrait of Attorneys at Work* (1985).

4. These concepts were formulated after the term *military-industrial complex*, coined by President Eisenhower in referring to the cold war situation, in which international tensions were fueled by the arms race and provided the military and defense establishments with great influence and the defense contractors with great profits. This complex had a vested interest in the continuation of the cold war. Another related term used lately is the "penitentiary-industrial complex" (Walters, 1991).

5. There are many jokes about the inefficiency of public sector workers; postal workers seem to be the most frequently selected group for these jokes.

6. The issue of ethics and morality is especially important in the case of corrections when punishment—the administration of "deliberate suffering"—is the focus of activity.

7. This perception of public sector employees is reflected in the often used term of "public servant" and the contrasting terms of "public service" versus "private business."

8. For example, unions of public correctional workers often thwart efforts to cut costs or to make the operation more effective. As most unions do, they tend to protect the behavior of their members even if it is not in line with the organizational goals of the institution. They are suspicious of outsiders, especially of social scientists who intend to do research in the institutions. For instance, in California, surveys of correctional personnel cannot be conducted without the agreement of the union.

9. There are often problems with providing incentives to career service personnel because many political appointees involve them in policy making. The lack of cooperation between policy making and policy execution affects the performance of government agencies and their ability to attract top managers (see Staats, 1988).

10. There are other new forms of budgeting suggested, for example, "output budgeting," "outcome budgeting," and "customer driven budgeting" (Osborne & Gaebler, 1992, pp. 162-163), which also allow more flexibility, but it seems that mission-driven budgeting is the most appropriate for prison operations although the others may be considered as well.

11. Between 1980 and 1988 the number of people under direct surveillance (probation, jails, prisons, and parole) increased from 1.8 million to 3.7 million, an increase of 104%. In the same period reported index crimes increased to 13.4 million (an increase of 4%) (Austin, 1990).

12. To illustrate this point, it should be mentioned that the U.S. Supreme Court on June 6, 1994 ruled in a 9-0 decision that prison officials can be held liable if they know that an inmate is in danger of assault, often rape, by other prisoners yet do nothing to prevent it (Savage, 1994). In another prison-related case, a U.S. District Court judge ruled in June, 1994 that in California prisons sweeping reforms in psychiatric care should be made because prison officials have deliberately been indifferent to thousands of mentally ill convicts (Hurst, 1994, p. A1).

13. As seen, there is a new trend in public management that tries among other aims to address the problem of incentives. This trend tries to provide more independence and autonomy to public workers and to create "self-interest cultures," which are based on the idea that "people work most effectively when there is a reasonable balance of effort and rewards. This concept requires explicit performance criteria, to which people will respond, given an appropriate set of incentives" (Lane & Wolf, 1990, p. 107).

14. Not all human service organizations and employees are receptive to these attempts. For example, in a recent article in the *NEA Higher Education Journal*, Parker and Slaughter (1994) claim that TQM programs "tend to emphasize elimination of 'variation'; prefer easily quantifiable outcomes; decrease employee control over working conditions and increase management control; [and] imply that employee needs are illegitimate and even antithetical to the institutions overall goals" (p. 6). It is very likely that similar objections will be heard also in regard to corrections as well as concerning other human services.

15. Would it be acceptable for the Air Force, Navy, or any other branch of the armed forces to be operated by a private corporation that promises more cost-effective, more flexible, and more efficient operation than under the supervision of generals, admirals, and their officers?

16. Consider, for instance, the failure of private charities to handle the homeless problem, or the health care crisis.

References

Adam Smith Institute. (n.d.). *Privatizing America*. Washington, DC: Author.

Adamson, C. R. (1983). Punishment after slavery: Southern state penal systems, 1865-1890. *Social Problems, 30*, 555-569.

Allen, F. (1981). *The decline of the rehabilitative ideal*. New Haven, CT: Yale University Press.

Allen, F. (1985). Criminal justice, legal values, and the rehabilitative ideal. In J. C. Murphy (Ed.), *Punishment and rehabilitation* (pp. 172-185). Belmont, CA: Wadsworth.

American Bar Association (ABA). (1986). *Section of Criminal Justice, Report to the House of Delegates*. Chicago: American Bar Association Division for Communications and Public Affairs.

American Friends Service Committee. (1971). *Struggle for justice*. New York: Hill and Wang.

Anderson, C. W. (1986). Pragmatic liberalism: Uniting theory and practice. In A. J. Damico (Ed.), *Liberals on liberalism* (pp. 201-219). Totowa, NJ: Rowman and Littlefield.

Anderson, J. W., Jr. (1989). *Corporate social responsibility*. Westport, CT: Quorum.

Anderson, P., Cavoli, C. R., & Moriarity, L. J. (1985). Private corrections: Feast or fiasco? *Prison Journal, 45*(2), 32-41.

Ascher, K. (1987). *The politics of privatization: Contracting out public services*. New York: St. Martin's.

Austin, J. (1986). Using early release to relieve prison crowding. *Crime & Delinquency, 32*, 404-502.

Austin, J. (1990, December). America's growing correctional-industrial complex. *NCDD Focus*.

Avila, D. A. (1992, June 24). Sheriff seen in a catch-22 on jail overcrowding. *Los Angeles Times*, p. B5.

Ayers, E. L. (1984). *Vengeance and justice: Crime and punishment in the 19th-century American South*. New York: Oxford University Press.

Babington, A. (1971). *The English Bastille: A history of Newgate gaol and prison conditions in Britain, 1188-1902*. London: MacDonald.

Ball, R. A., Huff, C. R., & Lilly, J. R. (1988). *House arrest and correctional policy: Doing time at home*. Newbury Park, CA: Sage.

Barnes, H. E., & Teeters, N. K. (1959). *New horizons in criminology*. Englewood Cliffs, NJ: Prentice Hall.

Bartollas, C., & Dinitz, S. (1989). *Introduction to criminology: Order and disorder*. New York: Harper & Row.

Bartollas, C., & Miller, S. J. (1978). *Correctional administration: Theory and practice.* New York: McGraw-Hill.

Bartollas, C., Miller, S. J., & Dinitz, S. (1976). *Juvenile victimization: The institutional paradox*. New York: Halsted.

Beattie, J. M. (1986). *Crime and the courts in England, 1660-1800*. Princeton, NJ: Princeton University Press.

Beccaria, C. (1819). *An essay on crimes and punishment*. Philadelphia: P. H. Nicklin.

Becker, C. L. (1945). *Freedom and responsibility in the American way of life*. New York: Vintage.

Becker, C., & Stanley, A. D. (1985, June 15). Incarceration Inc.: The downside of private prisons. *The Nation*, pp. 728-730.

Beetham, D. (1984). The future of the nation state. In G. McLennan, D. Held, & S. Hall (Eds.), *The idea of the modern state* (pp. 208-222). Milton Keynes, UK: Open University Press.

Beetham, D. (1991). *The legitimization of power*. London: Macmillan.

Bell, D. (1976). *The cultural contradictions of capitalism*. New York: Basic Books.

Bellah, R. N., Madsen, R., Sullivan, W. M., Swidler, A., & Tipton, S. M. (1985). *Habits of the heart: Individualism and commitment in American life*. New York: Harper & Row.

Bendick, M., Jr. (1989). Privatizing the delivery of social welfare services: An idea to be taken seriously. In S. B. Kamerman & A. J. Kahn (Eds.), *Privatization and the welfare state* (pp. 97-120). Princeton, NJ: Princeton University Press.

Benekos, P. J., & Hagan, F. E. (1990, November). *Too little, too late: Regulation and prosecution in the savings and loan scandal*. Paper presented at the annual meeting of the American Society of Criminology, Baltimore.

Benenson, R. (1985). Privatizing public services. *Editorial Research Reports, 11*(4), 559-576.

Bierstedt, R. (1978). Sociological thought in the eighteenth century. In T. Bottomore & R. Nisbet (Eds.), *A history of sociological analysis* (pp. 3-38). New York: Basic Books.

Black, D. (1976). *The behavior of law*. New York: Academic Press.

Blau, P. M., & Scott, W. R. (1962). *Formal organizations*. San Francisco: Chandler.

Blumstein, A. (1983). Selective incapacitation as a means of crime control. *American Behavioral Scientist, 27*(1), 87-108.

Bookspan, S. (1991). *A germ of goodness: The California state prison system, 1851-1944*. Lincoln: University of Nebraska Press.

Borna, S. (1986). Free enterprise goes to prison. *British Journal of Criminology, 26*, 321-334.

Bottoms, A. E. (1983). Neglected features of contemporary penal systems. In D. Garland & P. Young (Eds.), *The power to punish* (pp. 166-202). London: Heinemann.

Bowditch, C., & Everett, R. S. (1987). Private prisons: Problems within the solution. *Justice Quarterly, 4*, 441-453.

Bowker, L. H. (1980). *Prison victimization*. New York: Elsevier.

Bowker, L. H. (1988). Victimizers and victims in American correctional institutions. In R. Johnson & H. Toch (Eds.), *The pains of imprisonment* (pp. 63-76). Prospect Heights, IL: Waveland.

Bozeman, B. (1988, March-April). Exploring the limits of public and private sectors: Sector boundaries as Maginot Line. *Public Administration Review*, pp. 672-674.

Bradshaw, T., & Vogel, D. (Eds.). (1981). *Corporations and their critics*. New York: McGraw-Hill.

Braithwaite, J. B. (1989a). Criminological theory and organizational crime. *Justice Quarterly*, *6*, 333-358.

Braithwaite, J. B. (1989b). *Crime, shame and reintegration*. Cambridge, UK: Cambridge University Press.

Braithwaite, J., & Geis, G. (1982). On theory and action for corporate crime control. *Crime & Delinquency*, *28*, 292-314.

Brakel, S. J. (1988). Prison management, private enterprise style: The inmate's evaluation. *New England Journal of Criminal and Civil Confinement*, *14*, 175-244.

Brinton, C. (1950). *The shaping of modern thought*. Englewood Cliffs, NJ: Prentice Hall.

Bronick, M. J. (1989). *The Federal Bureau of Prisons' experience with privatization*. Washington, DC: National Institute of Justice.

Bureau of Justice Statistics. (1988). *Report to the nation on crime and justice*. Washington, DC: U.S. Department of Justice.

Bureau of Justice Statistics. (1992). *Correctional populations in the United States*. Washington, DC: U.S. Department of Justice.

Burger, W. E. (1983). Factories with fences. *Pace Law Review*, *4*(1), 1-9.

Butler, S. M. (1985). *Privatizing government services*. New York: Universe.

Calavita, K. (1983). The demise of the Occupational Safety and Health Administration: A case study in symbolic action. *Social Problems*, *30*, 437-448.

Calavita, K., & Pontell, H. (1990). "Heads I win, tails you lose": Deregulation, crime and crisis in the savings and loan industry. *Crime & Delinquency*, *36*, 309-341.

California Department of Corrections. (1987). Contract with Gary White Associates (Mesa Verde RTC), Sacramento.

California Senate Journal, fourth session. (1853). San Francisco: State Printer.

California Senate Journal, twelfth session. (1861). Annual Message of Governor John G. Downey. Sacramento: State Printer.

Camp, C. G., & Camp, G. M. (1984). *Private sector involvement in prison services and operations*. Washington, DC: National Institute of Corrections.

Camp, G. M., & Camp, C. G. (1985). *Prison gangs: Their extent, nature and impact on prisons*. Washington, DC: U.S. Department of Justice.

Cardenas, J. (1986). The crime victim in the prosecutorial process. *Harvard Journal of Law and Policy*, *9*, 357-398.

Carleton, M. T. (1971). *Politics and punishment*. Baton Rouge: Louisiana University Press.

Carnoy, M. (1984). *The state and political theory*. Princeton, NJ: Princeton University Press.

Carroll, B. J., Conant, R. W., & Easton, T. A. (Eds.). (1987). *Private means, public ends: Private business in social service delivery*. New York: Praeger.

Carroll, L. (1974). *Hacks, blacks and cons*. Lexington, MA: D. C. Heath.

Carroll, L. (1988). Race, ethnicity, and the social order of the prison. In R. Johnson & H. Toch (Eds.), *The pains of imprisonment* (pp. 181-203). Prospect Heights, IL: Waveland.

Castle, M. N. (1991). *Alternative sentencing: Selling it to the public.* Washington, DC: National Institute of Justice.

Cavadino, M., & Dignan, J. (1992). *The penal system.* London: Sage.

Champion, D. (1990). *Corrections in the United States.* Englewood Cliffs, NJ: Prentice Hall.

Chandler, R. C. (1986). The myth of private sector superiority in personnel administration. *Policy Studies Review 5,* 643-653.

Chitwood, O. P. (1961). *A history of colonial America.* New York: Harper & Row.

Christie, N. (1993). *Crime control as industry.* New York: Routledge, Chapman and Hall.

Cikins, W. I. (1986). Privatization of the American prison system: An idea whose time has come. *Notre Dame Journal of Law, Ethics and Public Policy, 4,* 445-464.

Cikins, W. I. (1993). Partial privatization of prison operations: Let's give it a chance. In G. W. Bowman, S. Hakim, & P. Seidenstat (Eds.), *Privatizing correctional institutions* (pp. 13-18). New Brunswick, NJ: Transaction.

Clear, T. R., & Cole, G. F. (1990). *American corrections* (2nd ed.). Monterey, CA: Brooks/Cole.

Clemmer, D. (1958). *The prison community.* New York: Holt, Reinhart & Winston.

Clinard, M. B. (1983). *Corporate ethics and crime: The role of middle management.* Beverly Hills, CA: Sage.

Clinard, M. B., & Yeager, P. C. (1980). *Corporate crime.* New York: Free Press.

Cody, W. J. M., & Bennett, A. D. (1987). The privatization of correctional institutions: The Tennessee experience. *Vanderbilt Law Review, 40,* 829-849.

Coffin v. Reichard, 143 F.2d 443 6th Cir. (1944).

Cohen, S. (1979). The punitive city: Notes on the dispersal of social control. *Contemporary Crises, 3,* 339-363.

Cohen, S. (1985). *Visions of social control.* Cambridge, UK: Polity.

Coleman, J. W. (1989). *The criminal elite: The sociology of white collar crime.* New York: St. Martin's.

Colvin, M. (1982). The 1980 New Mexico prison riot. *Social Problems, 29,* 449-463.

Conklin, J. E. (1977) *"Illegal but not criminal": Business crime in America.* Englewood Cliffs, NJ: Prentice Hall.

Conley, J. A. (1980). Prisons, production and profit: Reconsidering the importance of prison industries. *Journal of Social History,* pp. 257-275.

Conrad, J. (1984). Corrections and its constituencies. *Prison Journal, 64,* 47-55.

Cooper v. Pate, 378 U.S. 584 (1964).

Cornish, D. B., & Clarke, R. V. (Eds.). (1986). *The reasoning criminal: Rational choice perspectives on offending.* New York: Springer-Verlag.

Corrections Corporation of America. (1989). *Annual report.* Nashville, TN: Author.

Corrections Corporation of America. (n.d.). *Corporate profile: A look at CCA's business philosophy.* Nashville, TN: Author.

Council of State Governments and the Urban Institute. (1987). *Issues in contracting for the private operation of prisons and jails.* Washington, DC: National Institute of Justice.

Crants, D. R., III. (1991). Private prison management: A study in economic efficiency. *Journal of Contemporary Criminal Justice, 7*(1), 49-59.

Cressey, D. R. (1965). Prison organizations. In J. G. March (Ed.), *Handbook of organizations* (pp. 1023-1070). Chicago: Rand McNally.

Crouch, B. M. (1986). Prison guards on the line. In K. C. Haas & G. P. Alpert (Eds.), *The dilemmas of punishment* (pp. 177-206). Prospect Heights, IL: Waveland.

Crouch, B. M., & Marquart, J. W. (1990). Intervention and emergent order in Texas prisons. In J. J. DiIulio (Ed.), *Courts, corrections and the Constitution* (pp. 94-114). New York: Oxford University Press.

Crozier, M. (1984). *The trouble with America*. Berkeley and Los Angeles: University of California Press.

Cullen, F. T. (1986). The privatization of treatment: Prison reform in the 1980s. *Federal Probation, 50*(1), 8-16.

Cullen, F. T., Cullen, J. B., & Wozniak, J. F. (1988). Is rehabilitation dead? The myth of the punitive public. *Journal of Criminal Justice, 16,* 303-317.

Cullen, F. T., & Gilbert, K. E. (1982). *Reaffirming rehabilitation*. Cincinnati, OH: Anderson.

Cullen, F. T., Maakestad, W. J., & Cavender, G. (1987). *Corporate crime under attack: The Ford Pinto case and beyond*. Cincinnati, OH: Anderson.

Currie, E. (1985). *Confronting crime: An American challenge*. New York: Pantheon.

Daniels v. Williams, 474 U.S. 88 L.Ed.2d 662 (1986).

Dauber, E., & Shichor, D. (1979). A comparative exploration of prison discipline. *Journal of Criminal Justice, 7,* 21-36.

Davidson v. Canon, 474 U.S. 88 L.Ed.2d 677 (1986).

Davidson, R. T. (1974). *Chicano prisoners: The key to San Quentin*. New York: Holt, Reinhart & Winston.

de Beaumont, G., & de Tocqueville, A. (1979). *On the penitentiary system in the United States and its application in France*. Carbondale and Edwardsville: Southern Illinois University Press. (Original work published 1833)

DeHoog, R. H. (1984). *Contracting out for human services*. Albany: State University of New York Press.

DeLacey, M. (1986). *Prison reform in Lancashire, 1700-1850*. Stanford, CA: Stanford University Press.

Delaney, K. J. (1990). Power, intercorporate networks, and "strategic bankruptcy." *Law and Society Review, 23,* 643-666.

Dempsey, P. S. (1989). *The social and economic consequences of deregulation: The transportation industry in transition*. New York: Quorum Books.

DeWitt, C. B. (1986a, November). *Ohio's new approach to prison and jail financing* (Construction Bulletin). Washington, DC: National Institute of Justice.

DeWitt, C. B. (1986b, June). *Florida sets example with use of concrete modules* (Construction Bulletin). Washington, DC: National Institute of Justice.

DeWitt, C. B., & Binder, S. D. (1989). Problems of financing prison construction. In J. Sevick & W. Cikins (Eds.), *Facilities: Is there a role for the private sector?* Washington, DC: Brookings Institution.

Diederiks, H. (1992). Forced labor in the penal system, in the poor relief system, and in the Dutch colonies since the 18th century. *IAHCCJ Bulletin, 16,* 34-40.

DiIulio, J. J., Jr. (1986). *Prisons, profits, and the public good: The privatization of corrections* (Research Bulletin 1). Sam Houston State University, Criminal Justice Center.

DiIulio, J. J., Jr. (1987). *Governing prisons: A comparative study of correctional management*. New York: Free Press.

DiIulio, J. J., Jr. (1988). What is wrong with private prisons. *The Public Interest, 92,* 66-83.

DiIulio, J. J., Jr. (1990a). The duty to govern: A critical perspective on the private management of prisons and jails. In D. C. McDonald (Ed.), *Private prisons and the public interest* (pp. 155-178). New Brunswick, NJ: Rutgers University Press.

DiIulio, J. J., Jr. (1990b, March). Prisons for profit? *Commentary*, pp. 66-68.

DiIulio, J. J., Jr. (1991). *No escape*. New York: Basic Books.

Dix, D. L. (1967). *Remarks on prisons and prison discipline in the United States* (Reprinted edition). Montclair, NJ: Patterson Smith.

Donahue, J. D. (1988). *Prisons for profit: Public justice, private interests*. Washington, DC: Economic Policy Institute.

Donahue, J. D. (1989). *The privatization decision: Public ends, private means*. New York: Basic Books.

Donaldson, T. (1982). *Corporations and morality*. Englewood Cliffs, NJ: Prentice Hall.

Doran, R. E. (1977). Organizational stereotyping: The case of the adjustment center classification committee. In D. F. Greenberg (Ed.), *Corrections and punishment* (pp. 41-68). Beverly Hills, CA: Sage.

Drucker, P. J. (1973). *Management: Tasks, responsibilities, practices*. New York: Harper & Row.

Duffee, D. (1980). *Correctional management: Change and control in correctional organizations*. Englewood Cliffs, NJ: Prentice Hall.

Duffee, D., & Ritti, R. R. (1977). Correctional policy and public values. *Criminology, 14*, 449-460.

Duffy, S. M. (1984, May 14). Breaking into jail: The private sector starts to build and run prisons. *Barron's*, pp. 20-22.

Dunham, D. W. (1986). Inmate's rights and the privatization of prisons. *Columbia Law Review, 86*, 1475-1504.

Durham, A. M., III. (1988). Evaluating privatized correctional institutions: Obstacles to effective assessment. *Federal Probation, 52*(2), 65-71.

Durham, A. M., III. (1989). Origins of interest in the privatization of punishment: The nineteenth and twentieth century American experience. *Criminology, 27*, 107-139.

Dye, T. R. (1978). *Understanding public policy*. Englewood Cliffs, NJ: Prentice Hall.

Earnshaw, L., & Normandeau, A. (1986). *Privatization in corrections: The Canadian situation*. Montreal: University of Montreal, International Center for Comparative Criminology.

Ellison, W. J. (1986/1987). Privatization of corrections: A critique and analysis of contemporary views. *Cumberland Law Review, 17*, 683-729.

Elvin, J. (1985). A civil liberties view of private prisons. *Prison Journal, 65*(2), 48-52.

Empey, L. T. (1982). *American delinquency: Its meaning and construction*. Homewood, IL: Dorsey.

England, D. (1990). Developments in prison administration. In J. W. Murphy & J. E. Dison (Eds.), *Are prisons any better? Twenty years of correctional reform* (pp. 61-75). Newbury Park, CA: Sage.

Ericson, R. V., McMahon, M. W., & Evans, D. G. (1987). Punishing for profit: Reflections on the revival of privatization in corrections. *Canadian Journal of Criminology, 29*, 355-387.

Ermann, M. D., & Lundman, R. J. (1982). *Corporate deviance*. New York: Holt, Rinehart & Winston.

Ethridge, P. A., & Marquart, J. W. (1993). Private prisons in Texas: The new penology for profit. *Justice Quarterly, 10*, 29-48.

Etzioni, A. (1961). *A comparative analysis of complex organizations*. New York: Free Press.

Etzioni, A. (1964). *Modern organizations*. Englewood Cliffs, NJ: Prentice Hall.

Evans, B. B. (1987). Private prisons. *Emory Law Journal, 36*, 253-283.

Ezorsky, G. (Ed.). (1972). *Philosophical perspectives on punishment*. Albany: State University of New York University Press.

Farrington, K. (1992). The modern prison as total institution? Public perception versus objective reality. *Crime & Delinquency, 38*, 6-26.

Feeley, M. M. (1991). The privatization of prisons in historical perspective. *Criminal Justice Research Bulletin, 6*(2), 1-10. Huntsville, TX: Sam Houston State University, Criminal Justice Center.

Fenton, J. (1985). A private alternative to public prisons. *Prison Journal, 65*(2), 42-47.

Fisse, B. (1985). Sanctions against corporations: The limitation of fines and the enterprise of creating alternatives. In B. Fisse & P. A. French (Eds.), *Corrigible corporations and unruly law* (pp. 137-157). San Antonio, TX: Trinity University Press.

Fitzgerald, E. (1985). Prison discipline and the courts. In M. Maguire, J. Vagg, & R. Morgan (Eds.), *Accountability and prisons: Opening up a closed world* (pp. 29-45). London: Tavistock.

Flanagan, T. J., & Maguire, K. (Eds.). (1990). *Sourcebook of criminal justice statistics, 1989*. Washington, DC: Bureau of Justice Statistics.

Flanagan, T. J., & Maguire, K. (Eds.). (1992). *Sourcebook of criminal justice statistics, 1991*. Washington, DC: Bureau of Justice Statistics.

Fleisher, M. S. (1989). *Warehousing violence*. Newbury Park, CA: Sage.

Fogel, D. (1975). *". . . We are the living proof . . .": The justice model for corrections*. Cincinnati, OH: Anderson.

Folz, D. H., & Scheb, J. M., II. (1989). Prison, profits, and politics: The Tennessee privatization experiment. *Judicature, 73*(2), 98-102.

Fong, R. S. (1990). The organizational structure of prison gangs: A case study. *Federal Probation, 54*, 36-43.

Foucault, M. (1977). *Discipline and punish: The birth of the prison*. New York: Random House.

Fox, J. G. (1982). *Organizational and racial conflict in maximum-security prisons*. Lexington, MA: D. C. Heath.

Frank, N., & Lambness, M. (1988). *Controlling corporate illegality: The regulatory justice system*. Cincinnati, OH: Anderson.

Frankena, W. K. (1963). *Ethics*. Englewood Cliffs, NJ: Prentice Hall.

Fraser/Associates. (1980). *Political action for business: The PAC handbook*. Cambridge, MA: Ballinger.

Funke, G. (1985). Economics of prison crowding. *Annals of the American Academy of Political and Social Science, 478*, 86-99.

Galston, W. A. (1986). Liberalism and public morality. In A. Damico (Ed.), *Liberals on liberalism* (pp. 129-147). Totowa, NJ: Rowman and Littlefield.

Gandy, J., & Hurl, L. (1987). Private sector involvement in prison industries: Options and issues. *Canadian Journal of Criminology, 29*, 185-204.

Gardner, G. (1987). The emergence of the New York state prison system: A critique of the Rusch-Kirchheimer model. *Crime and Social Justice, 29*, 88-109.

Garland, D. (1990). *Punishment and modern society*. Chicago: University of Chicago Press.

Garsombke, D. J., & Garsombke, T. W. (1987). Strategic marketing of social services. In B. J. Carroll, R. W. Conant, & T. A. Easton (Eds.), *Private means, public ends: Private business in social service delivery* (pp. 119-134). New York: Praeger.

Geis, G. (1967). The heavy electrical equipment antitrust cases of 1961. In M. B. Clinard & R. Quinney (Eds.), *Criminal behavior systems* (pp. 139-151). New York: Holt, Rinehart & Winston.

Geis, G. (1987). The privatization of prisons: Panacea or placebo? In B. J. Carroll, R. W. Conant, & T. A. Easton (Eds.), *Private means, public ends: Private business in social service delivery* (pp. 76-97). New York: Praeger.

Gendreau, P., & Ross, R. R. (1987). Revivification of rehabilitation? Evidence from the 1980s. *Justice Quarterly, 4*, 349-408.

Gentry, J. T. (1986). The panopticon revisited: The problem of monitoring private prisons. *Yale Law Journal, 96*, 353-375.

Gettinger, S. (1982). Accreditation on trial. *Corrections Magazine, 8*, 7-19.

Giddens, A. (1971). *Capitalism and modern social theory: An analysis of the writings of Marx, Durkheim and Max Weber.* Cambridge, UK: Cambridge University Press.

Gilbert, M. J. (1992, March). *Ethical considerations about privatization, correctional practice, and the role of government.* Paper presented at the annual meeting of the Academy of Criminal Justice Sciences, Pittsburgh, PA.

Gittler, J. (1984). Expanding the role of the victim in a criminal action: An overview of issues and problems. *Pepperdine Law Review, 11*, 117-182.

Glasberg, D. S. (1981). Corporate power and control: The case of Leasco Corporation versus Chemical Bank. *Social Problems, 29*, 104-116.

Glasberg, D. S. (1989). *The power of collective purse strings: The effect of bank hegemony on corporations and the state.* Berkeley: University of California Press.

Glaser, D., & Fry, L. J. (1987). Corruption of prison staff in inmate discipline. *Journal of Offender Counseling, Services, and Rehabilitation, 12*(1), 27-38.

Glazer, M. P., & Glazer, P. M. (1989). *The whistleblowers: Exposing corruption in government and industry.* New York: Basic Books.

Goffman, E. (1961). *Asylums.* Garden City, NY: Anchor.

Goodsell, C. T. (1983). *The case for bureaucracy, a public administration polemic.* Chatham, NJ: Chatham House Publishers.

Goodwin, J. (1985). *Brotherhood of arms: General dynamics and the business of defending America.* New York: Times Books.

Gorham, W. (1983). Foreword. In H. P. Hatry (Ed.), *A review of private approaches for delivery of public services* (p. xi). Washington, DC: The Urban Institute.

Gottfredson, M. R., & Hirschi, T. (1990). *A general theory of crime.* Stanford, CA: Stanford University Press.

Gottfredson, S. D., & Taylor, R. B. (1987). Attitudes of correctional policymakers and the public. In S. D. Gottfredson & S. McConville (Eds.), *America's correctional crisis: Prison populations and public policy* (pp. 57-75). Westport, CT: Greenwood.

Greenwood, P. (1981). *Private enterprise prisons? Why not? The job would be done and at less cost.* Santa Monica, CA: RAND.

Greenwood, P. W., with Abrahamse, A. (1982). *Selective incapacitation.* Santa Monica, CA: RAND.

Greenwood, P., & Turner, S. (1993). Private presentence reports for serious juvenile offenders: Implementation issues and impacts. *Justice Quarterly, 10*, 229-243.

Gross, E. (1980). Organizational structure and organizational crime. In G. Geis & E. Stotland (Eds.), *White-collar crime: Theory and research* (pp. 52-76). Beverly Hills, CA: Sage.

Gurin, A. (1989). Governmental responsibility and privatization: Examples from four social services. In S. B. Kamerman & A. J. Kahn (Eds.), *Privatization and the welfare state* (pp. 179-205). Princeton, NJ: Princeton University Press.

Gurvitch, G. (1942). *Sociology of law.* New York: Philosophical Library.

Hackett, J. C., Hatry, H. P., Levison, R. B., Allen, J., Chi, K., & Feigenbaum, E. D. (1987). *Issues in contracting for the operation of prisons and jails.* Washington, DC: U.S. Department of Justice.

Hagan, J. (1994). *Crime and disrepute.* Thousand Oaks, CA: Pine Forge.

Hamilton, W. H. (1931). The ancient maxim caveat emptor. *Yale Law Review, 40,* 1133-1187.

Harding, C., Hines, B., Ireland, R., & Rawlings, P. (1985). *Imprisonment in England and Wales.* London: Croom Helm.

Hart, H. L. (1968). *Punishment and responsibility.* Oxford, UK: Clarendon.

Hasenfeld, Y. (1983). *Human service organizations.* Englewood Cliffs, NJ: Prentice Hall.

Hasenfeld, Y., & English, R. A. (Eds.). (1974). *Human service organizations.* Ann Arbor: University of Michigan Press.

Hatry, H. P., Brounstein, P. J., Levinson, R. B., Altschuler, D. M., Chi, K., & Rosenberg, P. (1989). *Comparison of privately and publicly operated corrections facilities in Kentucky and Massachusetts.* Washington, DC: The Urban Institute.

Hawkins, G. (1976). *The prison: Policy and practice.* Chicago: University of Chicago Press.

Hawkins, R., & Alpert, G. P. (1989). *American prison systems: Punishment and justice.* Englewood Cliffs, NJ: Prentice Hall.

Heilbroner, R. L. (1966). *The worldly philosophers* (12th paperback printing). New York: Simon & Schuster.

Held, D. (1984). Central perspectives on the modern state. In G. McLennan, D. Held, & S. Hall (Eds.), *The idea of the modern state* (pp. 29-79). Milton Keynes, UK: Open University Press.

Hepburn, J. R. (1989). Prison guards as agents of social control. In L. Goodstein & D. L. MacKenzie (Eds.), *The American prison: Issues in research and policy* (pp. 191-206). New York: Plenum.

Hewitt, J. D., Poole, E. D., & Regoli, R. M. (1984). Self-reported and observed rule-breaking in prison: A look at disciplinary response. *Justice Quarterly, 1,* 437-447.

Hinsley, F. H. (1986). *Sovereignty* (2nd ed.). Cambridge, UK: Cambridge University Press.

Hobbes, T. (1969). *Leviathan* (Abridged ed.). F. B. Randall (Ed.). New York: Washington Square Press. (Original work published 1651)

Hobhouse, L. T. (1964). *Liberalism.* Oxford, UK: Oxford University Press.

Hoffman, J. (1988). *State, power and democracy.* Sussex, UK: Wheatsheat.

Hofstadter, R. (1967). *Social Darwinism in American thought.* Boston: Beacon.

Hofstadter, R. (1974). *The American political tradition.* New York: Vintage.

Holley, C. E. (1988). Privatization of corrections: Is the state out on a limb when the company goes bankrupt? *Vanderbilt Law Review, 41,* 317-339.

Holt v. Sarver, 309 F.Supp. 362 ED Ark. (1970).

Hospers, J. (1978). Free enterprise as the embodiment of justice. In R. T. DeGeorge & J. A. Pickler (Eds.), *Ethics, free enterprise, and public policy.* New York: Oxford University Press.

Houghen, H. R. (1977). The impact of politics and prison industry on the general management of the Kansas State Penitentiary, 1883-1909. *Kansas Historical Quarterly, 43,* 297-318.

Hughes, W. S. (1958). *Consciousness and society.* New York: Vintage.

Ex parte, Hull. 312 U.S. 546 (1941).

Hurst, J. (1991, October 8). $1.5 billion savings seen as prison admissions drop. *Los Angeles Times,* p. A3.

Hurst, J. (1994, June 8). Psychiatric care of inmates needs reform, jurist rules. *Los Angeles Times*, p. A1.

Hutto v. Finney, 437 U.S. 678 (1978).

Hutto, T. D. (1990). The privatization of prisons. In J. W. Murphy & J. E. Dison (Eds.), *Are prisons any better? Twenty years of correctional reform* (pp. 111-127). Newbury Park, CA: Sage.

Ignatieff, M. (1978). *A just measure of pain*. New York: Columbia University Press.

Ingraham, B. L., Evans, M., & Anderson, E. (1978). Discretion and rehabilitation: Fads and fixtures? In M. Evans (Ed.), *Discretion and control* (pp. 89-106). Beverly Hills, CA: Sage.

Irwin, J. (1980). *Prisons in turmoil*. Boston: Little, Brown.

Irwin, J., & Austin, J. (1994). *It's about time: America's imprisonment binge*. Belmont, CA: Wadsworth.

Jackson v. Bishop, 404 F.2d 393 (1968).

Jacobs, J. B. (1977). *Stateville: The penitentiary in mass society*. Chicago: University of Chicago Press.

Jacobs, J. B. (1983). *New perspectives on prisons and imprisonment* (pp. 160-177). Ithaca, NY: Cornell University Press.

Jacobs, J. B., & Crotty, N. (1983). The guard's world. In J. B. Jacobs (Ed.), *New perspectives on prison and imprisonment* (pp. 133-141). Ithaca, NY: Cornell University Press.

Jacobs, J. B., & Kraft, L. J. (1983). Race relations in the guards' subculture. In J. B. Jacobs (Ed.), *New perspectives on prison and imprisonment*. Ithaca, NY: Cornell University Press.

Jacobs, J. B., & Zimmer, L. (1983). Collective bargaining and labor unrest. In J. B. Jacobs (Ed.), *New perspectives on prison and imprisonment* (pp. 142-159). Ithaca, NY: Cornell University Press.

Jamieson, K. M., & Flanagan, T. J. (1989). *Sourcebook of criminal justice statistics, 1988*. Washington, DC: Bureau of Justice Statistics.

Jankowski, L. W. (1992). *Correctional populations in the United States, 1990*. Washington, DC: Bureau of Justice Statistics.

Janus, M. (1993). Bars on the iron triangle: Public policy issues in the privatization of corrections. In G. M. Bowman, S. Hakim, & P. Seidenstadt (Eds.), *Privatizing correctional institutions* (pp. 75-89). New Brunswick, NJ: Transaction.

Jayewardene, C. H. S., & Talbot, C. K. (1983). Entrusting corrections to the private sector. *International Journal of Offender Therapy and Comparative Criminology, 26*, 177-187.

Joel, D. C. (1993). The privatization of secure adult prisons: Issues and evidence. In G. H. Bowman, S. Hakim, & P. Seidenstadt (Eds.), *Privatizing correctional institutions* (pp. 51-74). New Brunswick, NJ: Transaction.

Johnson, B. R., & Ross, P. P. (1990). The privatization of correctional management: A review. *Journal of Criminal Justice, 18*, 351-358.

Johnson, D. (1982). Morality and police harm. In F. Elliston & N. Bowie (Eds.), *Ethics, public policy, and criminal justice* (pp. 79-82). Cambridge, MA: Oelgeschlager, Gunn, and Hain.

Johnson, H. A. (1988). *History of criminal justice*. Cincinnati, OH: Anderson.

Johnson, R. (1987). *Hard time: Understanding and reforming the prison*. Monterey, CA: Brooks/Cole.

Johnson, T. A. (1987). Policy implications of private sector involvement in correctional services and programs. *Journal of Forensic Sciences, 32*, 221-224.

Johnston, V. R. (1990). Privatization of prisons: Management, productivity, and governance concerns. *Public Productivity and Management Review, 14*, 189-201.

Jones, D. A. (1981). *The law of criminal procedure: An analysis and critique.* Boston: Little, Brown.

Jordan, B. (1985). *The state: Authority and autonomy.* Oxford, UK: Basil Blackwell.

Kamerman, S. B., & Kahn, A. J. (1989). Conclusion: Continuing the discussion and taking a stand. In S. B. Kamerman & A. J. Kahn (Eds.), *Privatization and the welfare state* (pp. 261-270). Princeton, NJ: Princeton University Press.

Kay, S. L. (1987). The implication of prison privatization on the conduct of prisoner litigation under 42 U.S.C. Section 1983. *Vanderbilt Law Review, 40,* 867-888.

Keating, D. (1991, January 30). Monroe County sheriff gets back control of jail from Wackenhut. *Miami Herald,* p. 4B.

Keating, J. M., Jr. (1990). Public over private: Monitoring the performance of privately operated prisons and jails. In D. C. McDonald (Ed.), *Private prisons and the public interest* (pp. 130-154). New Brunswick, NJ: Rutgers University Press.

Kentucky Corrections Cabinet. (1985). *Changing faces, common walls: History of corrections in Kentucky.* Louisville: Author.

Keve, P. W. (1991). *Prisons and the American conscience: A history of U.S. federal corrections.* Carbondale and Edwardsville: Southern Illinois University Press.

King, R. D., & Maguire, M. (1994). Introduction: Contexts of imprisonment: An international perspective. *British Journal of Criminology, 34,* 1-13.

Kleinig, J. (1991). Punishment and moral seriousness. *Israel Law Review, 25,* 401-421.

Klofas, J. (1987). Patterns of jail use. *Journal of Criminal Justice, 15,* 403-411.

Knepper, P. (1991a, November). *Prison historiography and the maternity question.* Paper presented at the annual meeting of the American Society of Criminology, San Francisco.

Knepper, P. (1991b, November). *A Brief history of profiting from the punishment of crime.* Paper presented at the annual meeting of the American Society of Criminology, San Francisco.

Knight, B. B., & Early, S. T., Jr. (1986). *Prisoners' rights in America.* Chicago: Nelson-Hall.

Kramer, R. C. (1982). Corporate crime: An organizational perspective. In P. Wickman & T. Dailey (Eds.), *White collar crime and economic crime* (pp. 75-94). Lexington, MA: D. C. Heath.

Krause, J. D. (1992). The effects of prison siting practices on community status arrangements: A framework applied to the siting of California state prisons. *Crime & Delinquency, 38,* 27-55.

Krisberg, B., & Austin, J. (1980). *The unmet promise of alternatives to incarceration.* San Francisco: National Council on Crime and Delinquency.

Krisberg, B., DeComo, R., & Herrera, N. C. (1992). *National juvenile custody trends, 1978-1989.* Washington, DC: U.S. Department of Justice, Office of Justice Programs.

Kulis, J. C. (1983). Profit in the private presentence report. *Federal Probation, 14,* 11-15.

Lamott, K. (1961). *Chronicles of San Quentin: The biography of a prison.* New York: David McKay.

Lampkin, L. M. (1991). "Does crime pay?" AFSCME reviews the records on the privatization of prisons. *Journal of Contemporary Criminal Justice, 7*(1), 41-48.

Lane, L. M., & Wolf, J. F. (1990). *The human resource crisis in the public sector: Rebuilding the capacity to govern.* New York: Quorum.

Langan, P. A. (1991). America's soaring prison population. *Science, 251,* 1568-1573.

Lawrence, D. M. (1986). Private exercise of governmental power. *Indiana Law Journal, 61,* 647-695.

Leonard, W. N., & Weber, M. G. (1970). Automakers and dealers: A study of crimogenic market forces. *Law and Society Review, 4,* 407-424.

Lerner, M. (1937). Introduction. In A. Smith, *The wealth of nations* (Reprinted ed., pp. v-x). New York: Modern Library.

Levinson, R. B. (1985). Okeechobee: An evaluation of privatization in corrections. *Prison Journal, 45*(2), 75-94.

Lewis, O. F. (1967). *The development of American prisons and prison customs, 1776-1845*. Montclair, NJ: Patterson Smith. (Original work published 1922)

Lewis, W. D. (1965). *From Newgate to Dannemora*. Ithaca, NY: Cornell University Press.

Liebmann, G. W. (1975). Delegation to private parties in American constitutional law. *Indiana Law Journal, 50*, 650-719.

Lilly, J. R. (1991, November). *Power, profit, and penality: A beginning*. Paper presented at the annual meeting of the American Society of Criminology, San Francisco.

Lilly, J. R., & Knepper, P. (1991). Prisonomics: The iron triangle. *The Angolite, 16*(4), 45-58.

Lilly, J. R., & Knepper, P. (1992). An international perspective on the privatization of corrections. *Howard Journal, 31*, 174-191.

Linebaugh, P. (1992). *The London hanged: Crime and civil society in the eighteenth century*. New York: Cambridge University Press.

Linowes, David F. (1988). *Privatization: Toward more effective government*. Urbana and Chicago: University of Illinois Press.

Linowes, David F. (1990). The future of privatization. *National Forum, 52*(2), 2-4.

Lipson, M. (1975). *On guard: The business of private security*. New York: Quadrangle.

Litwin, G. H. (1968). Climate and behavior theory. In R. Tagiuri & G. H. Litwin (Eds.), *Organizational climate: Explorations of a concept* (pp. 35-61). Boston: Harvard Business School, Division of Research.

Locke, J. (1955). *On civil government*. Chicago: Henry Reguery. (Original work published 1692)

Lockwood, D. (1980). *Prison sexual violence*. New York: Elsevier.

Logan, C. H. (1987). The propriety of proprietary prisons. *Federal Probation, 51*(3), 35-40.

Logan, C. H. (1990). *Private prisons: Cons and pros*. New York: Oxford University Press.

Logan, C. H. (1991). *Well kept: Comparing quality of confinement in a public and private prison* (Executive summary). Washington, DC: National Institute of Justice.

Logan, C. H., & McGriff, B. W. (1989). *Comparing costs of public and private prisons: A case study*. Washington, DC: Department of Justice, National Institute of Justice Research in Action.

Logan, C. H., & Rausch, S. P. (1985). Punish and profit: The emergence of private enterprise prisons. *Justice Quarterly, 2*, 303-318.

Lombardo, L. X. (1981). *Imprisoned guards*. New York: Elsevier.

Lombardo, L. X. (1988). Stress, change, and collective violence in prison. In R. Johnson & H. Toch (Eds.), *The pains of imprisonment* (pp. 77-93). Prospect Heights, IL: Waveland.

Lukes, S. (1978). *Power: A radical view*. London: Macmillan.

Mabbott, J. D. (1939). Punishment. *Mind, 48*, 159-167.

Mabbott, J. D. (1967). *The state and the citizen*. London: Hutchinson University Library.

Machan, T. (1988). *Commerce and morality*. Totowa, NJ: Rowan and Littlefield.

Mack, M. P. (Ed.). (1969). *A Bentham reader*. New York: Pegasus.

Maghan, J. (1991). Privatization of corrections: Anticipating the unanticipated. In D. E. J. Macnamara & R. J. Kelly (Eds.), *Perspectives on deviance: Dominance, degradation, and denigration* (pp. 135-151). Cincinnati, OH: Anderson.

Mann, K. (1985). *Defending white-collar crime: A portrait of attorneys at work*. New Haven, CT: Yale University Press.

Manuel, F. E. (1951). *The age of reason*. Ithaca, NY: Cornell University Press.

Martin, S., & Ekland-Olson, S. (1987). *Texas prisons*. Austin: Texas Monthly Press.

Martindale, D. (1960). *The nature and types of sociological theory*. Boston: Houghton-Mifflin.

Martinson, R. (1974). What works: Questions and answers about prison reform. *Public Interest*, *35*, 22-54.

Mason, T. (1991, June 16). Many for-profit jails hold no profits—not even inmates. *Wall Street Journal*.

Matthews, R. (1989). Privatization in perspective. In R. Matthews (Ed.), *Privatizing criminal justice* (pp. 1-23). London: Sage.

Mayer, C. (1986). Legal issues surrounding private operation of prisons. *Criminal Law Bulletin*, *22*, 309-325.

McAfee, W. M. (1987). Tennessee's Private Prison Act of 1986: An historical perspective with special attention to California's experience. *Vanderbilt Law Review*, *40*, 851-865.

McAfee, W. M. (1990). San Quentin: The forgotten issue of California's political history in the 1850s. *Southern California Quarterly*, *52*(3), 235-254.

McAfee, W. M., & Shichor, D. (1990). An analysis of California's private prison experience in the 1850s. *Criminal Justice History*, *11*, 89-103.

McClintock, F. (1980). The future of imprisonment in Britain. In A. E. Bottoms & P. H. Preston (Eds.), *The coming penal crisis. A criminological and theological explanation* (pp. 126-136). Edinburgh, UK: Scottish Academic Press.

McConville, S. (1981). *A history of English prison administration, Volume 1, 1760-1877*. London: Routledge and Kegan Paul.

McCoy, C. (1981). The impact of Section 1983 litigation on policy making in corrections. *Federal Probation*, *45*(4), 17-23.

McDonald, D. C. (1989). The cost of corrections: In search of the bottom line. *Research in Corrections*, *2*, 1-25.

McDonald, D. C. (1990a). The costs of operating public and private correctional facilities. In D. C. McDonald (Ed.), *Private prisons and the public interest* (pp. 86-106). New Brunswick, NJ: Rutgers University Press.

McDonald, D. C. (1990b). When government fails: Going private a last resort. In D. C. McDonald (Ed.), *Private prisons and the public interest* (pp. 179-189). New Brunswick, NJ: Rutgers University Press.

McDonald, D. C. (1990c). Introduction. In D. C. McDonald (Ed.), *Private prisons and the public interest* (pp. 1-18). New Brunswick, NJ: Rutgers University Press.

McDonald, D. C. (1994). Public imprisonment by private means: The re-emergence of private prisons and jails in the United States, the United Kingdom, and Australia. *British Journal of Criminology*, *34*, 29-48.

McDonald, D. C., & Weisburd, D. (1992). Segregation and hidden discrimination in prisons: Reflections on a small study of cell assignments. In C. A. Hartjen & E. E. Rhine (Eds.), *Correctional theory and practice* (pp. 146-161). Chicago: Nelson-Hall.

McDonald, W. F. (1977). The role of the victim in America. In R. E. Barnett & J. Hegel, III (Eds.), *Assessing the criminal* (pp. 295-307). Cambridge, MA: Ballinger.

McKanna, C. V. (1987, March). 1851-1880: The origins of San Quentin. *California History*, pp. 49-54.

McKay, J. P., Hill, B. D., & Buckler, J. (1983). *A history of Western society*. Boston: Houghton-Mifflin.

McKelvey, B. (1936). *American prisons*. Chicago: University of Chicago Press.

McShane, M. D., & Williams, F. P., III. (1989). Running on empty: Creativity and the correctional agenda. *Crime & Delinquency, 35*, 562-576.

Medina v. O'Neill, 589 F.Supp. 1028 (1984).

Melossi, D., & Pavarini, M. (1981). *The prisons and the factory: Origins of the penitentiary system*. Totowa, NJ: Barnes and Noble.

Mendelson, M. A. (1974). *Tender loving greed*. New York: Alfred A. Knopf.

Merlo, A. V. (1992). Ethical issues and the private sector. In P. J. Benekos & A. V. Marlo (Eds.), *Corrections: Dilemmas and directions* (pp. 23-36). Cincinnati, OH: Anderson.

Messner, S. F., & Rosenfeld, R. (1994). *Crime and the American Dream*. Belmont, CA: Wadsworth.

Meyer, J. C., Jr. (1972). An action-orientation approach to the study of occupational crime. *Australian and New Zealand Journal of Criminology, 5*, 35-48.

Mintz, B., & Schwartz, M. (1985). *The power structure of the American business community*. Chicago: University of Chicago Press.

Mitchell, D. (1988, July 10). Private prisons guard wallets of taxpayers. *San Bernardino Sun*, p. D3.

Mitchell, R. L. (1978, February 7). A new idea: Private-enterprise prisons. *Los Angeles Times*, Pt. 2, p. 9.

Mizruchi, M. S. (1982). *The American corporate network*. New York: Vintage.

Moe, R. C. (1988, March-April). "Law" versus "performance" as objective standard. *Public Administration Review, 47*, 674-675.

Monahan, J. (1981). *Predicting violent behavior: An assessment of clinical techniques*. Beverly Hills, CA: Sage.

Montilla, M. R. (1978). *Prison employee unionism: Management guide for correctional administrators*. Washington, DC: U.S. Government Printing Office.

Moore, W. E. (1962). *The conduct of the corporation*. New York: Vintage.

Moos, R. H. (1968). The assessment of social climates of correctional institutions. *Journal of Research in Crime and Delinquency, 5*, 174-188.

Morgan, K. E. (1900, August 3). Waiting to vote on CCA's prisoner rate could have saved the country some money. *Chattanooga Times*, p. 14.

Morris, N. (1974). *The future of imprisonment*. Chicago: University of Chicago Press.

Mullen, J. (1985). *Corrections and the private sector* (Research in Brief). Washington, DC: National Institute of Justice.

Mullen, J., Chabotar, K. J., & Carrow, D. M. (1985). *The privatization of corrections*. Washington, DC: National Institute of Justice.

Murphy, J. G., & Coleman, J. L. (1984). *The philosophy of law: An introduction to jurisprudence*. Totowa, NJ: Rowman and Allenheld.

Murton, T. O. (1979). Prison management: The past, the present, and the possible future. In M. E. Wolfgang (Ed.), *Prisons: Present and possible* (pp. 5-53). Lexington, MA: D. C. Heath.

Nalla, M., & Newman, G. (1990). *A primer in private security*. Albany, NY: Harrow and Heston.

National Center on Institutions and Alternatives. (1987). *Prison privatization past and present: How privatization failed at San Quentin*. Alexandria, VA: Author.

Neese, R. (1959). *Prison exposures*. Philadelphia: Chilton Co.

Nelken, D. (1989). Discipline and punish: Some notes on the margin. *Howard Journal, 28*, 245-254.

Nelson, B. J. (1980). Purchase of service. In G. J. Washnis (Ed.), *Productivity improvement handbook for state and local government* (pp. 427-447). New York: Wiley.

Novak, D. A. (1978). *The wheel of servitude: Black forced labor after slavery*. Lexington: University Press of Kentucky.

Novey, D. L. (1985). Privatization in prisons: A potential forest fire across the USA. *Correctional Peacekeeper, 3*, 8.

Nozick, R. (1974). *Anarchy, state, and utopia*. New York: Basic Books.

O'Brien, P. (1982). *The promise of punishment: Prisons in nineteenth-century France*. Princeton, NJ: Princeton University Press.

O'Connor, J. (1973). *The fiscal crisis of the state*. New York: St. Martin's.

O'Hare, M., Leone, R., & Zegans, M. (1990). The privatization of imprisonment: A managerial perspective. In D. C. McDonald (Ed.), *Private prisons and the public interest* (pp. 107-129). New Brunswick, NJ: Rutgers University Press.

Osborne, D., & Gaebler, T. (1992). *Reinventing government*. Reading, MA: Addison-Wesley.

Packer, H. (1968). *The limits of the criminal sanction*. Stanford, CA: Stanford University Press.

Palmer, J. W. (1985). *Constitutional rights of prisoners* (3rd ed.). Cincinnati, OH: Anderson.

Palumbo, D. J. (1986). Privatization and corrections policy. *Policy Studies Review, 5*(3), 598-605.

Papadakis, E., & Taylor-Gooby, P. (1987). *The private provision of public welfare*. New York: St. Martin's.

Parker, M., & Slaughter, J. (1994). Beware! TQM is coming to your campus. *NEA Higher Education Journal, 10*(1), 5-30.

Parsons, T. (1951). *The social system*. New York: Free Press.

Parsons, T. (1970). How are clients integrated into service organizations? In W. E. Rosengreen & M. Lefton (Eds.), *Organizations and clients: Essays in the sociology of service* (pp. 1-16). Columbus, OH: Charles E. Merrill.

Patrick, A. L. (1986). Private sector—profit motive vs. quality. *Corrections Today, 48*, 68-74.

Pease, K. (1983). Penal innovations. In J. Lishman (Ed.), *Social work with adult offenders* (pp. 72-87). Aberdeen: University of Aberdeen Press.

Pearce, F., & Tombs, S. (1992). Realism and corporate crime. In R. Matthews & J. Young (Eds.), *Issues in realistic criminology* (pp. 70-101). London: Sage.

Pellicciotti, J. M. (1987). 42 U.S.C. Sec. 1983 correctional officials liability: A look to the new century. *Journal of Contemporary Criminal Justice, 3*, 1-9.

Pennings, J. M. (1980). *Interlocking directorates: Origins and consequences of connections among organizations' board of directors*. San Francisco: Jossey-Bass.

Pollock, F. A., & Maitland, F. W. (1898). *The history of English law before the time of Edward I* (2nd ed.). Cambridge, UK: Cambridge University Press.

Pollock, J. M. (1994). *Ethics in crime and justice: Dilemmas and decision* (2nd ed.). Pacific Grove, CA: Brooks/Cole.

Pomeroy, E. (1953). California 1846-1860: Politics of a representative frontier state. *California Historical Society Quarterly, 32*, 295-296.

Pontell, H. N. (1978). Deterrence: Theory versus practice. *Criminology, 16*, 3-22.

Poole, E. D., & Regoli, R. M. (1981). Alienation in prison: An examination of the work relations of prison guards. *Criminology, 19*, 251-270.

Poole, R. W. (1983, Spring). Objections to privatization. *Policy Review, 24*, 106-119.

Porter, R. G. (1990). The privatization of prisons in the United States: A policy that Britain should not emulate. *Howard Journal, 29*, 65-81.

Press, A. (1990). The good, the bad, and the ugly: Private prisons in the 1980s. In D. C. McDonald (Ed.), *Private prisons and the public interest* (pp. 19-41). New Brunswick, NJ: Rutgers University Press.

Pugh, R. B. (1968). *Imprisonment in medieval England*. Cambridge, UK: Cambridge University Press.

Quinney, R. (1977). *Class, state and crime: On the theory and practice of criminal justice*. New York: David McKay.

Rawls, J. (1971). *A theory of justice*. Cambridge, MA: Harvard University Press.

Rein, M. (1989). The social structure of institutions: Neither public nor private. In S. B. Kamerman & A. J. Kahn (Eds.), *Privatization and the welfare state* (pp. 49-71). Princeton, NJ: Princeton University Press.

Reiman, J. H. (1979). *The rich get richer and the poor get prison: Ideology, class, and criminal justice*. New York: Wiley.

Rhine, E. E. (1990). The rule of law, disciplinary practices, and Rahway State Prison: A case study in judicial intervention and social control. In J. J. DiIulio (Ed.), *Courts, corrections, and the Constitution* (pp. 173-222). New York: Oxford University Press.

Ring, C. (1987). *Contracting for the operation of private prisons*. College Park, MD: American Correctional Association.

Robbins, I. P. (1986, September). Privatization of corrections: Defining the issues. *Federal Probation, 50*, 24-30.

Robbins, I. P. (1989). The legal dimensions of private incarceration. *American University Law Review, 3*, 531-854.

Roberts, A. R., & Powers, G. T. (1985). The privatization of corrections: Methodological issues and dilemmas involved in evaluative research. *Prison Journal, 45*(2), 95-107.

Rogers, J. W. (1989). The greatest correctional myth: Winning the war on crime through incarceration. *Federal Probation, 53*(3), 21-28.

Rothman, D. J. (1971). *The discovery of the asylum*. Boston: Little, Brown.

Rothman, D. J. (1980). *Conscience and convenience: The asylum and its alternatives in Progressive America*. Boston: Little, Brown.

Rudovsky, D., Bronstein, A. J., Koren, E. J., & Cade, J. (1988). *The rights of prisoners: The basic ACLU guide to prisoners' rights* (4th ed.). Carbondale: Southern Illinois University Press.

Ruffin v. Commonwealth, 62 Va. (21 Gratt) 790 (1871).

Ruiz v. Estelle, F.2d 115 (1980).

Rusche, G., & Kirchheimer, O. (1939). *Punishment and social structure*. New York: Columbia University Press.

Russell, B. (1945). *A history of Western philosophy*. New York: Simon & Schuster.

Rutherford, A. (1990). British penal policy and the idea of prison privatization. In D. C. McDonald (Ed.), *Private prisons and the public interest* (pp. 42-65). New Brunswick, NJ: Rutgers University Press.

Ryan, M., & Ward, T. (1989). Privatization and penal politics. In R. Matthews (Ed.), *Privatizing criminal justice* (pp. 53-73). London: Sage.

Ryan, M. H., Swanson, C. L., & Buchholz, R. A. (1987). *Corporate strategy, public policy and the Fortune 500: How America's major corporations influence government*. Oxford, UK: Basil Blackwell.

Sadurski, W. (1991). Social justice and the problem of punishment. *Israel Law Review, 25*(3-4), 302-331.

Sagarin, E., & Maghan, J. (1985, January 12). Should states opt for private prisons? No. *Hartford Journal*, pp. E1-E4.

Samaha, J. (1983). *Criminal law*. St. Paul, MI: West.

Sampson, A. (1992, April 1). Crime and furbishment. *The Guardian*, p. 23.

Savage, D. G. (1994, June 7). High court opens door to rape suits by inmates. *Los Angeles Times*, p. A4.

Savas, E. S. (1982) *Privatizing the public sector*. Chatham, NJ: Chatham House.

Savas, E. S. (1985). The efficiency of the private sector. In S. M. Butler (Ed.), *The privatization option: A strategy to shrink the size of government* (pp. 15-31). Washington, DC: The Heritage Foundation.

Savas, E. S. (1987). Privatization and prisons. *Vanderbilt Law Review, 40*, 889-899.

Savas, E. S. (1990). Privatization: A strategy for structural reform. *National Forum, 70*(2), 9-13.

Schafer, S. (1977). *Victimology: The victim and his criminal*. Reston, VA: Reston.

Schiflett, K. L., & Zey, M. (1990). Comparison of characteristics of private product producing organizations and public service organizations. *Sociological Quarterly, 31*, 569-583.

Schrag, C. (1961). Some foundations for a theory of corrections. In D. Cressey (Ed.), *The prison* (pp. 309-357). New York: Holt, Rinehart & Winston.

Schuman, A. M. (1989). The cost of correctional services: Exploring a poorly chartered terrain. *Research in Corrections, 2*, 27-33.

Scull, A. T. (1977). *Decarceration: Community treatment and the deviant: A radical view*. Englewood Cliffs, NJ: Prentice Hall.

Sechrest, D. K. (1976). The accredition movement in corrections. *Federal Probation, 40*(4), 15-19.

Sechrest, D. K. (1992a). Locating prisons: Open versus closed approaches to siting. *Crime & Delinquency, 38*, 88-104.

Sechrest, D. K. (1992b, November). *The American Correctional Association and the accredition movement: Standards without principles*. Paper presented at the annual meeting of the American Society of Criminology, New Orleans, LA.

Sechrest, D. K., Papas, N., & Price, S. J. (1987). Building prisons: Pre-manufactured, prefabricated, and prototype. *Federal Probation, 51*(1), 35-41.

Sechrest, D., & Shichor, D. (1993a). *Evaluation of California's community correctional facilities*. Unpublished report submitted to the California Department of Corrections.

Sechrest, D., & Shichor, D. (1993b, September). Corrections goes public and private in California. *Federal Probation, 57*, 3-8.

Sellers, M. P. (1989). Private and public prisons: A comparison of costs, programs and facilities. *International Journal of Offender Therapy and Comparative Criminology, 33*, 241-256.

Sellin, J. T. (1944). *Pioneering in penology: The Amsterdam House of Corrections*. Philadelphia: University of Pennsylvania Press.

Sellin, J. T. (1976). *Slavery and the penal system*. New York: Elsevier.

Sevick, J. R. (1987). Introduction. In J. R. Sevick & W. I. Cikins (Eds.), *Constructing correctional facilities: Is there a role for the private sector?* (pp. 1-12). Washington, DC: Brookings Institution.

Shapiro, M. (1988). *Who guards the guardians? Judicial control of administration*. Athens: University of Georgia Press.

Shearing, C. D., & Stenning, P. C. (Eds.). (1987). *Private policing*. Newbury Park, CA: Sage.

Sheehan, S. (1978). *A prison and a prisoner*. Boston: Houghton Mifflin.

Shichor, D. (1978). The people changing v. people processing organizational perspective: The case of correctional institutions. *LAE Journal, 41*(3), 37-44.

Shichor, D. (1987). Penal policies: Some recent trends. *Legal Studies Forum, 11*(1), 55-78.

Shichor, D. (1989). On corporate deviance and corporate victimization: A review and some elaborations. *International Review of Victimology, 1,* 67-88.

Shichor, D. (1992a). Myths and realities in prison siting. *Crime & Delinquency, 38,* 70-87.

Shichor, D. (1992b). Following the penological pendulum: The survival of rehabilitation. *Federal Probation, 56*(2), 19-25.

Shichor, D. (1993). The corporate context of private corrections. *Crime, Law and Social Change, 20,* 113-138.

Shichor, D., & Bartollas, C. (1990). Private and public placements: Is there a difference? *Crime & Delinquency, 36,* 286-299.

Shichor, D., & Sechrest, D. K. (1992). Unpublished interviews in California public and private furlough facilities.

Shinnar, S., & Shinnar, R. (1975). The effects of the criminal justice system on the control of crime: A quantative approach. *Law and Society Review, 9,* 581-611.

Shover, N., Clelland, D. A., & Lynxwiler, J. (1986). *Enforcement or negotiation.* Albany: State University of New York Press.

Shover, N., & Einstadter, W. J. (1988). *Analyzing American corrections.* Belmont, CA: Wadsworth.

Silvester, D. B. (1990). Ethics and privatization in criminal justice: Does education have a role to play? *Journal of Criminal Justice, 18,* 65-70.

Singer, R. G. (1979). *Just deserts: Sentencing based on equality and desert.* Cambridge, MA: Ballinger.

Skinner, Q. (1978). *The foundations of modern political thought.* Cambridge, UK: Cambridge University Press.

Smart, B. (1983). On discipline and social regulation: A review of Foucault's genealogical analysis. In D. Garland & P. Young (Eds.), *The power to punish: Contemporary penality and social analysis* (pp. 62-83). London: Heinemann.

Smart, J. J. C. (1991). Utilitarianism and punishment. *Israel Law Review, 25,* 360-375.

Smith, A. (1937). *The wealth of nations* (Reprinted ed.). New York: Modern Library.

Sneed, W. C. (1860). *A report on the history and mode of management of the Kentucky penitentiary.* Frankfort, KY: J. B. Major.

South, N. (1988). *Policing for profit: The private security sector.* London: Sage.

Sparks, R. (1994). Can prisons be legitimate? Penal politics, privatization, and the timeliness of an old idea. *British Journal of Criminology, 34,* 14-28.

Spurlock, D. S. (1987). Liability of state officials and prison corporations for excessive use of force against inmates of private prisons. *Vanderbilt Law Review, 40,* 983-1021.

Staats, E. B. (1988, March/April). Public service and the public interest. *Public Administration Review,* pp. 601-605.

Starr, P. (1987). The limits of privatization. *Proceedings of the Academy of Political Science, 3*(3), 124-137.

Starr, P. (1989). The meaning of privatization. In S. B. Kamerman & A. J. Kahn (Eds.), *Privatization and the welfare state* (pp. 15-48). Princeton, NJ: Princeton University Press.

State of California. (1985). *Financial management handbook for private return-to-custody facilities.* Sacramento: Department of Corrections.

State of California. (1990). *Blue Ribbon Commission on Inmate Population Management* (Final Report). Sacramento, CA: Department of Corrections.

Stinchcombe, A. L., Adams, R., Heimer, C. A., Lane Schepple, K., Smith, T. W., & Taylor, D. G. (1980). *Crime and punishment: Changing attitudes in America.* San Francisco: Jossey-Bass.

Stone, C. D. (1975). *Where the law ends.* New York: Harper & Row.

Street, D., Vinter, R. D., & Perrow, C. (1966). *Organization for treatment.* New York: Free Press.

Stroud v. Swope, 187 F.2d 850 9th Cir. (1951).

Sullivan, H. J. (1989). Privatization of corrections and the constitutional rights of prisoners. *Federal Probation, 53*(2), 36-42.

Sutherland, E. H. (1956). Crime of corporations. In A. Cohen, A. Lindesmith, & K. Schuessler (Eds.), *The Sutherland papers* (pp. 78-96). Bloomington: Indiana University Press.

Sutton, A., & Wild, R. (1978). Corporate crime and social structure. In P. R. Wilson & J. Braithwaite (Eds.), *Two faces of deviance: Crimes of the powerless and the powerful* (pp. 177-198). Brisbane, Queensland, Australia: University of Queensland Press.

Sykes, G. M. (1958). *The society of captives.* Princeton, NJ: Princeton University Press.

Sykes, G. M. (1978). *Criminology.* New York: Harcourt Brace Jovanovich.

Sykes, G. M., & Messinger, S. L. (1960). The inmate social system. In R. A. Cloward, D. R. Cressey, G. H. Grosser, R. McCleery, L. E. Ohlin, G. M. Sykes, & S. L. Messinger (Eds.), *Theoretical studies in the social organization of the prison* (pp. 5-19). New York: Social Science Research Council.

Tagiuri, R. (1968). The concept of organizational climate. In R. Tagiuri & G. H. Litwin (Eds.), *Organizational climate* (pp. 11-32). Boston: Harvard Business School.

Talbot, C. K. (Ed.). (1981). *Privatization in Canadian corrections: A more economical and humane solution?* (Selected Readings). Ottawa: University of Ottawa, Department of Criminology.

Tennessee v. Garner, 105 S.Ct. 1694, 85 L.Ed.2d 1 (1985).

Thomas, C. W. (1991). Prisoners' rights and correctional privatization: A legal and ethical analysis. *Business and Professional Ethics Journal, 10,* 3-45.

Thomas, C. W., & Foard, S. L. (1991). *Private correctional facility census.* Gainesville: University of Florida, Center for Studies in Criminology and Law.

Thomas, C. W., & Hanson, L. S. C. (1989). The implications of 42 U.S.C. § 1983 for the privatization of prisons. *Florida State University, 16,* 933-962.

Thomas, C. W., & Logan, C. H. (1991, March). *The development, present status, and future potential of correctional privatization in America.* Paper presented at a conference of the American Legislative Exchange Council, Miami, FL.

Thomas, J., Keeler, D., & Harris, K. (1986). Issues and misconceptions in prisoner litigation. *Criminology, 24,* 775-797.

Thomas, J. C. (1987). Privatization of prisons: A new breed of liability. *Journal of Security Administration, 10,* 27-34.

Thompson, J. D. (1967). *Organizations in action.* New York: McGraw-Hill.

Thornberry, T. P., Tolnay, S. E., Flanagan, T. J., & Glynn, P. (1991). *Children in custody 1987: A comparison of public and private juvenile custody facilities.* Washington, DC: U.S. Department of Justice, Office of Juvenile Justice and Delinquency Prevention.

Tifft, L., & Sullivan, D. (1980). *The struggle to be human: Crime, criminology, and anarchism.* Over The Water, Sanday, Orkney, UK: Cienfuegos.

Toch, H., & Klofas, J. (1982). Alienation and a desire for job enrichment among correctional officers. *Federal Probation, 46*(1), 35-44.

Tolchin, M. (1985, April 21). Privately operated prison in Tennessee deports $200,000 in cost overruns. *New York Times.*

Tolchin, S. J., & Tolchin, M. (1983). *Dismantling America: The rush to deregulate.* Boston: Houghton Mifflin.

Tumulty, K. (1991, August 22). Private prisons may be nicer but cost savings are in doubt. Los Angeles Times, p. A5.

U.S. General Accounting Office. (1991). Private prisons. Washington, DC: U.S. Government Printing Office.

U.S. House of Representatives. (1985). Privatization of corrections hearings before the subcommittee on courts, civil liberties, and the administration of justice. Washington, DC: U.S. Government Printing Office.

U.S. Senate (1985). District of Columbia appropriations for fiscal year 1986 before a subcommittee of appropriations. Washington, DC: U.S. Government Printing Office.

Useem, M. (1984). The inner circle: Large corporations and the rise of business political activity in the U.S. and U.K. New York: Oxford University Press.

van den Haag, E. (1975). Punishing criminals. New York: Basic Books.

Vass, A. A. (1990). Alternatives to prison: Punishment, custody and the community. London: Sage.

Vaughan, D. (1980). Crime between organizations: Implications for victimology. In G. Geis & E. Stotland (Eds.), White-collar crime: Theory and research (pp. 77-97). Beverly Hills, CA: Sage.

Vise, D. A. (1985, September 22). Private company asks for control of Tennessee prisons. Washington Post, p. F1.

Visher, C. (1987). Incapacitation and crime control: Does a "lock'em up" policy reduce crime? Justice Quarterly, 4, 513-543.

von Hirsch, A. (1976). Doing justice. New York: Hill and Wang.

von Hirsch, A. (1985). Past or future crimes. New Brunswick, NJ: Rutgers University Press.

Walker, D. R. (1988). Penology for profit: A history of the Texas prison system 1867-1912. College Station: Texas A&M University Press.

Walker, S. (1980). Popular justice: A history of American criminal justice. New York: Oxford University Press.

Walker, S. (1989). Sense and nonsense about crime: A policy guide (2nd ed.). Pacific Grove, CA: Brooks/Cole.

Wallace, S. E. (1971). On the totality of institutions. In S. E. Wallace (Ed.), Total institutions (pp. 1-7). New Brunswick, NJ: Transaction.

Walters, D. (1991, July). The penitentiary-industrial complex. California Republic, p. 9.

Walzer, M. (1985, April 8). At McPrison and Burglar King, it's hold the justice. New Republic, pp. 10-12.

Wayson, B. L., & Funke, G. S. (1989). What price justice? A handbook for the analysis of criminal justice costs. Washington, DC: National Institute of Justice.

Webb, S., & Webb, B. (1963). English prisons under local government. Hamden, CT: Archon Books. (New impression of the 1922 edition)

Weber, M. (1964). The theory of social and economic organization. New York: Free Press.

Weber, M. (1958). The Protestant ethic and the spirit of capitalism. New York: Scribner.

Wecht, D. N. (1987). Breaking the code of deference: Judicial review of private prisons. Yale Law Journal, 96, 815-837.

Weinstein, H. (1990, February 28). Northrop, guilty in fraud case, is fined $17 million. Los Angeles Times.

Weintraub, D. M. (1993, January 17). Wilson seeks to reshape way state operates. Los Angeles Times, pp. A3, A34.

Weiss, C. H. (1973). Where politics and evaluation research meet. Evaluation, 1, 37-45.

Weiss, R. P. (1989). Private prisons and the state. In R. Matthews (Ed.), Privatizing criminal justice (pp. 26-51). London: Sage.

West v. Atkins, 815 F.2d 993 (4th Cir. 1987), rev'd 108 S.Ct. (1988).

White, L. A. (1949). *The science of culture*. New York: Farrar, Strauss, and Cudahy.

Williams, F., III, Shichor, D., & Wiggenhorn, A. (1989). Fine tuning social control: Electronic monitoring and surrogate homes for drug using parolees—A research note. *Journal of Contemporary Criminal Justice, 5*(3), 173-180.

Wilson, J. Q. (1975). *Thinking about crime*. New York: Basic Books.

Wilson, J. Q., & Herrnstein, R. (1985). *Crime and human nature*. New York: Simon & Schuster.

Wines, E. C., & Dwight, T. W. (1867). *Report on the prisons and reformatories of the United States and Canada made to the legislature of New York*. Albany, NY: Van Benthuysen and Sons.

Wolff v. McDonnell, 418 U.S. 539 (1974).

Wooden, K. (1976). *Weeping in the playtime of others: America's incarcerated children*. New York: McGraw-Hill.

Woolley, M. R. (1985). Prisons for profit: Policy considerations for government officials. *Dickenson Law Review, 90*, 307-331.

Ex parte, Young. 209 U.S. 123 (1908).

Young, M. A. (1990, June). *Legal reorganization in response to the savings and loan crisis*. Paper presented at the aannual meeting of the Law and Society Association, Oakland, CA.

Zimring, F. E., & Hawkins, G. (1991). *The scale of imprisonment*. Chicago: University of Chicago Press.

Index

About the Author

David Shichor is Professor in the Department of Criminal Justice at California State University, San Bernardino. He received his B.A. in sociology and history from the Hebrew University in Jerusalem, Israel, his M.A. in sociology from California State College, Los Angeles, and his Ph.D. in sociology from the University of Southern California. He previously taught at the Institute of Criminology, Tel Aviv University, Israel.

He has conducted research; presented professional papers; and published articles, book chapters, and books primarily in the areas of juvenile delinquency, corrections, criminological and penological theory, victimology, deviance, and white-collar crime. He reviewed books for publishers in these fields and was reviewer for several professional journals. Recently, he completed an evaluation study, with his colleague Dale Sechrest, of private and public proprietary confinement facilities (community correctional facilities) for the California Department of Corrections. His recent publications appeared in *Sociological Quarterly; Crime, Law and Social Change; Crime & Delinquency; Federal Probation;* and the *International Review of Victimology*. Currently, he is researching the various aspects of criminal justice privatization and victim-offender reconciliation and is involved in a project studying victimization by a telemarketing scam.